Finding Fogerty

Finding Fogerty

Interdisciplinary Readings of John Fogerty and
Creedence Clearwater Revival

Edited by Thomas M. Kitts

LEXINGTON BOOKS
Lanham • Boulder • New York • Toronto • Plymouth, UK

Published by Lexington Books
A wholly owned subsidary of The Rowman & Littlefield Publishing Group, Inc.
4501 Forbes Boulevard, Suite 200, Lanham, Maryland 20706
www.rowman.com

10 Thornbury Road, Plymouth PL6 7PP, United Kingdom

British Library Cataloguing in Publication Information Available

Library of Congress Cataloging-in-Publication Data
Finding Fogerty : interdisciplinary readings of John Fogerty and Creedence Clearwater
Revival / edited by Thomas M. Kitts.
    pages cm
  Includes bibliographical references and index.
  ISBN 978-0-7391-7483-8 (cloth : alk. paper)—ISBN 978-0-7391-7485-2 (pbk. : alk.
paper)— ISBN 978-0-7391-7484-5 (electronic) 1. Fogerty, John, 1945—Criticism and
interpretation. 2. Creedence Clearwater Revival (Musical group) I. Kitts, Thomas M.,
1955- editor of compilation.
  ML420.F64F56 2012
  782.42166092—dc23   2012043796

Printed in the United States of America

To the happy and peaceful residents
and guests of Casa Kittsberg

Contents

~

Acknowledgments

I would like to thank a number of people who helped make this book possible. Janice Shaman, who has worked with me for several years now, was her usual competent and generous self, for which I am very grateful. She always comes through in crunch time. Melissa King, my graduate assistant, was immensely helpful in fact checking, finding sources, and proofing. Her initiative in so many aspects involving this collection is greatly appreciated. Many others willingly gave their time and insights, especially Craig Baron, Steven Hamelman, and Peter Rinaldi, and some contributors like Stephen Paul Miller, Nick Baxter-Moore, and Larry Pitilli took on extra tasks.

Special thanks must go to Jeff Sellars for not only helping to create the title of the book but also for designing and maintaining the book's website: http://findingfogerty.wordpress.com/2011/11/09/finding-fogerty/. Please visit and add any comments you might have on the essays, CCR, or Fogerty.

I also had the good fortune to work with Lenore Lautigar at Lexington, who was especially patient and extended her sound advice and guidance throughout the process of assembling this collection. She was very helpful and a pleasure to work with.

Finally, I have to thank my family. My wife Lisa Rosenberg was very patient as I worked on some beautiful summer days that we should have spent together at the beach or, at least, relaxing together in our backyard. I also thank our children—Hayley, Dylan, Julia, and Holly—who make our work meaningful and keep our lives interesting.

~

Introduction

As I was working on this collection, I had a conversation about Creedence Clearwater Revival with Chris Byrne, formerly of Black 47 and now leading Seanchai and the Unity Squad. "One of my all-time favorite bands," Chris said. "But you know they were never considered 'cool' or 'hip.' They were thought of as an AM band, a singles group."

Byrne is right. Few knew the band was one of the headliners at Woodstock. Leader John Fogerty was dissatisfied with their performance and so withheld the necessary permissions from the filmmakers and record producers—certainly a missed opportunity for some counterculture credibility. Even though CCR produced counterculture anthems like "Fortunate Son" and "Who'll Stop the Rain," there was something less than radical about the band. Their lifestyle and work ethic somehow seemed a bit too middle class. They worked all the time, releasing hit after hit. . . too many for their counterculture good. From 1968 through 1972, CCR produced 10 top-ten singles and seven gold albums of new material—no live albums or greatest hits collections. Over the same period, Woodstock stars Sly and the Family Stone produced four top-ten singles and five albums (one a greatest hits collection) and The Who released no top-ten singles and five albums (but two compilations and one live record).

For many in the counterculture, CCR were too prolific, too successful, too middle class, and too clean. Fogerty, in fact, has been called "the notorious Puritan of rock."[1] In 1976, he explained to Cameron Crowe: "I suppose I should be ashamed [of never taking acid] or something. But I didn't want to be 30 and driving down the freeway when suddenly a little part of it hits me again. No drinkin' and no dopin'—that's always been my policy."[2]

Perhaps predictably, CCR began life in the suburban community of El Cerrito, California, located five miles from Berkeley, another five miles from Oakland, and another five from San Francisco. In 1958, three junior high school students, three-quarters of what would eventually evolve into Creedence Clearwater Revival, formed a combo. John Fogerty played guitar; Stu Cook played piano, and Doug Clifford drums. None was brave enough to sing. Throughout high school and still without a regular vocalist, the Blue Velvets, as they called themselves, got every sock hop and youth gig in town. "It's funny, we were the only band in junior high, we were the only band in high school," said Cook. "We were the only kids we knew who were playing."[3] El Cerrito has never been a hotbed of music. Carole King and Gerry Goffin could have been writing and the Monkees could have been singing about El Cerrito in "Pleasant Valley Sunday," with "charcoal burning everywhere," weekend squires mowing lawns, and roses blooming, but only the Blue Velvets were "trying hard to learn their song." Remember, this is pre-Beatles.

Missing from the Blue Velvets was later Creedence member Tom Fogerty, John's older brother by 3½ years. Tom had developed his own musical path through high school, and by his 1959 graduation, he was fronting Spider Webb & the Insects, a band that flirted with success. By the fall of 1961 after the Insects disbanded, Tom took note of his kid brother's band. They weren't bad and they needed a vocalist. Tom joined for occasional gigs and used the Blue Velvets as his backing band for recording sessions at Orchestra Records. One of the failed singles, "Have You Ever Been Lonely" (1962), marked John's debut as a songwriter. Before long Tom joined the band as a permanent member and assumed leadership.

The band struggled on for several years trying different musical and fashion styles and names (the Visions, the Golliwogs) and occasionally releasing singles that sold poorly. However, as time passed, John's ambition began to take hold, especially after he took work as a shipping clerk at Fantasy Records. He began to assert himself more and more within the band, and by 1965, he was the lead vocalist and the leader of the band—a point solidified with the Golliwogs' fourth single, a derivative bluesy rocker called "Brown-Eyed Girl" (not Van Morrison's). "This was really the first record by John," states Paul Rose, an unofficial A&R man for Fantasy. "The whole sound was different. Now we really got into more involved sessions, where we overdubbed John on everything. We'd use Doug and Stu on the basic tracks but didn't record Tom's instrument at all, he would just sing. John also played organ and occasionally bass on some of those sessions too. So Doug was sometimes the only other musician."[4]

"Brown-Eyed Girl" became a local hit, selling over 10,000 copies and putting the band on the California highways. They may have toured the state but they were still largely a cover band. "I don't recall playing our early singles live," comments Clifford, "though we would play our 'hit.' We did the popular songs like 'Gloria' and 'Satisfaction' that were on the jukebox, to keep our audience."[5] The next single in February 1966, "Fight Fire," may have failed but featured John's fuzz-tone guitar and indicated another crucial ingredient in the Creedence sound—an interest in sonic experimentation which would make John's simple hypnotic riffs dynamic and flexible in songs like the soon-to-come "Suzie Q" or "Born on the Bayou" and, near the end of CCR, "Heard It Through the Grapevine."

In 1966, John and Doug entered the Army Reserves. Soon after their discharge the following year, the band rededicated themselves and changed their name to Creedence Clearwater Revival—*Creedence* from a coworker of Tom's friend, Credence Nuball, with an added *e* to suggest creed and commitment; *Clearwater* from an advertisement for Olympia Beer and indicative of the band's environmental concerns; and *Revival* reflective of the band's renewed energy. In the first days of January 1968, the band re-signed with Fantasy, which had been purchased by a group led by Saul Zaentz, who was very encouraging at the time. The CCR sound took a leap forward with the 8:36 remake of Dale Hawkins's "Susie Q," which locks into a dark grove and flirts with San Francisco psychedelia, reverberations, snake-like guitar runs (not dissimilar from the later "Run Through the Jungle" or "The Old Man down the Road"), John's voice from a megaphone, fuzz tone, and feedback. Released as a single, with the song split on the A and B side, it reached #11 on the national charts and introduced CCR to the world. They were off and running with John Fogerty in charge.

In 1971, Tom, feeling underappreciated, quit CCR, and by 1972, the band collapsed. In short, Tom, Stu, and Doug found John increasingly domineering and overbearing. They wanted more input into the music and they wanted to record their own songs under CCR. John—who on previous albums had been credited as composer, producer, and arranger—yielded on the band's final album, the disastrous *Mardi Gras*, which Jon Landau in *Rolling Stone* called "the worst album that I have ever heard from a major rock band."[6]

After the break-up, all continued careers in music. Tom had only minor success with his solo albums and as part of the band Ruby. Doug "Cosmo" Clifford, who also released a solo album, continued to play with Stu Cook in the Sir Douglas Quintet and then the Don Harrison Band. Cook joined Southern Pacific, a country rock band that enjoyed success on the country charts in the 1980s. In 1995, Clifford and Cook found commercial success with Creedence Clearwater *Revisited*, a project that riled Fogerty into filing an injunction to prohibit the use of the name. (The injunction was overturned.) The band drew large crowds and, in 1998, released a live album, *Recollection*, which featured old CCR hits. After almost ten years of constant sales, the album was certified platinum.

Since the demise of CCR, John Fogerty has had an uneven solo career, one requiring two major comebacks after decade-long absences from the music scene. Fogerty has released ten solo albums from *Blue Ridge Rangers* in 1973 to *Wrote a Song for Everyone*, scheduled for release in the fall of 2012, on which he and guest stars perform CCR classics. Fogerty's solo work, while inconsistent in commercial and artistic success, has been, nonetheless, consistently adventurous and ambitious. He has continued to provide insights into his two favorite topics: America and himself. He celebrates both while revealing his country's inequities and hypocrisies and exposing his own frustrations and self-torment. Only late in his career does he reveal some consistent self-contentment. He has risen from a kid in a local suburban band to become a forceful American artist.

Surprisingly, Fogerty's work with and apart from CCR has not received significant scholarly attention. *Finding Fogerty: Interdisciplinary Readings of John Fogerty and Credence Clearwater Revival* begins to correct this neglect. This book stands as a tribute to one of America's great rock bands and one of the rock era's great songwriters and vocalists and one of its underrated guitarists and producers. *Finding Fogerty* pulls together scholars from various disciplines and approaches to argue for the musical and cultural contributions of Fogerty and CCR—an argument easily won.

Section One opens with "'Born on the Bayou': CCR and the Evocation of Place" by Jeff Sellars who focuses on CCR's signature song, examining its "swamp gumbo," its origins, its distinctive sound and grove, its images, its sense of history and myth, and its evocations of place, time, and memory, all of which combine to transport the listener to Fogerty's secret world. Stephen Paul Miller's "Reviving the Pre-Sixties: Creedence on a Sixties/Seventies Cusp" argues that CCR was the first major late sixties rock group to found its success upon an anxiety of influence toward sixties rock and the sixties itself. Miller states that the bayou, the central site of CCR, represents the Vietnam war, a valid cultural escape from it, and the cusp between them, a cusp that runs parallel with that between the loosely codified realities of the sixties and the increasingly codifying realities of the seventies. In "John Fogerty: Middle-

Class Poet," Jake Sudderth interprets Fogerty as a product and chronicler of middle-class America and, in "Down to the River: Narrative, Blues, and the Common Man in John Fogerty's Imagined Southern Gothic," Bob McParland investigates Fogerty and CCR's appeal to southern iconography and the southern musical tradition of rockabilly and the blues, while also examining Fogerty's evocation of an America both haunted and harmonious.

With "'Devil's on the Loose': Creedence Clearwater Revival and the Religious Imagination," Ted Trost begins Section Two with an investigation of the deep undercurrents of danger, moral questioning, and the awareness of injustice that characterize the band's entire song catalogue. These persistent concerns, "religiously" considered, suggest how the band's songs helped to articulate conflicts in American identity during a period of agonizing reappraisal. Timothy Gray, in "Flying the Flannel: An Americana Salute to Creedence Clearwater Revival," considers CCR's lasting influence on today's alt-country types by devising a top ten, actually twelve, list of CCR songs that matter, not only because they showcase the multiple influences the band accepted, but also because they speak to a flannel-clad fan's understanding of American independence. In "The 1969 Creedence Clearwater Revival Recording Contract and How It Shaped the Future of the Group and Its Members," CCR biographer Hank Bordowitz analyzes one of rock's most infamous record contracts, which led to lawsuits, internal band conflicts, and personal and professional distress for especially John Fogerty.

In "Centerfield," Section Three, Larry Pitilli focuses on Fogerty's love for Americana, his struggles with writer's block, and his creation of the Blue Ridge Rangers in "America as Patron and Muse: The Creation of the Blue Ridge Rangers," while Tom Kitts considers "The 1980s Comeback of John Fogerty" with close readings of *Centerfield* and *Eye of the Zombie*. The section closes with "Multimodal Fogerty: Scoring and Scaffolding the Music of CCR to a Vietnam War Literature Unit," in which Chris Goering and Will Sewell suggest strategies for using CCR and Fogerty to teach about the Vietnam War and literary devices such as metaphor, imagery, and narrative voice.

In the final section, "Keep on Chooglin'," Lee Cooper contextualizes the CCR leader within the rock tradition in "John Fogerty and America's Three Rock Generations." William Miller and Jeremy Walling study Fogerty's complicated relationship with the political world and the impact of politics on his music from his days with CCR to the present in "The Political Legacy of Fogerty: Forty Years of Parallel Messages." The collection ends with Nick Baxter-Moore's assessment of Fogerty as a songwriter, guitarist, and vocalist in "'Rockin' All Over the World': John Fogerty's Place in American Popular Music," a place which Fogerty himself has seemed to sabotage from time to time.

The sweep of this collection reflects Fogerty's largeness and largess. He is both rock's puritan and rock's Walt Whitman. Fogerty hails not from El Cerrito, California, but from America: the North, South, East, and West and everywhere in-between. He translates America in all its beauty, force, and contradictions, its optimism and fear, its past times, like baseball and war, and its rural vacations and poverty—just look at the covers of successive albums *Green River* and *Willy and the Poor Boys*. In inducting CCR into the Rock and Roll Hall of Fame in 1993, Bruce Springsteen referred to the "music's power and its simplicity. ... Hits filled with beauty and poetry and a sense of the darkness of events and of history, of an American tradition shot through with pride, fear, and paranoia, and they rocked hard."[7] In short, Fogerty exudes America.

Notes

1. Hank Bordowitz, *Bad Moon Rising: The Unauthorized History of Creedence Clearwater Revival* (Chicago: Chicago Review Press/A Cappella Books, 2007), 210.

2. Cameron Crowe, "John's Clearwater Credo: Proud Fogerty Post-Creedence," *Rolling Stone*, May 6, 1976, 9.

3. Alec Palao, "Pre-Creedence: The First Decade," *Creedence Clearwater Revival*, booklet accompanying box set, Fantasy Records, 2001, 23.

4. Ibid., 27.

5. Ibid., 28.

6. Jon Landau, Rev. of *Mardi Gras*, *Rolling Stone*, May 25, 1972, 63.

7. Bruce Springsteen, "On Creedence Clearwater Revival," Speech from the Rock and Roll Hall of Fame Induction Ceremony, January 1993, in *The Rock and Roll Hall of Fame: The First 25 Years*, ed. Holly George-Warren (New York: Collins, 2009), 79.

PART I

"BORN ON THE BAYOU"

~

CHAPTER ONE

"Born on the Bayou": CCR and the Evocation of Place

Jeff Sellars

It is certainly no secret that Creedence Clearwater Revival is famous for its unique rock stylings—often called "swamp rock." Possibly the quintessential song in their catalog to convey this style of music is "Born on the Bayou." The song evokes a vivid sense of place and history, and the music and lyrics are deceptively simple—but both betray an expressive profoundness. In this essay, I want to examine the way in which "Born on the Bayou" creates a vivid sense of place in the mind of the listener through an examination of lyrical and musical content and economy. Through this examination, I will attempt to draw attention to the way in which John Fogerty and CCR transport the listener through simple and profound soundscapes and lyrical imagery. I want to examine the economy of the musicianship and the approach of a simple or minimalist aesthetic. I also want to examine some of the devices and economy of Fogerty's poetics.

From the ominous drone that begins the song, to the first plucks of the richly toned, deeply echoing, twangy, slow vibrato E7 chord, we are transported from wherever we are to the back porch of CCR's swampy home—smelling the smells, hearing the sounds, seeing the sights, and, also, somehow sensing the deep back history of the bayou. It is in this imaginative evocation (through the simple fingering of a few notes) that we find the music, people, and culture of the bayou—it's the "cultural baggage [of] back-porch sounds of scrapping fiddles and percussive guitars, wheezy squeezeboxes and scratched rubboards; high nasal vocals arched over modified waltzes and simple but driving two-step dance rhythms."[1] We find this history just outside New Orleans, between Baton Rouge and the Louisiana-Texas border. … [It's the] swampy, water-laced countryside familiar from films like *The Big Easy*. It's called the bayou, and from the mid-1700s on it became a refuge for the French-speaking inhabitants of the Canadian province Acadia. The British government began uprooting them after the French loss of Canada; though the Crown tried to resettle them elsewhere, many successfully fled to New France, where they reestablished their communities and culture and became known as Cajuns.[2]

The bayou's other settlers, the French speaking black Creoles (who were descended from runaway and freed slaves), were part of this dynamic cultural mix. This mix of influences created a unique musical sound, and the Creole and Cajun culture developed along similar lines in many areas, like cuisine; in music, they crossfertilized to the point that their sounds were frequently interchangeable stylistically, with instrumentation, rhythms, and mournful vocals in idiosyncratic French staying fairly constant across the color bar. This was the case at least until the '20s and '30s, when other influences on the music's development entered the bayou via records and later radio. For Cajuns, the key new entrant was country music—the early raw hillbilly kind derived from the Anglo-Celtic folk traditions of jigs and reels and ballads, not Nashville's corporate product. For Creoles it was blues, which thrived along the Mississippi River in bustling ports and on backwoods plantations alike. Not surprisingly, these musical strains continued to cross talk, with Creoles picking up on country stylings and Cajuns adapting blues elements.[3]

All of this history and these influences are squeezed into "Born on the Bayou"—even just in the first guitar figure at the beginning of the song. John Fogerty plays his own version of the blue note, hinting at the history of that non-western scale, the sliding notes of African work songs and Irish and English folk music. The evocation is so deep that it is almost as if John Fogerty has distilled the essence of the swamp down to those few notes, even if Mr. Fogerty never lived there. The simple bluesy bending notes of that first guitar figure lays the foundation for what comes after. The band drops in and follows suit. Each member of the band is working in the tradition of the blues, a swampy blues, derived from the mud of the Deep South. This tradition found its way through the rock music that also influenced the band. Their music came from, as Doug Clifford has said, their

musical tastes growing up. We all had similar tastes. We all bought the same records. We listened to the same radio stations. Most of that was the roots of Rock 'n' Roll … the music of Fats Domino, Little Richard, a lot of the great singing groups from that era. Bo Diddley. And then the Sun Records folks … Elvis Presley, Carl Perkins. Elvis Presley was a big influence.[4]

This tradition can be found in each of the band members' playing styles. For John Fogerty, this tradition is found in his singing as well as his playing. For instance, in Fogerty's singing we hear the employment of the blues technique of rasp. We can hear clearly the tear and stress on his vocal cords—the proof is in the hearing, in this instance, and the emotional cry, or belt, and twang of his voice is nearly undeniable. The skill of twang is a common one, found in many gospel and blues singing: "*Twang* [is] heard frequently in gospel and blues singing. [It includes] in [its] physical set a tilted thyroid which stretches the vocal folds to thin them. ... *Twang* is evident in most of the blues and gospel singers' vocal deliveries."[5] The twang in Fogerty's voice is unmistakably evident in "Born on the Bayou," not least when he sings the song's title and stretches out the phrase (especially, the word "bai-u"). The heavy belt of John's voice, imploring the listener to feel along with him, is present throughout "Born on the Bayou." Belt is a special technique, seen as a development from "the 'shouting' style of ... field hollers. ... Equally, the influence of the preaching style of delivery within the gospel tradition has affected vocal performance. ... The vocal requirements of pre-amplification deliveries demand a large physical component and certain vocal qualities render the voice more audible. ... Here, elements of *belt* and *twang* may be deliberately employed to aid projection."[6] Fogerty picks up on belt quite readily in "Born on the Bayou." But John's belting style is not merely a musical technique to project (but it is that as well—for even the amplified singer needs the power of projection), but it is also a metaphorical technique for projection: the listener may now be more attentive to the voice and lyrics and the emotion that is conveyed; Fogerty's not just singing, he's preaching. With Fogerty's guitar playing, we see the common use of the sliding and bending notes of the blues scale, as well as the finger picking style of many old blues players. The finger plucking of the intro chord to "Born on the Bayou" is evidence of this inheritance, and John's use of the dominant 7th chord is also a clear reference to this blues tradition, run through the likes of Sun Records players like Sonny Burgess, Scotty Moore, and Carl Perkins. In fact, Scotty Moore's finger picking technique (which combined the use of fingers and a pick) is evident when watching John play this song live.

In Doug Clifford's drumming, we see the simple pulse of a 4/4 beat, handled with gusto and a good, solid, heavy hand. Clifford's drumming here on "Born on the Bayou" reminds one of the classic hard driving blues drumming found on numerous blues recording artists—such as Muddy Waters, Howlin' Wolf, or Elmore James—as translated through classic rock artists (for example, the drumming of D.J. Fontana or Jerry Allison). Coupled with the deep thunderous drumming is the bottom of Stu Cook's bass. The two combine for a dynamic backbeat that holds the song together and drives it onwards. Stu's bass is focused in on the root notes of the song, occasionally sliding around to hit accentuations and adding variation—even climbing up into the high scale of his instrument for effect. Added to this background is the steady rhythm of Tom Fogerty's guitar. Tom holds down the root chords—from E7 to D/D6 to A and back to E7—while John is powering through and augmenting the root playing of Tom.

The musicianship of the band is such that it always works for the song: there is no "showing off" which would distract the listener from the song itself; the skill and musicianship displayed are working towards a common musical goal. When the group is working together for a common purpose something greater than the sum of the parts arises—this is when the music transcends and grooves. This group effort provides a compelling approach to the valuation of a musical style: the transcendence that can occur when following such an approach can be emotionally affective and effective, as well as intellectually satisfying. It adds to the evocation of place: if they can provide that transcendence, it takes a person out of the norm, out of where he or she is currently, and it transports the person to a *somewhere*, a *somewhere* that the music dictates. If one wants a groove or feel, it is not the best thing to have players off on other tangents (playing for show or some other end). Even if one has the chops to play wildly technical flourishes, the discipline of restraint comes into play: the adding of gratuitous flourishes does not necessarily contribute anything to the song, the feel, the emotion, or the groove; in fact, it can be simply distracting and counter-productive to the ends of a song. In this aesthetic, the "chops" of the player should be used for the song and not the other way around. This does not mean, however, that flourishes and technique and the like are simply banished—that "going off" does not have its place. But it does mean that these things are subsumed under the aegis of "for the song." They must be working for the bigger goal, striving to help create the soundscape, or they fall short: they become mere solipsistic shouts, mere rants of ego, that fail to yield nourishing fruits. As Fogerty says, "Even though I have often recorded alone, I still feel the best music is made by musicians playing off each other."[7] CCR creates their groove in just this aforementioned way. The drums and bass are working together in concert, holding down the backbeat. Stu Cook and Doug Clifford hold to a simple aesthetic and that aesthetic gives them their unique place in rock music:

> When you talk about classic rhythm sections, you probably think about John Bonham and John Paul Jones or Jack Bruce and Ginger Baker. But Doug Clifford and Stu Cook, drummer and bass player, respectively, for Creedence

Clearwater Revival, were responsible for recording some of the most driving and potent rhythm tracks ever laid down on tape. Clifford was a very simple drummer, but had a feel that perfectly complemented the songs of John Fogerty.[8]

The no-frills attitude is reflected in Doug Clifford's comments on his history with Stu Cook:

Well, he plays bass and I play drums. ... It's ridin' a bicycle and that's what we're doing; we're out there enjoying riding that old tandem bike and keepin' it chuggin' the way it should be. ... We've been doing it for so long that, yeah, it's pretty automatic. There's something going on. Let's put it this way, I'm not worried about Stuey, and we just get the thing done.[9]

Additionally, we could certainly make a distinction between the "simple" and the "basic" or "unsophisticated"—where the "simple" is the honing of one's craft, the decidedly profound, thoughtful, and purposeful encapsulation of an artist's work, and the "basic" or "unsophisticated" is an operation of "dumbing down." We can here push against the common notions of the simple: Is simplicity necessarily to be equated with "dismissible," "undemanding," "effortless," or "unintelligent"? It is the contention here that the aforementioned notions of the "transcendence of groove" and "working for the song" make just such a case for the simple—and, as just one example, it resides in the connection between economy of playing and evocation of place. It is the simplicity of playing, of working together to make a groove, that leads to transcendence, that helps to transport one to another place. We might then let the simple do its work and confound the wise. John Fogerty also notes this sense of the simple, and its importance, along with his philosophy of beauty: "But I think beautiful is simple and elegant, like a ballad with simple harmony."[10]

And we see this economy of playing displayed beautifully in CCR's musicianship in "Born on the Bayou." Just in the first notes of the song, the twanging of the vibrato guitar makes a straightforward case for an economy of playing: again, it isn't how many notes one plays but which notes one plays. The drums drop in simply, with Doug Clifford's distinctive CCR sound: tubby, flat, crisp, tight—laying a steady beat, driving the song forward. The deepness and thickness of Stu Cook's bass guitar holds a strong anchor to the backbeat, slipping up to higher notes periodically. The wash of the guitars, counter balancing each other, each distinguishable yet complementing each other with a seemingly effortless precision. And the guitar solo: understated, harmonious and evocative, played with a restrained energy. John Fogerty's beautiful voice rises above it all: muddy, gravelly, raspy, downright dirty and determined, authentic, soulful. The combination is exciting, rousing, and suggestive. The soul of the band is on display. There is no pretending at groove here—it is there in abundance. There is no, what record producer Jerry Wexler has called, "oversouling" it.[11]

The way the songs of CCR were recorded also plays a big part of their ability to create a sense of place. There was a general consistency to their recording techniques. Engineer Russ Gary "set up his mics in a consistent manner, one that Fogerty took to immediately from the first 'Green River' session. 'He came in, I got everything miked up and listened to them play a little bit, then John came into the booth and we went through it. My approach was not to add any EQ; just bring it up and go from there.'"[12] In this way, the natural sounds of the instruments were highlighted. This natural sound is also found with Doug Clifford's drums:

> Each piece of Clifford's Camco drum kit was also miked with an SM56, though the snare required a second mic, a Sony C37 condenser. "Doug used a big Camco snare. It was a *big* wooden snare, and the rattles were so far down below that the mics could barely hear it." ... At Fogerty's request, the snare was recorded through one of Heider's echo chamber returns—from Chamber 4, Gary's favorite. "I printed the return right in with the snare," he says. "If we wanted something and we knew it was right, we'd do it." Another unique part of the CCR drum sound was Clifford's large-diameter hi-hat. "That was an 18-inch hi-hat," Gary says. "I've never recorded anyone who used cymbals that large. And if you hear Doug and Stu play with their band today, you can really tell that identifying sound between those guys." Gary placed a Sony C37A on the crash and a U87 on the ride. Another U87 was placed about six feet behind the drum kit for ambience. "When you're close-miking, everything sounds real up-front. Not only did the room mic capture ambience from the drums, it captured some of the other instruments, as well."[13]

The methods of recording reflect a general sense of letting the instruments and players do the "talking." All of this adds up to a very native sound, where the timbre and character of the music shines through and gives an unaffected air to the records. These techniques certainly added to the earthy, backwoods feel of the band's music. There was very "little EQ on Creedence recordings—or any other trickery for that matter." However, even when they did use some effects they worked towards the recall of the "old sounds" of their inherited musical tradition:

> there was one signature effect that appeared on nearly every Creedence recording. "When we first worked together, John asked, 'Can you give me some

slap-back?' I said, 'Yeah, sure.'" Gary had grown up on Elvis and Sun Records recordings, as had Fogerty. Gary achieved the CCR slap using a pair of Ampex 440 2-track machines and the studio's echo chambers. "During most mixing sessions, both 2-track machines would be running and I would delay the signal going to the chamber to get it slapping and bouncing around, and then there would be one to mix on."[14]

This simple, minimalist aesthetic is also continued, in its own way, in Fogerty's lyrical play. Fogerty's poetics are clean and effective in "Born on the Bayou": the tales of childhood, politics, and the other-worldly all work together to transport the listener and evoke a striking sense of place. This is Fogerty's swamp myth. Fogerty effectively places us somewhere through the narratival device of memory: he concocts a past that implicitly gives the listener a sense of history, of time and space. For example, Fogerty's use of the term "the man" is itself a profound transporter and effective conveyer of history. The phrase "the man" conjures up a complex history. As Howard Zinn noted, the phrase gets its start in the Populist movement of the late 1800s:

> When the Texas People's party was founded in Dallas in the summer of 1891, it was interracial, and radical. There was blunt and vigorous debate among whites and blacks. ... When someone suggested there be separate white and black Populist clubs which would "confer together," R.H. Humphrey, the white leader of the Colored Alliance, objected: "This will not do. The colored people are part of the people and they must be recognized as such." ... Blacks and whites were in different situations. The blacks were mostly field hands, hired laborers; most white Alliance people were farm owners. ... Racism was strong, and the Democratic party played on this, winning many farmers from the Populist party. When white tenants, failing in the crop-lien system, were evicted from their land and replaced by blacks, race hatred intensified. ... It was a time that illustrated the complexities of class and race conflict. ... The Populist movement also made a remarkable attempt to create a new and independent culture for the country's farmers. ... The Populists poured out books and pamphlets from their printing presses. ... Hundreds of poems and songs came out of the Populist movement, like "The Farmer Is the Man."[15]

Of course, in common parlance this phrase has come to denote an oppressor, or someone who holds authority, or, more generally, the establishment. And its use here in this song, in the '60s, paints a vivid picture, in two short words, of the general unrest of the times and of the history that led up to it. Implicit in this is a commentary on class, race, politics, government, and unease and disagreement with "the establishment" and older generations—and Fogerty's phrase of not letting "the man" do what he did because he will "get you" makes an implicit argument for the younger counterpart in the lyric to watch out for these larger powers, to keep them in check if possible, and to fight these larger powers when and where one can.

Additionally, Fogerty is tapping into a profound mystery when he utilizes the device of memory. To employ the theological evaluation of Augustine, the "power of memory is great, very great. ... It is a vast and infinite profundity. Who has plumbed its bottom?"[16] The images of various points of entry into the mind are available to us in our memories, and if these images "were not present in [our memories, we] would not know what [we were] talking about."[17] Fogerty's use of simple phrases and simple rhymes (again, reflecting the aesthetic of the band as a whole, eschewing unnecessary flourishes and distractions) puts these images in the forefront of our minds—allowing us to transport ourselves with him to his created landscape. We see this reflected in Fogerty's own words about his song:

> "Born on the Bayou" was vaguely like "Porterville," about a mythical childhood and a heat-filled time, the Fourth of July. I put it in the swamp where, of course, I had never lived. It was late as I was writing. I was trying to be a pure writer, no guitar in hand, visualizing and looking at the bare walls of my apartment. Tiny apartments have wonderful bare walls, especially when you can't afford to put anything on them. "Chasing down a hoodoo." Hoodoo is a magical, mystical, spiritual, non-defined apparition, like a ghost or a shadow, not necessarily evil, but certainly other-worldly. I was getting some of that imagery from Howlin' Wolf and Muddy Waters.[18]

Fogerty's visualizations and borrowed blues imagery create a short-hand for the audience, allowing the mood to develop within the listener. Fogerty creates a world within this song, and, much like a work of literary fiction, the song requires us to "'open up' ... to an 'outside' that it projects before itself and offers to critical appropriation by a reader. ... This opening consists in the pro-position of a world capable of being inhabited."[19] Fogerty lays a foundation of cultural history, of a memory that is accessible to the listener. This foundation allows us to project ourselves into his created world.

The mention of Howlin' Wolf and Muddy Waters is telling. While John Fogerty does not point out which songs in particular "Born on the Bayou" was "borrowing from," some songs come directly to mind—for example, and in particular, "I Ain't Superstitious." Written by Willie Dixon, the song, as performed by Howlin' Wolf in 1961, shares some similarities with "Born on the Bayou." There is a half-tempo feel to the song that is reminiscent of "Born on the Bayou"—though it is certainly not an exact matching tempo. The song also shares the lyrical content that John Fogerty mentions in passing in the above quote. Specifically, the song speaks of various superstitions and calls up notions of "hoodoo": that there are forces at work in the world that are not always seen but they are known. The song also speaks of dogs howling, which Fogerty's "hound dog barking" clearly echoes. Fogerty connects, if this song was in his mind, the ideas of the howling dog and the hoodoo—connecting the dog (and its "sixth sense") with the mysterious forces that haunt the world.

Again, Fogerty does not mention specific songs, but certain songs of Muddy Waters come directly to mind as well, and, in particular, Muddy Waters's "Got My Mojo Working" is another good candidate for consideration. The song was written by Preston Foster (made popular by Muddy Waters in 1957), and Foster's original lyrics and Muddy Waters's lyrical change-ups both echo Fogerty's lyrics. For example, Foster's lyrics talk about "hoodoo ashes" and various spells, and Waters's lyrical change-ups speak of "going down to Louisiana" to get a "mojo hand." Fogerty's reference to hoodoo and the connection with spells again highlights this "other-worldliness" that pervades these songs; Fogerty also mentions going back to the bayou, to New Orleans, with his Cajun Queen—which gives both songs a shared place.

Within this connection of the quasi-spiritual aspect of the song's lyrics, there is a relationship that can also be drawn between the idea of spiritual transcendence and a sense of place. I want to indulge a bit here and explore this philosophical-theological connection between Fogerty's lyrics and the idea of creating a place, a world. Connected to Fogerty's use of memory is his use of time. In Fogerty's use of time (for example, his simple line in "Born on the Bayou" of remembering the Fourth of July and running through backwoods), he sets up a temporal sequence that allows us to "be in the world" his lyrics create. Again, in Paul Ricoeur's words, this type of "fictive experience" is

> the temporal aspect of this virtual experience of being-in-the-world proposed by the text. It is in this respect that the literary work, escaping its own closure, "relates to...," "is directed toward ...," in short, "is about ...." Short of the reception of the text by the reader and the intersection between this fictive experience and the reader's actual experience, the world of the work constitutes ... a transcendence immanent in the text.[20]

Tangled up in this idea of transcendence is the connection between memory and time. As Augustine noted, we deal with three common notions of time: past, present, and future. But it is clear "that neither future nor past exists, and it is inexact language to speak of three times—past, present, and future."[21] The past exists as a retelling in the present of past events: "When a true narrative of the past is related, the memory produces not the actual events which have passed away but words conceived of images of them."[22] With the future, even when we forecast something that will happen, we forecast *in the present*:

> I look at the dawn. I forecast that the sun will rise. What I am looking at is present, what I am forecasting is future. It is not the sun which lies in the future (it already exists) but its rise, which has not yet arrived. Yet unless I were mentally imagining its rise, as now when I am speaking about it, I could not predict it. ... So future events do not yet exist, and if they are not yet present, they do not exist; and if they have no being, they cannot be seen at all. But they can be predicted from present events.[23]

But what are we to make of time that is created fictively? When we are in the process of creating a narrative fiction, then, might we be implicitly involved in what Augustine called extension? For Augustine, the present does not appear to have extension because it is always divided into what has happened (the past) and what will happen (the future): in itself, the present has no space.[24] However, we do measure past periods of time so that we can say that one period is twice as long as another or equal to it. ... Therefore ... we measure periods of time as they are passing, and if anyone says to me "How do you know?" I reply: I know because we do measure time and cannot measure what has no being; past and future have none. But how do we measure present time when it has no extension? It is measured when it passes, but not when it has passed, because then there will be nothing there to measure. When time is measured, where does it come from, by what route does it pass, and where does it go? It must come from the future, pass by the present, and go into the past; so it comes from what as yet does not exist, passes through that which lacks extension, and goes into that which is now non-existent.[25]

Augustine finds his answer to this mystery in the mystery of memory and of God—it is in the memory, where the past "sticks" and stays fixed in the mind: "So it is in you, my mind, that I measure periods of time"; and it is in God that we are

> gathered to follow the One, "forgetting the past" and moving not towards those future things which are transitory but to "the things which are before" me, not stretched out in distraction but extended in reach, not by being pulled apart but by concentration. . . Then shall I find stability and solidity in you, in your truth which imparts form to me. . . Let them therefore see that without the creation no time can exist, and let them cease to speak that vanity (Ps. 143: 8). Let them also be "extended" towards "those things which are before" (Phil. 3: 13), and understand that before all times you are eternal Creator of all time.[26]

For Augustine, we ultimately find our being in the grounding of God's Being. The present, which does not have extension, finds its extension, its permanence, in God. For the creation of narrative, this can have far reaching implications: when we create an imaginative world we are "extending," and when doing so we are "extending" in to something—a requirement of transcendence arises here through this imaginative extension.

Now, coming back again to Fogerty's construction and evocation of place, we can note that the mere act of creating a world opens up the possibility of transcendence and of transportation: it creates a sense of timelessness within time. By creating a sense of history, Fogerty's "swamp myth" fulfills just such a role: it is a mode of transportation, of intellectually and emotively moving the listener to a designated place. For example, Fogerty's image of a little boy standing to his daddy's knee recalls the wistful days of youth, when cares were few. Just the image of the bayou brings forth a variety of mental pictures and ideas: the wildness of the area, the freedom to be found as a young child running through backwoods, bare. The freedom of the image creates a sense of the timelessness of youth: why is it that this particular time in life seems not to have the "pushing quality" found when one is older? This time of life can also be fraught with difficulties: childhood is certainly not perfect and even as children we can experience tragedies, and Fogerty's lyrics give warning that the "golden age" of youth must make the transition to the tough realities of the world—the lyrics thus recount the boy's father warning his child about the oppression that might come. The man, as we have seen, is a loaded phrase which also brings forth the idea of danger—the freedom we so desperately cling to as children can be taken away (or simply misunderstood as ever having been ours to begin with). Coupled with this idea of freedom is Fogerty's use of the Fourth of July. Of course, it places us directly in America, with connotations of what this freedom means, with the accompanying images of fireworks, war, heroes, and more. But there is also the sense of the oppressed, of those who have not attained the promised freedom of America. There has been in the past a trend to "define America too narrowly," and this historical trend, telling the stories of "American heroes" and "American creativity" and the "American entrepreneurial spirit" has often been told through a grand narrative that excludes "the 'uprooted' from Africa, Asia, and Latin America"—as well as excluding the stories of Native Americans and various other immigrants.[27] This history is reflected, also, in the stories of our railroads, of our "freight trains." Of course, as any fans of popular music can tell us, the use of freight train imagery in classic rock and blues music is certainly not uncommon: the image conjures up notions of commerce and economics, class and societal divides, poverty, rhythm, homelessness, travelling, scenery, expansion, industrialization, relocation, displacement, extermination, and much more. The history of the railroad stretches across the continent and across cultures:

> As its tracks traversed the continent, the railroad was ushering in a new era. . . Horses and also Indians would have no place in modern America. As the railroad crossed the plains and reached toward the Pacific coast, the iron horse was bringing the frontier to an end. … As the railroad advanced to the Pacific, this mighty engine of technology was bespangling towns and cities across America, their lights glowing here and there on the horizon. Behind the "resistless" railroad were powerful corporate interests, deliberately planning the white settlement of the West and the extension of the market.[28]

Needless to say, the freight train image brings with it a vast trail of cars, extending back through the history of this country. And the freight train and its tracks run through so much of classic blues music that its importance cannot be underestimated: for instance, the railroad has connections to the transmission of blues and folk songs through logging lines and has links with barrelhouses and juke joints.[29]

This is undoubtedly just a narrow portrayal of the vast history behind these lyrics and a narrow interpretation and representation of the vivid images in "Born on the Bayou," but Fogerty's use of simple, unfettered, and very charged lyrics has a way of transporting the listener, almost with the power of suggestion—notions of America, politics, race, celebration, youth, superstition, religion, the South, and more all come crashing together in lightning-flash images: a little boy standing to his daddy's knee, the man, the Fourth of July, a hound dog barking, a Cajun Queen, a freight train, New Orleans, a hoodoo. These images move together in a mythic amalgamation, a phantasia, transcending themselves while retaining their particularity, pointing beyond themselves while being rooted in their place.

It is certainly true that "Born on the Bayou" has become an enduring rock classic. This is so for a number of reasons, not least of which is the artfulness of the playing, singing and writing. This classic-ness, this timelessness, is in part due to the unique stylings of the group, to the merits of creating a distinctive sound and groove. The creation of this timeless sound and groove lies, again in part, in the band's ability to work together, to maintain an economy of playing, to transport the listener and transcend the mere components of the particular instrumental make-up of the song. It is also, in part, due to Fogerty's ability to maintain this economy in his lyrical play. The devices of memory and time utilized in his lyrics also add special ingredients to his musical "swamp gumbo": they give the music and story a sense of history, of myth and phantasia, and help to transport the listener to Fogerty's created world; they help the listener to transcend the mere make-up of the song and enter a realm of extended time and space. CCR's enduring musical legacy attests to the worth and work of the band—and while CCR may not be to everyone's taste, they have certainly carved out a distinctiveness that few would dare deny.

Notes

1. Gene Santoro, *Dancing in Your Head: Jazz, Blues, Rock, and Beyond* (New York and Oxford: Oxford University Press, 1994), 29.

2. Ibid., 28–29.

3. Ibid., 29.

4. Gary James, "Gary James' Interview with Doug Clifford of Creedence Clearwater Revival," http://www.classicbands.com/CCRInterview.html. (April 24, 2012).

5. Allan Moore, ed. *The Cambridge Companion to Blues and Gospel Music* (Cambridge: Cambridge University Press, 2002), 106.

6. Ibid., 113.

7. John Fogerty, "John Fogerty Quotes," http://www.brainyquote.com/quotes/authors/j/john_fogerty.html. (April 24, 2012).

8. Steven Rosen, "The Popdose Interview: Doug Clifford," June 23, 2009, http://popdose.com/the-popdose-interview-doug-clifford/.

9. Ibid.

10. John Fogerty, "John Fogerty Quotes."

11. "The great Jerry Wexler—who produced both Ray and Aretha—coined a great term. . . 'oversouling.' He described it as 'the gratuitous and confected melisma' that hollows out a song and drains it of meaning. Wexler, who knew more about soul than any producer before or since, said: 'Time and again I have found that flagrantly artificial attempts at melisma are either a substitute for real fire and passion or a cover-up for not knowing the melody. . . Please, learn the song first, and then sing it from the heart'" (John Eskow, "Christina Aguilera and the Hideous Cult of Oversouling," *Huffington Post*, February 8, 2011, http://www.huffingtonpost.com/john-eskow/christina-aguilera-and-th_b_819979.html).

12. Matt Hurwitz, "Classic Tracks: Creedence Clearwater Revival 'Fortunate Son,'" *Mix Magazine: Professional Audio and Music Production*, March 1, 2009, http://mixonline.com/recording/tracking/classic-tracks-creedence-clearwater-revival-fortunate//index1.html, 2.

13. Ibid.

14. Ibid.

15. Howard Zinn, *A People's History of the United States: 1492-Present* (New York: HarperCollins Publishers, 2003), 290–92.

16. Augustine, *Confessions*, trans. Henry Chadwick (New York and Oxford: Oxford University Press, 1998), 187.

17. Ibid., 192.

18. John Fogerty, "TK's Factory: 'Born on the Bayou,'" http://www.backonstage .halmstad.net/tk/fogindex.htm. (October 31, 2011).

19. Paul Ricoeur, *Time and Narrative, Volume 2*, trans. Kathleen McLaughlin and David Pellauer (Chicago and London: University of Chicago Press, 1985), 100.

20. Ibid., 100–101.

21. Augustine, *Confessions*, 235.

22. Ibid., 234.

23. Ibid., 234–35.

24. "If it has duration, it is divisible into past and future. But the present occupies no space" (Ibid., 232).

25. Ibid., 234.

26. Ibid., 242–44.

27. Ronald Takaki, A *Different Mirror: A History of Multicultural America* (New York: Little, Brown and Company, 1993), 6–7.

28. Ibid., 101–102.

29. One such look at the history behind railroads and blues music can be found in Max Haymes, *Railroadin' Some: Railroads in the Early Blues* (Eden Prairie, MN: Gazelle Distribution, 2006).

~

CHAPTER TWO

Reviving the Pre-Sixties: Creedence on a Sixties/Seventies Cusp

Stephen Paul Miller

With its January 1969 release of *Bayou Country*, Creedence Clearwater Revival becomes the first major late sixties rock group to found its success upon an anxiety of influence toward sixties rock and the sixties itself. Others, including Bob Dylan, had already registered this anxiety, and it is not surprising that Dylan called "Proud Mary" from *Bayou Country* his favorite song of the year.[1] Dylan's acoustic and sparse late 1967 *John Wesley Harding* and the Beatles' initial 1968 plans to release a relatively unproduced proto-punk and raw version of *Let It Be* speak to a desire to move past sixties expectations of perpetual innovation and overproduction. However, this desire is obviously not the founding impulse inspiring Dylan and the Beatles. The Band's *Music from Big Pink* also predates *Bayou Country*. However, *Music from Big Pink* is not so much anxious about sixties rock as it runs parallel to it while productively incorporating it into its more traditional American musical roots.

In 1966, John Fogerty and drummer Doug Clifford were able to enlist in the reserves rather than follow the usual draft procedures, which would have most likely led them to Vietnam.[2] This facilitates a clean break from the band's many prior incarnations that date back to the late fifties, providing an interregnum between the group as the more modish and sixties sounding Golliwogs and their last incarnation as Creedence Clearwater Revival. In 1968 John Fogerty manages to fulfill his military commitment by serving in the United States Army Reserve at three Southern locations: Fort Bragg in North Carolina, Fort Knox in Kentucky, and Fort Lee in Virginia, and Clifford satisfies his obligation within the United States Coast Guard Reserve.

Although Fogerty's reserve duties are sometimes confined to weekends, they preoccupy Fogerty and present obstacles to songwriting, practicing with the band, performing, and recording.

In July of 1968 Fogerty and Clifford complete their military duties and begin to work more steadily with their El Cerrito, California, band. After Fogerty's military hiatus from Northern California counterculture, John becomes the group's primary songwriter, lead singer, and lead guitarist, wresting control of the group from his elder brother Tom. John Fogerty fully commits himself and the group to sound mining and to creatively using southern black and white origins of rock and roll.

Fogerty seemingly must, for however briefly, escape his Northern Californian roots and upbringing as well as his sixties San Francisco Bay Area home. San Francisco is, after all, often thought of as the sixties' capital. Yet El Cerrito is not San Francisco or Berkeley, but rather an unfashionable working-class suburb. Perhaps military service is in keeping with Fogerty's El Cerrito identity and acts as a catalyst for Fogerty to express resentment toward San Francisco and its rock counterculture. Tellingly, Fogerty loves baseball but is not a San Francisco Giant or, closer to East Bay El Cerrito, an Oakland Athletic but rather a New York Yankee fan.

Much more significantly, Fogerty finds his and the group's identity well outside the mid-sixties San Francisco rock scene. Either consciously or unconsciously, whether or not being in the South exposes him to southern music, Fogerty's army reserve tour in the South facilitates a convincing shift in his and the group's identity from a derivative sixties British invasion related sound to one related to southern proto-black rock and rockabilly, divorcing itself from most evocations of its true counterculture Bay Area identity. Indeed, if CCR does not claim to be a southern group their songs, particularly their hits, do.

There are many possible explanations for this development. As a child, Forgerty's mother sang him Stephen Foster songs. A familiarity with not only pre-rock music but also pre-modern American popular music may have facilitated a search for roots as a response to a contemporary sixties California music that did not appear to serve him adequately.

Creedence's first hit covers Louisiana proto-rockabilly Dale Hawkins's 1957 hit, "Susie Q," initially recorded in Shreveport, Louisiana, and incorporating the guitar lick of both future Rock and Roll and future Rockabilly Hall of Fame guitarist James Burton, whom Fogerty identifies as one of his greatest guitar playing influences. CCR's version of "Susie Q" (retitled "Suzie Q") lightly combines a Northern California mode of extended jamming with a sophisticated knowledge of the pioneering Louisiana rock recording's background linking the work of black and white musicians.

In a 1993 *Rolling Stone* interview, Fogerty points out that the Creedence version of "Susie Q" was written with the San Francisco rock audience in mind since it was designed to be played on the proto-American progressive rock station, San Francisco's KMPX. Fogerty felt that the station would play "weird things. I told the other guys that the quickest way we could get on the radio, therefore get more exposure and get this thing going was to specifically go in and record an arrangement of 'Suzie Q' that could get played on that station. It's been said that what we were doing seemed very far removed from the rest of San Francisco, but that's not quite true. 'Suzie Q' was designed to fit right in. The eight-minute opus. Feedback."³

Paradoxically, the "San Franization" of "Susie Q" calls deserved attention to the song's precursors. In 1957, "Susie Q" drew upon Howlin' Wolf's 1956 recording of "Smokestack Lightning." "Susie Q" is driven by a similarly explosive yet contained backbeat. However, "Susie Q" is a more broadly assimilatable, a "whitening" of Howlin' Wolf's rougher and more explosively expressive and powerful sound. Acknowledging Howlin' Wolf's contribution to "Suzie Q," CCR's recording emphasizes the "wildly understated" "Susie Q" backbeat that is even more prominent in "Smokestack Lightning." Presumably this is at least partially drummer Doug Clifford's contribution, who, much like John Fogerty, seems to have been aided by getting away from El Cerrito so as to be able to form a stronger alternative musical vision.

This vision bonds with early fifties black roots of rock and roll. John Fogerty often cites Howlin' Wolf as one of his most important influences. It seems to be no accident that a little more than two minutes into CCR's 1968 version of "Susie Q," it very nearly reduplicates the guitar lick starting Wolf's 1956 recording of "Smokestack Lightning," a model for the 1957 "Susie Q." Remarkably, the CCR "Suzie Q" redoes the distinctively high-pitched pings of Wolf's "Smokestack Lightning." However, CCR, unlike other versions such as the 1964 Rolling Stones and the 1965 Johnny Rivers "Susie Q" covers, reinforces and furthers the uncannily streamlined and minimal if somewhat syncopated sound and structure of the original "Susie Q."

"Suzie Q" advances on CCR's prior incarnation as the Golliwogs. As CCR's "Suzie Q" makes the beat of the song more efficient and yet more exhilarating than it had ever been before, after the group's pause for two of its members' military commitments, Creedence dynamically tightens the Golliwog's rhythm and song structure. CCR redoes its 1966 Golliwogs single "Walking on the Water" as "Walk on the Water" on its self-titled first album, *Creedence Clearwater Revival*, which includes "Suzie Q." Although about a minute and a half shorter, the Golliwogs version of "Walking on the Water" is more segmented, more ornate and less driving, and more mid-sixties in style, More than half of Creedence's "Walk on the Water" is a driving concluding instrumental. Listening in retrospect, one can hear a signature CCR dynamic drive in the song's long finish. Both Fogerty brothers are credited with writing the song, but, according to Tom, it is the elder brother's composition. Since John had already or soon would become the group's leader, comparing "Walking on the Water" and "Walk on the Water" provides an interesting window into John's input and John's remaking of the group previously led by Tom. A tight drive based upon fifties blues and rockabilly riffs becomes paramount.

The name Creedence Clearwater Revival itself bespeaks reliance upon a credible, clear, and fluent spirit. However, if a fifties' rock-and-roll spirit is to be revived, the addition of the extra *e* in the spelling of *creedence* suggests the adding of subterfuge within this true gospel. After all, CCR's breakthrough album is called *Bayou Country*, which begins with the song "Born on the Bayou." Clearly, the group was taking on a Louisiana or southern working or fictional identity that John Fogerty seems to feel fits its image. However, Fogerty also seems to feel that this is truly who they are. Tellingly, Fogerty identifies this fictive life as his reality: "I know that buried deep inside me are all these little bits and pieces of Americana. It's deep in my heart, deep in my soul. As I learned in English 101, write about what you know about."[4] Ironically what Fogerty knew was not what he experienced but what he felt deeply about the America he had assimilated.

Of course, Fogerty did not literally believe himself to be southern. However, he may have felt that his music and lyrics were derived from a certain American vision of the South. Somehow Fogerty's vision of southern culture overcomes racial strife and is able to accommodate both black and white culture. If Fogerty's southern rebirth is not entirely based in personal experience it is nonetheless, from a creative and musical perspective, sincere, genuine, and lasting. If this transformation represents a prescient post-sixties urge to escape anxieties of sixties' influence, it is nonetheless at least partially rooted in a strong sense of sixties authenticity. Further into the seventies, however, the donning of personae become much more cynical and seemingly calculated, or in any case postmodern and inauthentic. For instance, David Bowie's and Madonna's seventies and eighties, like Lady Gaga's twenty-first century professional reformulations, do not appear as authentic as those of John Fogerty and CCR.

"I made a conscious effort to stop imitating other groups. That was my philosophy in '68," said John Fogerty.[5] Fogerty felt a tremendous pressure to be heard in a purer formulation of his sound than "Suzie Q" presented. "Although the group managed to nearly crack the Top Ten with 'Susie Q' (*sic*) from the first Creedence Clearwater Revival album, the second single failed to see the sunny side of the Hot 100," Joel Selvin maintained. "He was afraid the band was going to fall off the face of the earth and he would have to go back to work at the car wash."[6]

According to John Fogerty, he needed to look into a void to write "Born on the Bayou": "I would sit there, kind of look at the blank wall in my little apartment. ... Now around this same time, because of 'Suzie Q' getting played on the underground radio station, we played the Avalon Ballroom, in San Francisco. We were onstage for a two-minute sound check. I started doing this thing with the guitar, and I started screaming into the microphone what would later become a refined melody but at that moment was just noise, and I had Doug and Stu just play along. I just wanted to hear this energy thing. Anyway, that mythical thing that I was dreaming up at night and that burst of energy on the stage at the Avalon came together. 'Born on the Bayou' is almost the Gordian knot or the key to what happened later. As I was writing it, it occurred to me that there was more power than just this one song."[7] In a sense then, as a world-class artist, Fogerty is "born on the bayou," even if it is his unique version of the bayou. He does not merely write songs about it.

Part of Fogerty's reaction to the sixties includes a desire to brand Creedence Clearwater songs with a kind of uniformity. Not only the whole of *Bayou Country*, but also their following albums needed to align with the group personae of *Bayou Country*. Whereas Paul McCartney's concept album vision of *Sgt. Pepper's Lonely Hearts Club Band* could incorporate the diverse styles of songs by other band members, Fogerty insisted on his own musical dynamics informing every song. This portends a post-sixties sense of uniform branding that increasingly grows stronger.

Part of this concern with branding, that is perhaps not always as predominant after CCR, fosters quality control. Fogerty refused to release singles with inferior B sides. Most CCR singles were double-sided hits. CCR's first two major songs coming close to the top of the charts are the single-sharing "Proud Mary" and "Born on the Bayou." Both songs reach number two on the *Billboard* charts. Indeed, Fogerty's doubling up of the releasing of hit songs might be the reason that CCR is ironically the greatest maker of singles hits of its time yet they never had a number one hit.

It is fitting that CCR's first major single, nearly topping the charts, is the double-sided "Proud Mary" and "Born on the Bayou." "Proud Mary" is in a sense the origin tale of CCR's *Bayou Country* sound. Fogerty maintains that although he was working upon "Proud Mary," "Born on the Bayou," and "Keep on Chooglin'" while serving in the Army Reserves, these songs came together when Fogerty received his release from his obligation. This is particularly true about "Proud Mary." According to Fogerty, he wrote the lines with "left a good job in the city" and "working for the man every night and day" in response to being done with the military. It is as if leaving the Reserve allowed Fogerty to reenter sixties culture in a new way. Adding this element of leaving a job to "Proud Mary" transformed it from a song about a proud woman named Mary who held menial jobs to one about an idyllic life on the river rolling on a riverboat. The subject of the song became an everyman's working-class utopia as the people who live on the river are happy to give and to help others alleviate worries. The subject of a riverboat wheel enters when Fogerty believes it describes the sound of the chorus. The song's evocation of "rollin' on the river" paraphrases something Fogerty had heard Will Rogers say in a film. "Proud Mary" presses various strains of Americana into something new, yet traditional. Although the utopic aspect of the song recalls sixties sensibilities it also bespeaks Stephen Foster's "Old Folk's at Home." The sixties become rooted in a phantasmagoria of American cultural and musical tradition.

"Proud Mary" makes possible the controlled swamp rock dynamism of "Born on the Bayou," and as the subsequent "Run Through the Jungle," which conflates nightmares and true idyllic wisdom, makes obvious, the central site of Creedence Clearwater—the bayou—represents the Vietnam war, a valid cultural escape from it, and the cusp between them. For CCR this cusp runs parallel with the cusp between the loosely codified realities of the sixties and the increasingly codifying realities of the seventies.

Notes

1. Hank Bordowitz, *Bad Moon Rising: The Unauthorized History of Creedence Clearwater Revival* (Chicago: Chicago Review Press/A Cappella Books, 2007), 58.
2. Fogerty explains, "I got drafted. And I managed to get in [the Reserves], because I had contacted them before." Ralph Gleason, "John Fogerty: The *Rolling Stone* Interview," *Rolling Stone*, February 21, 1970, 18.
3. Michael Goldberg, "Fortunate Son," *Rolling Stone*, February 4, 1993, 48.
4. Ibid.
5. Goldberg, 77.
6. Joel Selvin, liner notes to expanded reissue of *Bayou Country*, Creedence Clearwater Revival, CD, Fantasy Records, 2008.
7. Goldberg, 48.

CHAPTER THREE

~

John Fogerty:
Middle-Class Poet

Jake Sudderth

As Pearl Jam lead singer Eddie Vedder accepted the award for the Best Hard Rock Performance at the 1996 Grammy Awards, his shaking right hand, born of nicotine withdrawal, itched his right temple as he shared his initial thoughts with a puzzled expression on his face: "I don't know what this means. We just came to relax. We just wanted to watch the show. I don't know what this [award] is. I don't think this means anything." Protected by understanding bandmates and panned by critics, Vedder was misunderstood. He had trouble identifying with an award for artistic expression. Who makes art? What does it mean? More importantly, does it mean anything if nobody can identify with the artist's words, music, or imagery?[1]

Creedence Clearwater Revival was a headliner at Woodstock, an unknown fact to many owners of their albums or viewers of the concert on video. The band's artistic ringleader, John Fogerty, joined by reluctant bandmates, foiled the release of a performance he considered subpar. Notoriety, fame, and even history were not important to Fogerty, who just wanted a clean, outstanding set. Playing one big show left him as disinterested as Vedder was after music television accolades.

Growing up in El Cerrito, CA, one of five boys with divorced parents, Fogerty lived the life of the American middle. His high school was even built by the WPA. He tells fans that his music is simple and provides unassuming commentary when fielding compliments and outlining his interests. Beneath this folksy veneer is an intense man focused on craftsmanship. Fogerty's behavior personifies American pragmatism, that mythical cultural strain that runs like a spine across the nation and implies that Jefferson, de Tocqueville, and William James were describing common traits of observation, testing, and practice that American empiricists cherish.

Fogerty uses this technique when delivering advice to the doer, the person actually experiencing work through sensory perception, as if the wisdom of the practitioner trumps the theories of the intellectual. He dispenses common sense advice and connects best with fans who enjoy recalling common middle-class experiences. While he does not sound arrogant or idealistic, we know Fogerty is competitive, unyielding, and willing to challenge detractors or move legal obstacles in his path. His art is paramount and his domineering attitude ultimately undermined his band and made reunions nearly impossible. Fogerty was such a brick wall that the other two surviving members of the band, Stu Cook and Doug Clifford, formed Creedence Clearwater *Revisited* in 1995 to build from a discarded past. Fogerty lost his brother and fourth member of CCR, Tom, to a calamitous tuberculosis infection in 1990 after the HIV virus, contracted from blood transfusions for back ailments, weakened him.[2]

"But the truth is, I would write the song and then the producer in me would take over and write the arrangement and I would show everybody exactly how it went," admitted Fogerty when discussing his process during the Creedence years. "You know that if you're going to go in and record you've got to have everybody having a specific part, otherwise you have a train wreck—you're just going to have noise. So I arranged everything, quite specifically, very much in the same way that Benny Goodman did with his swing band."[3] CCR was hardly a bunch of young wild men pumping out intense music in a freeform environment. They were managed and composed by a master at combining lyrics and rhythms at an alarming rate. In just three years (1968-1970) they amassed enough hits to become rock-and-roll legends without relying on psychedelia or deep philosophy to explain their motives. Compared to Jefferson Airplane and the Merry Pranksters, CCR was downright boring. Their artistic leader, John, kept them on track.

Few artists capture the American middle like he. Morality, work ethic, human spirit, community activism, redemption, and baseball are all wrapped up in song. His powerful music fueled the protest against the Vietnam War, and his rugged brand of individualism distanced him from joining a generational album (*Woodstock*) that both the voiceless and boorish cherished.

This essay defines middle class in Weberian terms, individuals and families between the working and upper classes. John Fogerty is introduced as the poet laureate of a generation. He was never a sex symbol; he wore flannel. He admired Ricky Nelson and Carl Perkins and drew inspiration from places that others treated as cultural wastelands. Fogerty shines when including the public in verse. His personal tales incorporate common feelings and attitudes. When he describes watching a dream end in Dallas and the loss of innocence, lusty images of President Kennedy snap listeners to attention. "I Saw It on T.V." conjures up imagery of shared activities, ubiquitous symbols that freeze our brains when the screen lights up.

"Centerfield" has become so iconic that the tune and the artist were honored at the Baseball Hall of Fame in 2010. Fogerty's career began after his discharge from the service. After denigrating war, supporting soldiers, fighting lawsuits over lost fortunes, and divorcing and remarrying, Fogerty has lived a full middle-class life while presenting highs and lows to the public via music. Like John Updike's fictional Harry "Rabbit" Angstrom, a middle-class man frustrated with the sterility of the modern world, Fogerty tells stories using phraseology that the common man recognizes.[4]

Updike scholar Jack DeBellis, described Angstrom as, "the late 20th-century man who summed up, for many, what happened in the American consciousness from Eisenhower through the Clinton administrations." Fogerty provides similar insight. His frustrations in song are unsettling and romantic and like Angstrom's character, "we can sympathize and ultimately gravitate toward him."[5] Angstrom's life in and around a fictional version of Reading, Pennsylvania, Updike's hometown, an ideal setting for the cultural middle, is reminiscent of Fogerty's coming of age in El Cerrito. The town was a haven for the needy after refugees from the 1906 San Francisco earthquake established residency. The original name for the village, Rust, symbolizes Fogerty's hardscrabble philosophy. Local citizens did not recast the town to mean "little hill" until World War I.[6] Only five miles from the University of California Berkeley campus, the 3.7-square-mile community is nestled alongside Albany and Kensington to the south and Richmond annex to the east. The little knoll is only sixty-nine feet above sea level and feels nothing like the wine-and-cheese crowd in the Berkeley Hills. El Cerrito is perfectly suited for easy access to the Bay Area in a subdued, middle-class environment while exuding a separatist feel—where the real people live. Heavy metal power band Metallica even set up a studio in the city to harness the vibe.

There were five Fogerty brothers living around working-class families turning screws and chipping off rust in local factories and shipyards booming during World War II. John was the middle brother born at the twilight of the national build-up. He fondly recalls his oldest brother Jim being a great R&B fan and listening to distant acts on local radio. Elvis was king but John wanted to be Carl Perkins, "He was a real musician."[7] Second-eldest Tom was also an aspiring musician, proficient with the violin and accordion, and a jock, a halfback for the local high school until injuring his leg. John was the brooding thinker among the clan. When the Fogerty parents divorced in the 1950s, single mother Lucille struggled to raise five sons, ages spanning sixteen years. Working full time and studying for a degree that certified her to teach handicapped youngsters, she relied on musical skill and interest to motivate her boys.[8] A folk music junkie, she dragged her sons to see Pete Seeger and Ramblin' Jack Elliot concerts in Bay Area festivals. After tinkering with old guitars lying around the house John and Tom paid $5 a month to rent a cheap electric version and try something new. They were hooked.

Labeling the middle class is tricky. Politicians habitually expand the definition of the subset and many Americans revel in explaining they are from working-class backgrounds, as if such a designation indicates they have accomplished more with less. In socio-economic terms, the middle class is the broad grouping of people who fall between the working and upper classes. United States families featuring primary earners employed in a blue-collar or semi-skilled job consider themselves middle class. While this sector of the working public does not live up to the British middle-class designation, which references people that have a good education, own a family house, and hold a managerial or professional post, it is the American condition, and Fogerty bridges the gaps with his music.[9]

Wealth is the causation of middle-class definition in America, and Creedence Clearwater Revival drew upon nuances above and below the mean. In "Fortunate Son," children of the wealthy are compared to the common soldier; the backs of the least powerful, yet most productive, Americans carried the burdens of the Vietnam War. "I ain't no senator's son" is a rally cry still used as a colloquial phrase by radio DJs and by protesters at political rallies. Fogerty describes welfare lines in "Wrote a Song for Everyone," while in "Penthouse Pauper" he features a protagonist who survives with nothing to his name. The instrumental "Poor Boy Shuffle" addresses survival in the face of plenty—a wealthy nation that cannot assist her own, a unique song that one critic said reminds him of a jug band.[10] This comparison of best-selling CCR to a group of pickers using homemade instruments was perfect, leading to an inevitable message: if you want something done, you need to do it yourself. Individualism and self-determination are primary subjects for Fogerty and his middle-class identity. "Proud Mary" brings independence on the Mississippi after eschewing a standard working life in the city. Imagination and unfulfilled dreams were a large part of the Creedence repertoire. "Lookin' Out My Back Door" draws the listener into fantasy in a plebian yard. The ubiquitous American symbol for journeys to nowhere, the train, is used in several songs, "Hideaway" the most prominent. Working life, the source of middle-class pride, is a persistent theme.

"Midnight Special" chimes in at the beginning with a work bell and mentions trouble with "the man." Listeners are warned: "danger lurks for those who protest too much." Fogerty's love for a folk song (he did not write) credited to prisoners of the American South is telling.[11] In "The Working Man," Fogerty builds on this theme in his own words. He tells of working hard and earning one's own way. The chorus is haunting, a reminder of the internal clock that keeps the laboring man on a schedule. "Don't take me on Friday, lord, 'cause that's when I get paid," is just the beginning. Listeners are taken through the trials and tribulations of a work week—the very ups and downs that most of us face—and the song culminates with a request for the narrator to die on a Saturday night so he does not have to face the burdens of life again. The band also released "Door-to-Door" which outlined the highs, lows, pains, and pressures of a door-to-door sales rep—"Place your order early 'cause you know I'm in a hurry." It was timely; the song was on the CCR *Mardi Gras* album only a few years after the powerful Albert and David Maysles and Charlotte Zwerin documentary, *Salesman*, showed up in avant-garde film houses.

During an era when capitalist methods were being questioned and students were debating the impact of technology and growth while clutching essays from E.F. Schumacher, who published *Small is Beautiful: Economics as if People Mattered* the following year, CCR was one of several bands grappling with societal transitions.[12] The generational view that capitalism was reducing people to insignificant cogs in a perceived machine (hence the sad story of the traveling salesman or Harry Chapin's mythical taxi driver in his "Taxi" from 1972) did not alter the future of business. Middle-class ethos was shifting and the era initiated environmentalism, growth management policies, nuclear proliferation protests, community gardening, and a host of similar responses to economic devices that artists believed overwhelmed the power of individuals to make a difference.[13] "Your neighbor's in her doorway, won't you sign right here?" finished "Door-to-Door" and reminded the listener of the constant pressure on the sales rep and the target. Who was to blame for transactions based on compassion and sadness?

Nostalgia, longing, and trepidation about returning home also defined attachment to the American center. In "Green River," childhood remembrances include catfish, desolate river roads, barefoot girls, ropes on trees, and skipping rocks—the ultimate summertime experience. "Up Around the Bend" implies American innocence and a meeting by a tree on the side of the highway. Such songs make the entire nation feel like a nostalgic small town. In "Lodi," the author seeks fame and fortune on the road, but once the dream becomes expensive and troublesome, home looks better. In "Green River," childhood is too spectacular to forget. When asked about his inspiration for the song Fogerty opened up: "Well, that's very much a true story—other than the fact that the stream was called Putah Creek, which is up by a Northern California town called Winters. We sometimes called it 'our green river,' and there was a descendant of Buffalo Bill Cody who owned the property and the cabin my family always rented there. This was about 1949, and I'm about four years old, and this guy Cody, who looked to be about 90 years old, quite likely could have been the son of Buffalo Bill Cody. I never talked about 'Green River' much, but all that stuff is true. There was an old Cody Junior, and that creek is where I would swing from a rope, and where I learned to fish and swim and skip rocks. It's a very idyllic memory for me."[14]

CCR music sounds like a bunch of guys gathering to jam on a porch on a summer day. This child-like simplicity, combined with adult lyrics, blends bourgeois experiences. Aptly named Fantasy Records distributed the music and Tom and John Fogerty even worked for the label as shipping clerks while honing their music, the classic hard-working kids laboring in the back room lobbying for a record contract and a chance to do something special.[15] The tale sounds like something out of the movie *That Thing You Do*.

Self-preservation (via advice and introspection) in the face of pressure is another primary theme. In "Ninety-nine and a Half," another cover, Fogerty needs "someone's love." "Pagan Baby" speaks of moving past the religious set and into the West Coast groove, while seeking truth and understanding. In "Before You Accuse Me," a remake of a Bo Diddley song, he recommends self-honesty in the face of conflict. Listening is a form of therapy. And Fogerty is unmatched when describing the small and massive problems that impact the common citizenry on a daily basis. "Ramble Tamble" is synonymous with the frustrations of everyday life, the proverbial "wolf at the door" metaphor spun at coffee tables and lunch counters. Mud in the water, a roach in the cellar, bugs, garbage, encroaching highways, car payments, problems that haunt the common man and the White House is singled out for selling independence, focusing only on the famous, and taking out a mortgage on the ordinary breadwinner's life.

The impact on the rest of America is why John Fogerty's voice is so important. What the middle class prefers is coveted by those in power. Greater numbers equal greater authority in American politics and nebulous middle-class values are trumpeted as the key indicators of where the nation should be headed, and where it used to go. Fogerty blends this recipe with biting lyrics; his talent presents both viewpoints. Whether protesting, inspiring, tugging memories of old ball fields or summertime fun, his talent for painting mental pictures is extraordinary; it speaks to people of all ages. "Centerfield" drew old and young alike to bob along to the music and it is still played illegally (without royalties) at small baseball venues across America. It is the quintessential dreamy pastime song for our national game. Politics are very much about history, nostalgia and bringing the best ideas of the past to the future—and Fogerty fits well into this schema.

To establish the middle there must be a top social layer, and Fogerty makes this comparison clear. His protest anthem, "Fortunate Son," provides a poignant comparison between haves and have-nots. Middle America lived in relative wealth compared to their worldwide brethren during the height of Creedence Clearwater Revival's fame, yet he makes the middling sound powerless in the face of elected leaders. This technique is as relevant to the United States as Marxism is to socialist theory. "It has ever been my hobbyhorse to see rising in America an empire of liberty, and a prospect of two or three hundred millions of freemen, without one noble or one king among them," wrote John Adams in a 1786 letter.[16] The American condition of promoting equality through rhetoric and building from a veneer of oppression is a tradition Fogerty cribbed from blues artists like Muddy Waters, early country acts, and Woody Guthrie.

Fogerty's influence on fellow artists Bruce Springsteen and John Mellencamp is palpable. He paved the way for a working man's revival and deconstructing the name of the band illustrates this double meaning: honoring the everyman and building his self-esteem. Their famous moniker was derived from three elements, the name of a co-worker of Tom Fogerty's friend, Credence Nuball, clear water from an advertisement for Olympia Beer (which fans later related to the band's commitment to ecology), and the rebirth of the group. When dissected, the imagery is pedestrian, no detectable snobbery. Paul Newman's rugged individualist logger character, Hank Stamper, drinks Olympia Beer in *Sometimes a Great Notion*, a 1971 movie based on the 1964 novel of the same name by Ken Kesey—himself of an artistic persuasion focused on drug-induced scenes of enlightenment. CCR's connection with beer presented as the drink of an everyman character represents their common persuasion.

Fogerty's fascination with American icons began with Elvis, a quixotic, romantic dreamer, more distant than the rock-ribbed Fogerty. Although hailing from rural Mississippi, unlike CCR's Bay Area culture house, Presley always loomed above his audience, as if too mysterious and distant to touch. He was also painfully shy in his early life, famously reclusive at the end, and heavily protected in the middle by his manager. Unlike the recalcitrant Fogerty, Elvis lived in a bubble. The latter read an interview with Carl Perkins that altered his perspective, plaintively explained new theory, and propelled him with a more natural philosophy that required little thinking. "He said his goal was just to dance and sing and play the guitar. To me, that's the whole point of being a rock & roller."[17]

"I was probably pretty much a middle class white boy. Because of the music I loved, it grew into this, into the way I wanted to express myself," Fogerty told John Blackstone of CBS.[18] In "Fortunate Son," the artist disassociates himself from millionaires and senators and paints the less powerful (everybody else) as people pulled into war. His sentiments comprise a middle-class anthem, more on this later. In "Effigy," he references the "silent majority" (the term for the great majority in America championed by Nixon and Agnew) not keeping quiet anymore and a decaying empire with fire spreading to the palace door. Presenting leadership that is out of touch with the largest social grouping in the nation underscores the feelings of disconnect that have permeated America during Fogerty's lifetime. As he meanders toward social security, national debates pinpoint separation between the powerful and the rest of the country and his music is relevant again.

Working on his craft and traveling for purposes of discovery, learning on his own rather than using experts and trainers, sets Fogerty apart, connecting him with the common fan. He seems genuinely curious, never distant in a fame-encircled bubble. An interest in various regions around the nation pulled him closer to American roots. His quest for deeper understanding of musical influences and ancestors led him to the Mississippi Delta in 1990. Long before he connected with that area he formed opinions of what made the music special. "It was the first time I knew I was in Mississippi. That's kind of strange. I'd been in Tennessee a lot; I'd been in Louisiana a lot. So it was just sort of a gap in my knowledge."[19] His terminology backed up his investigation. His use of language implies an understanding of countrified American rock and blues. "When rock and roll guys become amazing players, it's almost like they're not rock and roll anymore. They become too high falutin.' Cause rock and roll folks kind of have an attitude and a sound with some dirt in it."[20] His viewpoint took shape as a fan of music. Another Elvis comparison sealed the artist's view of style versus substance, classic American pragmatism:

When I was young I was smitten by Elvis and Duane Eddy. But there came a point when I could tell the difference between their roles—Elvis on the Dorsey show was just strumming his guitar. I've had renewed respect for him in later years—he sure strummed it great, he could really mash the guitar and those old Sun Records have a great acoustic sound—but still, there came a time when I knew there were other guys who could play with a lot more technique and finesse.[21]

Attributing hard work as the key to success is Fogerty's nature. Unlike much of the world, U.S. success stories begin with work and toil instead of spiritual power or inspiration. This national condition worked perfectly for the artist. "Every night I worked on writing songs from about 9 o'clock until about 4 o'clock in the morning. I had a routine, or a discipline, that went on for about two years. All the songs weren't great. I used to say for every song you heard I'd probably written 10 that were no good."[22] This focus continued after commercial success. Fogerty exuded classic middle-class nervousness when accolades followed him. He was not born into fame. "You've got the spotlight and everyone says 'Well?' but if what you do is crap, then they go 'Right. I knew that.' and they move on, and you never get the spotlight again, ever."[23]

Fear of failure pushed him as the band received recognition. "I had kind of looked around at our situation. 'Suzie Q' was a hit, something you pray all your life for. We finally got a hit! But then you're basically a one-hit wonder, and we were the classic version: a cover song with a unique arrangement, in the spotlight. That's the classic one-hit wonder syndrome. I looked around and thought, 'God, I sure don't want that to happen to me!'"[24] The goal became the music for a while. "I determined, we're on the tiniest record label in the world, there's no money behind us, we don't have a manager, there's no publicist. We basically had none of the usual star-making machinery, so I said to myself I'm just going to have to do it with the music. I looked within my own band and wondered about our chances. What I saw was people that could make music that was basically coming from me. I don't mean that to sound full of myself; it was just an honest appraisal."[25] He also said, "And I took that seriously, really, I just didn't want to go back to the carwash."[26] His choice of professions gives Fogerty away. His aspirations were modest. If music did not work out, he harbored no back-up plans. He never went back to a working-class job because his popularity was surprisingly fertile as his music compared the middle to those at the top during draft-era USA. This is what really established Fogerty: the ability to channel the common man in struggle.

November 16, 1969, Fogerty and the rest of Creedence Clearwater Revival performed "Fortunate Son" on the *Ed Sullivan Show*. Lucky for the artists, show producers did not censure any of the lyrics or disable the meaning of the song, eschewing strong reactions to acts like the Doors and the Rolling Stones. Fogerty's short, full-bore power song blurred lines and race and appealed to citizens who supported uniforms and the American flag, but questioned the fairness of the system. It is the quintessential protest tune of late twentieth-century USA, and still grips listeners with metaphoric comparisons between the powerful and the rest of us. The same rhetoric that incites protestors to claim membership among the bottom ninety-nine percent and decry the fiscal reach of the upper one percent is evident in this song.

Fogerty was joined by Bruce Springsteen in New York's Madison Square Garden to play "Fortunate Son" in late October 2009 at the twenty-five-year anniversary Rock and Roll Hall of Fame concert. Overt power grabs that roil middle-class citizens are neatly described in one small package: forced military service, tax collections, and the ultimate perceived protection in American democracy—being the son of a powerful politician, or the son of a wealthy family. The exact nature of this relationship is spelled out in the lyric, "I ain't no senator's son." The metaphor follows its generation and was used numerous times by President George W. Bush's detractors.

When Springsteen introduced the song, he called Fogerty the "Hank Williams of our generation." This is high praise among musicians. "I became aware that in Hank's recorded songs were the archetype rules of poetic songwriting," wrote Bob Dylan in his memoirs, *Chronicle: Volume One.* "The architectural forms are like marble pillars."[27] "Fortunate Son" is an anti-establishment song of defiance and blue-collar pride, both anti-Washington and anti-war. John Fogerty and Doug Clifford entered the army reserves in 1966 and were discharged in 1967, so they had experience watching the machinery in action. The vast majority of the American people supported American intervention in Vietnam. But as the war dragged on, the number of ground troops increased precipitously and televised body bags turned support into horror. When moderates questioned leadership, the middle-class foundation cracked. On October 15, 1969, two million Americans participated in a nationwide protest known as the Moratorium and up to half a million young men defied the Selective Service draft, some of them burning their draft cards in large demonstrations.[28]

When investigative journalist Seymour Hersh broke the story of the 1968 Mỹ Lai massacre on November 12, 1969, only four days before CCR played the Sullivan show, initial skepticism followed. The news was disseminated by a small left-leaning wire (Dispatch News Service) that had few followers. "No one believed it," said Washington bureau reporter Mike Roberts, who worked for Cleveland's *Plain Dealer,* and remembered that copies of the story were slipped under office doors in the National Press Building. "Bill Ware, the [*Plain Dealer's*] executive editor, called; he wasn't sure if we should go with it."[29] His concern was assuaged when Sergeant Ron Haeberle, a local resident and former combat photographer, heard about the story and showed up at the paper with disturbing evidence related to U.S. Army's Charlie Company. The non-fortunate sons were finally challenging authority and they were not crazy left-wingers; they had served their time like Fogerty and Clifford. "A clump of bodies," read the description on the front page of the *Plain Dealer* on November 20, 1969. Black-and-white photographs of slaughtered women, children, and old men in a Vietnamese village confirmed the worst and anger grew by the day.[30] The Sullivan performance suddenly carried extra weight as moderates around the nation began questioning political remedy in Vietnam.

When asked what inspired him to write "Fortunate Son," Fogerty explained that "Julie Nixon [then-President Nixon's daughter] was hanging around with David Eisenhower [former-President Eisenhower's grandson], and you just had this feeling that none of these people were going to be involved with the war."[31] Fogerty's assumption was actually incorrect. David Eisenhower would volunteer for military service in 1970, serving a total of three years as an officer in the U.S. Naval Reserve, far more time than Fogerty himself spent in the Army Reserve.[32] However, his feelings summarized tensions among classes.

As a historian, the Creedence front man is not always accurate, but his poetic vision and ears are sharp. In true Fogerty fashion, he deflected comparisons with Hank Williams when considering his impact on other people, using self-deprecating humor while reminiscing about a series of events that culminated with him on stage with Springsteen in his trademark flannel shirt. When asked about singing "When Will I Be Loved" by the Everly Brothers with one of rock's icons he reflected, "I had done the basic tracks and had a complete list of what I thought was going to be on this album, and then my wife, Julie, suggested this song. And she said, 'I think it would be great if you record this and then sing it with Bruce Springsteen.' It's almost like saying, 'Why don't you become a lawyer and then run for president?' I looked at her with big eyes and said, 'Sure, honey, that's a great idea.'"[33]

Fogerty's ear for nostalgia is perhaps his best interaction with the middle class and his constant tinkering symbolizes what it truly means to be members of the American center. Liberty, freedom, and popular sovereignty are the pillars upon which the common man honors the nation's alleged exceptional framework. The country's mythical man-made greatness subjugates individuals and ideas, and tinkering with the past, as U.S. politicians do, acknowledges only slight changes should be made to a glorious past. He loves honoring songs that reach him emotionally. Fogerty has tipped his hat to Ricky Nelson ("Garden Party"), Buck Owens ("I Don't Care"), John Denver ("Back Home Again") and "Paradise," the John Prine classic that Fogerty originally heard Denver perform. He even convinced former Eagles stars Don Henley and Timothy B. Schmit to provide harmonies when recording "Garden Party."

Fogerty and members of Creedence even briefly reunited and jammed at their 1983 high school reunion, like something out of a movie.

Childhood memories are always with the middle-class muse; they haunt him in a positive way. When asked what he remembered about encountering an instant classic in his youth, emotion flowed: "I was riding in my brother Tom's car—I was still too young to drive—and the Everly Brothers' 'When Will I Be Loved' came on the radio. It was one of those times where we just looked at each other with that thing in our eyes—a great big smile."[34] The moment had serious ramifications. Actor Tim Meadows likes to tell interviewers that he was serious about playing the saxophone professionally until he listened to a Charlie Parker album given to him by his father. He then turned off the stereo and put his saxophone back in its case; the dream was over. Most of us have similar reactions when confronted with mind-boggling talent, but Fogerty took the challenge. "It was one of those moments as a human being when you either wave a hand across your face, like swatting a fly, 'Nah,' or you receive it as a gauntlet being thrown down: 'I'd better get busy,' which is what I did. So I've been quite serious about my own daily improvement ever since."[35]

Baseball, the American institution by which people as different as Norman Mailer and George Will can unite, was also honored by Fogerty with "Centerfield." The tune captured the attention of fans of all ages in 1985. His inspiration for the work was identifiable by every red-blooded sports-crazed youngster in the U.S. "The first book I can remember reading was called *Lou Gehrig: Boy of the Sand Lots*. I think I was in the third grade. I actually have a copy of it now, although it isn't the one that I checked out of my school library. I got it in my mind when I was going to make *Centerfield* that it was a comeback of sorts and decided, well, what is really important to you? I have always felt my whole life that springtime and spring training is the most hopeful time. It's almost a metaphor for life. Everything is brand new, you're going to start all over. Everybody is in first place on Opening Day. So I tried to get that sense of hopefulness, almost like a motivational speaker."[36]

Self-produced albums was one way Fogerty managed his own sound. He saw the technique as a way to compete. With their folksy groves and heavy chords, CCR's albums sound laid-back and carefree. The opposite is true: they are carefully orchestrated and pieced together in methodical fashion. Fogerty wrote nearly every note that was played, and in many cases played most of those notes himself, alternately playing guitar (acoustic and electric), Dobro, saxophone, harmonica, and vocals. "The guys [rest of the band] used to say 'it seems like John was born with an eight-track machine in his head.'" To explain, Fogerty harked back to "Who'll Stop the Rain." "I wrote that on my electric guitar, but not plugged in so it sounded very acoustical. Remember, I'm a guy in a little two-room apartment and you can't be rocking out because your neighbors would let you know about it. So I would be doing that late at night and it would have a very acoustical sound, so I could imagine an acoustical sound for the song. And you just start imagining what will work."[37]

After Creedence disbanded, Fogerty continued with his self-made man syndrome and refused to honor his contract with Fantasy and produce at least eight more albums. The impasse was resolved only when Asylum Records' David Geffen bought Fogerty's contract for $1,000,000. He released *The Blue Ridge Rangers* in 1973—which yielded the Top-40 hit "Jambalaya"—and Fogerty delivered his first official solo album two years later, *John Fogerty*. Shortly thereafter, a series of protracted lawsuits developed with Fogerty battling Fantasy, former CCR accountants, and even his one-time bandmates.

Fogerty detached from the mainstream and moved to a farm in Oregon in 1976, an action that would make egalitarian Jefferson proud. He ceased making commercial music until *Centerfield* in January, 1985. That big hit was followed by *Eye of the Zombie*, which received only a lukewarm response. Another long hiatus followed as Fogerty returned to his artistic hiding zone. He admits to destroying unreleased material because he believes songs have a way of haunting [you] in the future. Finally, Fogerty released the Grammy winning *Blue Moon Swamp* in 1997 and was inducted into the Songwriters Hall of Fame. He even started playing Creedence songs in concert. Then Fogerty's militant façade of defiance regressed in 2005 when he re-established ties with Fantasy Records after 30-something years of estrangement, subsequently releasing the CD, *The Long Road Home* and a companion DVD, *The Long Road Home—In Concert*. A change in ownership initiated the move. The twist was that Fogerty arranged the meeting—he had grown up. A once angry middle-class boy matured and acknowledged the mechanics of contracts and commerce. After the Concord Music Group, partly owned by legendary TV producer Norman Lear, bought Fantasy, they restored his rights to royalties, signed away decades before to escape the label.

The animus between Fogerty and former Fantasy owner Saul Zaentz was a public soap opera centered on two respected visionaries seeking total control. Neither man would accept such an assessment because they each felt personally attacked. Zaentz started working in sales at Fantasy, the largest independent jazz label for years, in 1955.[38] In 1967 he and partners purchased the label from Max and Sol Weiss. The firm signed CCR and controlled distribution and publishing rights for the group. Perhaps constant pain and conflict helps Fogerty build a poet's notebook and bridge different generations with words. The twenty-five-song disc that announced his new collaboration with

Fantasy combined CCR hits with Fogerty solo material. Like a beacon from the late 1960s, the anti-Iraq war song "Deja Vu (All Over Again)" relived memories of the great protest years. Lyrics like "They told me, 'Don't go walkin' slow 'cause devil's on the loose,'" made "Run Through the Jungle" mysterious and haunting. "Another Momma's crying, she's lost her precious child to a war that has no end" made "Déjà vu" just as haunting. Comparing conflict in Iraq to war in Vietnam was powerful symbolism.

In 2005, Fogerty re-signed with Fantasy, which was under new ownership. "There's no way to overstate how cool this is," said the artist at the announcement. Middle-class aversion to lawyers and restraints on independence is part of the American social fabric and sometimes enjoyment is easier the second time around. "It's turned out to be, for me, a very, very happy, wonderful time in my life and career," reflected the artist. "Even a year ago I could not have envisioned this."[39] Then Fogerty described how his artistic process was undermined, deconstructing the long pauses in his career. "Every time I'd get into a songwriting groove by playing something I'd just do naturally, a little gremlin would pop up on my shoulder, and, looking very much like a lawyer, would go, 'No, no, no. You can't sound like that or I'm going to sue you.' Inevitably, that would piss me off, and whatever inspiration I had would just wither and die."[40] His good feelings did not initially extend to Doug Clifford and Stu Cook, CCR's other surviving members, whom Fogerty himself sued for performing as Creedence Clearwater Revisited. He compared them to a rattlesnake. "They bit me very badly in the same way that the old folks at Fantasy did. That hasn't changed, so I will continue to give them a very wide berth."[41]

November 2007 saw the debut of *Revival*—a collection of songs that included "Creedence Song." "I was working on a song for the new album one day—just sitting there doing my swampy thing on guitar—and the idea of calling it 'Creedence Song' suddenly came to me. I started to have a very warm feeling about my early days, and I was getting into this cool groove, and, this time, when the gremlin popped up like it always did and started saying to me, 'Creedence song? You can't say that or I'm going to sue you.' I just shouted out, 'Go away! I don't want you here anymore. Get out of my life.' And for the first time it just went *poof*, and was gone. My soul was healed from all the garbage I'd been through, and it was sort of like I was 23 again, and none of the bad stuff had happened."[42]

"I always thought that people that love rock and roll aren't necessarily stupid," reminisced Fogerty one time. "You know, if you can write a really good song and add as icing good lyrics, then it would be even better, as long as you didn't sacrifice the ethic of rock and roll in the first place."[43] The grand poet of post-World War II American abundance, good times, and protest understands that artistic thought comes from the heart and promotes the power of individuals, the ideal symptom for what Tom Wolfe called the Me generation. Without the middle-class connection, Fogerty is not a major American poet. He needs those at the top to defy and those in the middle to champion a cause. During a 2007 concert he announced he wrote "Who'll Stop the Rain" after Woodstock. The tune references five-year plans and new deals "wrapped in golden chains," programs designed to solve intricate problems while basic concerns, like rain, seem insolvable. In the face of such limited impact, people are the most important resource.

"He [Rabbit] tries to picture how it will end, with an empty baseball field, a dark factory and then over a brook in a dirt road, he doesn't know. He pictures a huge vacant field of cinders as his heart goes hollow."[44] In Rabbit Run, Rabbit Angerstrom is not sure how a crumbling America is going to rebound in the future. Evoking a field of play and the American pastime, a game for a patient man, makes him reconsider his frenetic pace.

Fogerty may not be more positive than he was over forty years ago as age has kept his poetry hard while softening his demeanor. Like Eddie Vedder he still might not know what artistic awards mean, but his travels introduce him to numerous fields of play and watching other people share good times makes his music more understandable. His songs evoke dreams and explain the potholes along the way—the very sinew of the middle class.

Notes

1. The 38th Annual Grammy Awards, Shrine Auditorium, Los Angeles, California, February 28, 1996, http://www.youtube.com/watch?v=AHEYs0CMe4U.

2. Phil Davies, "Tom Fogerty," in This Is My Story, 1993, http://www.rockabilly.nl/references/messages/tom_fogerty.htm (June 18, 2012).

3. Daniel J. Levitin, "Blue Moon Rising: The John Fogerty Interview," Audio Magazine, January 1998, 6.

4. Updike's Rabbit Series, which began with Rabbit, Run in 1962, was the author's response to Kerouac's On the Road, which he felt did not depict how people get hurt when someone with responsibilities just leaves. The series covered four books and a novella.

5. Bruce R. Posten, "Will the real Harry Angstrom please stand up?" readingeagle.com, February 1, 2009, http://readingeagle.com/article.aspx?id=123669.

6. David L. Durham, California's Geographic Names: A Gazetteer of Historic and Modern Names of the State (Sanger, California: Quill Driver Books, 1998), 628.

7. Davies.

8. Ibid.

9. "Middle class," used as a phrase or term, appears in literature for the first time in the 1911 United Kingdom Register—General's *Report* (published in 1913), in which statistician T.H.C. Stevenson identified the middle class as that falling between the upper class and the working class. Also see Reinhard Bendix, *Max Weber: An Intellectual Portrait* (Berkeley, California: University of California Press, 1977).

10. Stephen Thomas Erlewine, "Willy and the Poor Boys Review," in *Allmusic*, November 1, 2004, http://www.allmusic.com/album/willy-and-the-poor-boys-mw0000193432.

11. John Avery Lomax and Alan Lomax, *American Ballads and Folk Songs* (Mineola, New York: Courier and Dover Publications, 1994), 71.

12. E.F. Schumacher, *Small is Beautiful: Economics as if People Mattered* (London: Blond and Briggs, 1973).

13. For an outline of this process and transition, see Adam Rome, *The Bulldozer in the Countryside: Suburban Sprawl and the Rise of American Environmentalism* (New York: Cambridge University Press, 2001).

14. Art Thompson, "John Fogerty Summons his Creedence-Era Spirit on Revival," *Guitar Player*, February 2008, 9.

15. Craig Werner, "John Fogerty," *Goldmine*, July 18, 1997, http://riverising.tripod.com/john-interviews/GoldmineFirst.html. John Hollowell references this story as well in *Inside Creedence* (New York: Bantam Books, 1971).

16. Adrienne Koch, ed., *The American Enlightenment: The Shaping of the American Experiment and a Free Society*, Letter from John Adams to Count Sarsfield, February 3, 1786 (New York: George Braziller, Inc., 1965), 191.

17. Cameron Crowe, "John's Clearwater Credo: Proud Fogerty Post-Creedence," *Rolling Stone*, May 6, 1976, 14.

18. Sean Alfano, interview by John Blackstone, "John Fogerty's Musical Revival," on *Sunday Morning*, February 11, 2009, CBS TV.

19. Werner.

20. Ibid.

21. Levitin, 2.

22. Joshua Klein, "John Fogerty," *Pitchfork*, November 27, 2007, http://pitchfork.com/features/interviews/6737-john-fogerty/.

23. Alfano.

24. Klein.

25. Ibid.

26. Alfano.

27. Bob Dylan, *Chronicles, Volume One* (New York: Simon and Schuster, 2004), 96; and Alan Light, "Stars Add New Tunes to Country King's Lyrics," *New York Times*, September 23, 2011, http://www.nytimes.com/2011/09/25/arts/music/bob-dylan-assembles-the-lost-notebooks-of-hank-williams.html?pagewanted=all.

28. Mark Atwood Lawrence, *The Vietnam War: A Concise International History* (New York: Oxford University Press, 2010), 142.

29. Evelyn Theiss, "My Lai photographer Ron Haeberle exposed a Vietnam massacre 40 years ago today in *The Plain Dealer*," cleveland.com, November 20, 2009, http://www.cleveland.com/living/index.ssf/2009/11/plain_dealer_published_first_i .html.

30. Ibid.

31. "Fortunate Son Meaning," *shmoop*, http://www.shmoop.com/fortunate-son/ meaning.html (June 25, 2012).

32. Ibid.

33. Jeffrey Pepper Rodgers, *Acoustic Guitar* Magazine, John Fogerty Interview, January 2010, 2.

34. Ibid.

35. Ibid, 3.

36. Sean Daly, "Interview: John Fogerty on dissing Canseco, rocking Tropicana Field and picking that totally badass Louisville Slugger guitar," *Tampa Bay Times*, April 22, 2010, http://www.tampabay.com/blogs/poplife/content/interview-john -fogerty-dissing-canseco-rocking-tropicana-field-and-picking-totally-badass-lo.

37. Levitin, 6.

38. "Zaentz Heads Fantasy Sales," *Billboard*, March 12, 1955, 26.

39. David Bauder, "Fogerty is back with Fantasy."*Associated Press*, October 24, 2005, http://news.google.com/newspapers?nid=1298&dat=20051028&id=ZzEzAAA AIBAJ&sjid=1AgGAAAAIBAJ&pg=6699,8381401.

40. Art Thompson, "John Fogerty Summons his Creedence-Era Spirit on Revival," *Guitar Player* Magazine, February, 2008, 2. Fogerty addressed the same subject matter first with Mark Brown, "Q&A with John Fogerty,"*Rocky Mountain News*, September 29, 2007, http://m.rockymountainnews.com/news/2007/Sep/29/qa-with -john-fogerty/.

41. Bauder.

42. Thompson, 3.

43. Levitin, 12.

44. John Updike, *Rabbit, Run* (New York: Alfred A. Knopf, 1960), 324.

~

CHAPTER FOUR

Down to the River: Narrative, Blues, and the Common Man in John Fogerty's Imagined Southern Gothic

Robert McParland

The public life of John Fogerty began with an E7 chord. It produced a sultry sound born of the Delta blues. A four-man band from El Cerrito, California, lost in a sound check at the Avalon Ballroom, began to play what John Fogerty later called "the riff and attitude of 'Born on the Bayou' without the words."[1] Upon this foundation, John Fogerty set out to "conjure a Cajun swamp" and began inventing the simple and direct southern rhythm and blues/rockabilly sound of Creedence Clearwater Revival's gold albums: *Bayou Country*, *Green River*, *Willy and the Poor Boys*, and *Cosmo's Factory*. This essay will investigate John Fogerty and Creedence Clearwater Revival's appeal to southern iconography and the southern musical tradition of rockabilly and the blues and to what Barry Walters in *Rolling Stone* called Fogerty's "imagined Southern Gothic strengths." I am interested here in Fogerty's narrative voice and his musical voice and how these draw upon Delta blues singers. In this essay, I will look at how John Fogerty "blended anxious soul rhythms with loose country twang to embody a haunted but harmonious America."[2]

The key words here are "haunted" and "harmonious." CCR represents a generation's coming of age amid the high hopes of Woodstock and the shadows of Vietnam and racial tensions. From the first CCR album, John Fogerty's personal imagery connected with broader American cultural interpretations. In "Proud Mary," says Mark Kemp, Fogerty "characterized working class southerners of an undetermined race as compassionate people. The song suggested, however, that to understand this compassion, one had to visit the South and interact with its people."[3] This imagined South was harmonious, a community sometimes down on its luck but a community all the same. More than this, the community represented here was America, for there could be no binary distinction between this imagined South and Creedence's American audience. Fogerty was the common man, identifying with these working people, singing, as Kemp observes, "with the exaggerated vowels and slurred consonants of shouting southern bluesmen."[4]

"Born on the Bayou" began *Bayou Country*, the band's second studio album. Set in swampy rockabilly chords, the lyric mentions the Fourth of July, with a hound dog chasing an apparition. From images in "Proud Mary" of working people who are pleased to give of themselves to his covers of Leadbelly's "Cotton Fields" and "Midnight Special" on *Willy and the Poor Boys*, John Fogerty brought his listeners into a world of roots rock, jangling guitars, repetitive phrases, the rhythm guitar of his brother Tom, and the steady rhythm section of Doug Clifford (drums) and Stu Cook (bass). He told us that down on the bayou are rollicking good times, but there is also the "Bad Moon Rising." Creedence was very aware of the Vietnam conflict and the violence in America during their most commercially successful years, 1969-1971. Fogerty asked, "Who'll Stop the Rain?" and raised the question of what would become of the not so "Fortunate Son" and the shadows of Vietnam. Implicit in the question of the first title is the belief that someone, a nation's legislators in Washington, perhaps—needed to take action. Couched in the second was a critique of class privilege, in which the fortunate are spared military combat, while the unfortunate are drafted and sent overseas.

Green River seems to typify the movement from pastoral beauty to nightmare. The desire is expressed to return to cool water, a longing that opens the album with the title track. E chords open rockabilly, leaning on D, with bass, drum, and tambourine pushing the rhythm forward. We hear the vocal break in: "Well…" The images of shallow water, sounds of the bullfrog, and the moonlight's rays upon a girl dancing barefoot fill the opening verse. The lead guitar runs down the notes within an octave: EDBAE. The guitars brightly answer each other in repeating riffs. An infectious rhythm cuts into double-time on "Commotion." By the third song, we are hearing about tombstones and shadows. These shadows, landing on the path before the singer, or falling on his back, seem to be haunting the singer. Whenever there seems to be good news, something brings disenchantment. We are now in a blues pattern, with a gypsy man, a bending of strings, guitars humming together like an angry swarm of bees. The rhythm section is steady.

After a pause, the tempo slows a bit. A solo guitar begins and is joined by bass and drums. "Wrote a Song for Everyone" sounds a lament. The singer says he has encountered himself coming and going. He writes songs for everyone in a world in which communication has broken down. Following a very tasteful guitar lead, we hear that people are imprisoned and nothing has changed across time. The "pharaohs" and spin doctors avoid the truth. The song seeks universality and truth but the dislocation seems profound.

The lyrics turn grimmer, despite Fogerty's bright up-tempo music. The spirited romp of "Bad Moon Rising" carries a dark, apocalyptic lyric. The music lifts one, but the warning from the narrator is more terrifying than anything Barry McGuire could sing about in "The Eve of Destruction." One might imagine people dancing on their way to disaster. You can tap your foot to this one, like the dance band on the *Titanic*.

Then follows "Lodi," a song in which Lester Bangs distinctly hears disenchantment. The hope of the quest for fortune dissolves into disillusion. The song opens in the signature of B flat. One is deflated in Lodi, where ambition and dream have met immobility. Bangs writes of "that drab mood Fogerty conjured up so well in 'Lodi' which is a point at which ... the pointlessness of it all renders the musician utterly tired, surly, and above it all to the once unthinkable point of actually hating music itself of just about any kind."[5] All that is constant is the return to that last repeating line. The scene becomes a place of singing for drunks—the kind that perpetually asks a performing musician for his cover of "Stairway to Heaven" or "Sweet Home Alabama." He would escape, if he could, but he is stuck. The music nearly gets stuck too: for on the bridge it surprisingly slows down. As if momentarily bewildered but still persisting, it modulates to C.

In "Cross-Tie Walker" rockabilly chugs and churns like the freight train referred to in the lyric. A descending bass line adds an additional hook. A propulsive shuffle begins the song as the speaker goes down to the station. On the second verse the bass starts doing its catchy descending pattern. The music breaks into rockabilly guitar and then returns to the verse. Following the bass, the guitar returns to its arpeggio break. After this jubilant energy, the dissonant opening riff of "Sinister Purpose" brings us back to something more ominous. We hear that the sky has gone gray and that the moon is now "hate." The guitar lead's pull of notes edge out into a background feedback on the instrumental bridge, concluding with the bass and guitar riff.

The album's final song, a cover of Ray Charles's "The Night Time Is the Right Time," begins in a soulful blues E7. The song is structured in a call and answer form in which Fogerty's strong vocal is echoed by background vocals. The guitar kicks into a Chuck Berry-like grinding lead—playing several strings at once on the high strings, with tremolo on the end of the phrases. With this song we seem to have come way down river to visit the old bluesmen. "But his green river is alive with the noise of all the drowned souls it carries," wrote Rob Sheffield.[6] The big wheel that turned on the Mississippi carries Gothic images like those in Twain's *Huckleberry Finn*, ones of families in conflict or a raft capsized, and more recent images of the ghosts of Hurricane Katrina.

Fogerty's river may parallel Twain's famed river in several ways. Twain writes in *Life on the Mississippi* of two different ways of viewing the Mississippi River. The first is with a boyish awe, one of enchanted rapture or naïve poetic wonder at the beauty of the river. The young spirit is moved to delight by shimmering water, mysterious currents, and vivid sunsets. Then, as he grows older, wishing to become a riverboat captain, he is drawn toward a serious study of the river. His perspective changes: the river is seen with a cold, hard, and knowing gaze for all of its potential menace. The encounter seems to parallel that of some young artists with the music business. The young artist gigs with youthful wonder and enthusiasm and the more seasoned professional is aware of potential perils and the need for businesslike realism. It is all too easy for a big machine to crash into a musician's hopes of industry success—just as the paddle boat in *Huckleberry Finn* collided into Huck and Jim's fragile raft and their dreams of freedom. Fogerty suggested the perils of the American dream in the late 1960s. The America of his imagined South and beyond was never beyond redemption. It was filled with energy and humanity. Like Twain, Fogerty celebrated the imagery of the Mississippi Delta. However, both suggested America's shadows. A vision of the Greening of America held a hope.[7] Beside the green river a girl could dance barefoot in the moonlight. Yet, amid the shadows, the green river had its bends and its depths.

The big wheel of fortune turned around on Fogerty. Despite their stunning string of gold record singles and albums, Creedence became, in Woodstock memory, the invisible band of Woodstock history. This cultural amnesia was occasioned by the lack of documentary footage of the band's performance. CCR played at 3 a.m. at Woodstock, after a long jam set by the Grateful Dead. John Fogerty was less than thrilled with the performance and refused any reproduction of it on record or film. Later, Greil Marcus criticized San Francisco radio station KSFX for the omission of CCR in the documentary *The Rock Years: Portrait of an Era*. CCR, he said, "was perhaps omitted because of the influence of Howlin' Wolf, a certified black person, on lead singer John Fogerty's vocal style."[8] Meanwhile, people on the river were happy to give ... but Fantasy Records wanted to take and take some more away from Fogerty and the band. For years, Fogerty's own music was submerged because of lawsuits. (Is "Travelin' Band" a version of "Good Golly Miss Molly"? What if David Geffen hadn't made a deal for Fogerty with

Fantasy Records?) The career of Creedence Clearwater Revival and of John Fogerty, much like the southern Gothic, reflects that inversion of home that spills into what Freud called the *unheimlich* or the *uncanny*.[9] Creedence's own career portrays the journey from dreams of the garden and pastoral beauty to an America that remains a nation of the common man and woman trying to work things out. John Fogerty is representative of this tenacity and this hope.

In 1969, Creedence Clearwater Revival became an extraordinary singles machine. In Pete Fornatale's book *Back to the Garden*, Jerry Garcia, Bob Weir, and Leslie West all comment on this.[10] Fornatale points out that Creedence singles could be turned over: "Green River" and "Commotion," "Down on the Corner" and "Fortunate Son," "Travelin' Band" and "Who'll Stop the Rain." Side one and side two, in several cases, both became hits on radio airplay. In the top ten were also "Proud Mary," "Bad Moon Rising," and "Lookin' Out My Back Door." The high-spirited sound that was so successful commercially owes much to where country meets rock and roll in rockabilly. We may hear in it echoes of the guitar-based riff and tremolo sounds of Duane Eddy. All of this was complemented well by Stu Cook on bass and Doug Clifford on drums. We hear reworked rockabilly sounds in "Born on the Bayou." Fogerty gives us guitar chord driven songs, a distinctive sound, and fluent, clever lyrics.

Creedence seems to represent a point in time. In 1969, they were immensely successful. In 1971, Tom Fogerty left the band. Creedence ended in October 1972. In a cultural sense, they represent a time when the vivid hope of an American generation that gave rise to dreams of getting back to the garden was also plagued by violence and civil unrest. Much like this, the bucolic allure of the South, dreams of an antebellum culture that was "gone with the wind," gave way to stark realities. Indeed, Fogerty's own southern myth was plagued by carpetbaggers who essentially stole his songs and delayed his own "reconstruction" for several decades. Yet, his songs are enduring. The sound of Creedence Clearwater Revival and subsequent Fogerty songs remains very much alive. One reason for this is that John Fogerty, like a risen phoenix, has remained consistent. He is a consistent craftsman of the popular song.

To Creedence Clearwater Revival, John Fogerty brought a consistent narrative persona. On *Green River*, the brightness of chord driven rockabilly meets some dark, even apocalyptic shadows. We are reminded that Fogerty's CCR songs might be situated where folk poetry meets the blues. The southern Delta landscape is evoked and with this come the ghosts of blues history.

The first blues were sung in fields and their lyrics were a call to a communal understanding. In them was an invitation to a message, a code, or a bit of news about the situation that the community was living in. Fogerty's songs for Creedence were an analogue to the times, 1968–70, in which they were written and performed. The very question of whether the rain could be stopped described both Woodstock and the war in Vietnam. Fogerty took his audience outdoors to a mythic relationship with America. There were generous people on the river in "Proud Mary." One feels the sense of a multiracial people, working people, and one can almost feel the heat of the Delta. There is no time for memories that would downcast a man in worry. The engine, the flow of the ever-moving river and the music just keeps rolling on. If played in C, the verse lingers on the tonic, holding surely within that C chord for many measures before moving to a G major chord and down to the F chord before hitting the chorus back on the C. Then we hear that distinctive break—Bb-G-Bb-G-Bb-G-F—before we get back to that driving C. (Of course, one could move this all up a step to D, where the same progression applies.)

Rhythms propel "Proud Mary," like a turning wheel in motion pushing an engine. Lingering behind the chords are high grass, mosquitoes, and hot sun. As in many of Fogerty's songs, this one plays upon the hypnotic effects of a simple structure: a series of chiming chords, driving rhythms. In these songs we hear from a narrator who was "Born on the Bayou." We are transported somewhere down near the devil's crossroads to edges of vivid narratives of voodoo, bayous, and soulful endurance. Lurking behind Creedence's catchy songs seems to be those haunted travelers: Howlin' Wolf, Sonny Boy Williamson, Robert Johnson.

John Fogerty recognizes in "Proud Mary" that people who live along the river are often hospitable. Yet, in other songs, he recognizes the dark shadows along the river. Merrill Skaggs once suggested that southern hospitality may be the direct result of the isolation in which many southerners lived. Rural life separated people. They looked forward to occasions where they could spend time with other people in groups—gossiping, inventing narratives, and telling stories. Perhaps Fogerty's invention of a bluesy southern Delta and his energetic concerts are a similar antidote.

With CCR, Fogerty conjured a mythic South. While he was not born on the bayou, the narrative voices in many of his songs certainly were. Fogerty appears to have captured in his songs several features of the South that Wilbur Cash identified in his important study *The Mind of the South*. The South has often been positioned as a mythic land apart, or as Cash phrased it, "another land," one with "a remarkable homogeneity."[11] Yet, in *Green River*, John Fogerty and Creedence Clearwater Revival seem to be embracing all of a diverse America. What is "calling" to the narrator of the song "Green

River" is a dream, a hope of something better that is offset by a sometimes threatening landscape that includes "Commotion," "Tombstone Shadow," and a "Bad Moon Rising." In Fogerty's lyrics, America and this imagined South are not poles of a binary but are mutually linked. The discourse of the South as an internal other requires a broader look at national identity. Fogerty's imagined bayous are not so much an "internal other" as they are linked to American culture.

John Fogerty was part of a generation that sought hope, a nostalgia for freedom and to "get back to the garden." His songs on *Green River* and elsewhere act as metaphor: we see in them the gypsy man, the man down and out on the welfare line, the one who has sought a pot of gold and gotten mired in Lodi, losing connection. He writes not of another place, but of this place: America. One might suggest that in the 1960s' generation lay a romanticism that reflected traits that W.J. Cash observed in the South, which had gone, he said, "from the present toward the past"; it expressed "an intense individualism," and had a tendency toward romanticism.[12] Cash, meanwhile asserted that "violence ... has always been a part of the pattern of the South."[13] Such romanticism and violence appears to have been in the air of 1960s America. The bad moon on the rise lifted its sickly glow on the horizon of political assassinations, Vietnam, and civil unrest. The South, with its racial tensions, its homespun goodness, its high moral Biblical codes exemplified the broader internal conflict of America. John Fogerty, in 1968-71, wrote within a resonant metaphor. Within his own medium of rock music, he was not unlike America's finest Southern writers—William Faulkner, Eudora Welty, Thomas Wolfe, Robert Penn Warren, Flannery O'Connor among them— who each recognized Gothic elements, the inversions of the sublime, in a southern tradition that imagines an antebellum world of honor, beauty, and wholeness. The historian C. Vann Woodward called this myth of explaining this decline and nostalgia for the old South "a legend of incalculable potentialities."[14] The myth made the world more romantic, more sentimental.

John Fogerty, in his CCR period, tended to drop the sentimentality for realism. He was a spokesman for the cultural hopes and fears of a generation. His songs of this period weave social critique with story and offer a blend of romance with realism. They act as a metaphor for America at this time. Music with vigorous ebullience might bring on imaginative and spirited lyrics like "Lookin' Out My Back Door." However, other songs are possessed with intimations of darkness. One may "Run Through the Jungle" of an America of hand guns and urban blight. Fantasy may spring from the secure back doorway of one's home (or the poetic doorway of one's subconscious mind). In the comic and eccentric mode, the dreams of these songs are like tambourines and elephants on the lawn. In the tragic mode, they are the shadows and tombstones deep under the pulse of *Green River*.

The hit songs that John Fogerty produced with CCR are familiar, like a steady river within radio airplay. We need to pull them out from time to time and listen to them as if for the first time. Fogerty's songs merit our attention not only because they are popular but also because they say much about what it means to be human. The CCR-Fogerty song is not poetry. It is completely tied to oral tradition and to music. The song is meant to be heard, felt, performed, and moved to. In it, rhythm, words, chords, and melody are all fused. Indeed, it is a fuse, like that of a firecracker—once lit it burns for three minutes of fiery energy, bang, and goes out. Darkness may lurk behind some of these songs but often enough sorrow is cancelled out by a groove. Musically, we are talking about something catchier than the common cold. Fogerty uses simple and very effective combinations of chords, often I-IV-V, and this works well. Rhythm is present in the narrative, where he uses plain words and focuses on common people, much like Wordsworth once did.

What is essential about CCR is something more than their "tunefulness," or their place in that vast digital archive that people carry around on their MP3 players. Their rhythms and sound, this guitar-chord driven thing, is the voice of the common man and woman. Fogerty's special genius is linked to all of us. He is a meeting place for America: rock, folk, roots country, and blues. One expects no less from John Fogerty than a clear and steady gaze, a confident voice, jeans and a plaid shirt, and no pretense, only dedication. Behind his songs are an inner voice and a drive to find the form to put that voice into.

Notes

1. Austin Scaggs, Born on the Bayou: Creedence Clearwater Revival, 1969," in "100 Greatest Guitar Songs," *Rolling Stone*, June 12, 2008, 57 .

2. Barry Walters, "*Bayou Country* Reissued," *Rolling Stone*, October 2, 2008, http://www.rollingstone.com/music/albumreviews/bayou-country-reissue-20081002?print=true.

3. Mark Kemp, *Dixie Lullaby: A Story of Music, Race, and Beginnings in a New South* (New York: Free Press, 2004), 91.

4. Ibid.

5. Lester Bangs, "from Untitled Notes, 1981," *Psychotic Reactors and Carburetor Dung* (New York: Alfred A. Knopf, 1988), 375.

6. Rob Sheffield, "Creedence Clearwater Revival: 'Green River,'" *Rolling Stone*, May 11, 2000, http://www.rollingstone.com/allaccess.

7. Charles Reich, *The Greening of America* (New York: Bantam, 1971), argued that the youth generation was engaged in a transformation of consciousness.

8. Greil Marcus, *Ranters and Crowd Pleasers* (New York: Doubleday, 1993), 202.

9. Sigmund Freud, *The Uncanny*, trans. David McClintock (London and New York: Penguin Modern Classics, 2003).

10. Pete Fornatale, *Back to the Garden: The Story of Woodstock and How It Changed a Generation* (New York: Simon and Schuster, 2009), 158–59.

11. Wilbur J. Cash, *The Mind of the South* (New York: Alfred A. Knopf, 1940), 11.

12. Ibid., 14, 44, 57.

13. Ibid, 412.

14. C. Vann Woodward, *Origins of the New South* (Baton Rouge: Louisiana State University Press, 1931), 152–53.

PART II

"RUN THROUGH THE JUNGLE"

CHAPTER FIVE

~

"Devil's on the Loose": Creedence Clearwater Revival and the Religious Imagination

Theodore Louis Trost

Religion is not the first subject that comes to mind in connection with the songs John Fogerty wrote during his tenure as leader of Creedence Clearwater Revival. Granted, the band's name conjures up numerous associations with American-style religiosity of a particularly southern variety. Still, it would be a stretch to suggest that a song like "Hey Tonight," for example, is especially revelatory in a recognizably "religious" sense—even if it does declare at one point that Jody, the song's protagonist, is "gonna get religion" throughout the night. Still, in a rather profound way that this chapter examines, the songs of Creedence Clearwater Revival do make use of a characteristically American religious rhetoric. I am particularly interested in how a basically unobtrusive religious appeal or appeal to religion manifests itself in the context of 1960s rock-and-roll music and how certain CCR songs build upon this inheritance. In what follows, I will consider, first, the contested divide between church and state in America and speculation about the "end of religion"; second, the persistence of religious rhetoric in the public sphere, particularly in the recorded music featured on the radio; third, the ways a particular American myth or narrative pattern is reproduced in American song during the 1960s; and finally, the place of CCR in the context of these themes. While CCR is often revered for saving AM radio with their breezy hits, I want to insist that deep undercurrents of danger, moral questioning, and an awareness of injustice characterize the band's entire song catalogue. These persistent concerns, "religiously" considered, suggest how the band's songs helped to articulate conflicts in American identity during a period of agonizing reappraisal.[1]

The Divide between Sacred and
Secular in American Culture

Tensions between "sacred" and "secular," between "church" and "state," have always existed in American culture. There is a conflict, perhaps even a contradiction at the heart of the nation's myth of origin and this conflict in various permutations has been passed on from one generation of Americans to the next. The Puritans left England to pursue freedom from the established religion; upon reaching these shores, they established a society strictly regulated by religious dogma. Dissent was not tolerated. The minister Roger Williams was banished from the Massachusetts Bay Colony in 1646 for challenging the Puritan orthodoxy that regulated civic life. Among other things, Williams called for freedom of religion and argued that a "wall of separation" should divide the "garden of Christ" from the "wilderness of the world"; in other words, the precepts of the established church should not regulate relationships among the people.[2] Williams subsequently established a settlement he called "Providence" on land purchased from leaders of the Narragansett tribe. Other dissenters soon joined him in the colony that became Rhode Island.

During periods of cultural crisis, the story of America's origin is often recast for modern times. And so *The Scarlet Letter* (1850), by Nathaniel Hawthorne, explores the themes of sin, guilt, and freedom in the tumultuous period leading up to the Civil War through the lens of the colonial era. During the McCarthy Era, Arthur Miller represented the charged atmosphere generated by the House Committee on Un-American Activities with resort to the Salem witch trials in his play *The Crucible* (1952). Even the Eagles, in the aftermath of the 1960s, returned to Providence ("the one in Rhode Island") to inaugurate their own epic exploration of American identity in the song "The Last Resort" (*Hotel California*, 1976).

The concern for religious freedom as articulated by Roger Williams was codified in the United States Constitution's First Amendment, which states in part: "Congress shall make no law respecting an establishment of religion, or prohibiting the free exercise thereof." The first clause prevents the national government from advancing the cause of one religious group over another; the second clause denies the government the power to prevent citizens from practicing the religion of their choice. Freedom from, and freedom of, religion were unique rights for Americans in the eighteenth century. The nations of Europe continued to operate on the principle *cuius regio, eius religio*: "whose realm, his religion." This principle was arrived upon at the end of the bloody Thirty Years War in the "Treaty of Westphalia" (1648).[3] It meant that citizens were required to practice the religion that the ruler of the region followed. When regimes changed through war or by the religious conversion of the emperor, so did the religion of the realm. Frequently, this led dissenters (or "heretics") as well as practitioners of the formerly established religion to emigrate from hostile environments to friendlier territory. Many of these religious refugees found their way to America.

In part because the success of the American experiment with regard to religious freedom was repeated in Europe during the modern era, members of the intelligentsia began to speculate about the end of religion's hold on the citizenry. In a famous address delivered near the beginning of the twentieth century, German sociologist Max Weber advanced his "secularization thesis": as societies come of age, according to Weber, they become less religious. Therefore, in a progressive society, religion is relegated to the private realm and enlightened reason alone shapes the discourse in the public sphere. Weber referred to this process as the "disenchantment of the world." The German word for disenchantment, *Entzauberung*, suggests the elimination of magical elements from the social mix: breaking the spell of dogmatic, irrational, or fantastic forces; to put it in Fogerty terminology: chasing down—indeed, chasing out—some hoodoo.[4]

For those seeking evidence of disenchantment, one confirmation of the thesis might be presidential candidate John F. Kennedy's remarks before a group of evangelical ministers in Houston, Texas, in September 1960. In that speech, Kennedy affirmed his belief in an America "in which the separation of church and state is absolute" and no politician takes marching orders from a church council or pope.[5] The implications of this separation played out significantly during Kennedy's tenure in office. And so in the case of *Abington Township, Pennsylvania v. Schempp* (1963), the Supreme Court ruled that Bible reading in public schools fundamentally violated the State's position of neutrality in matters of religion. While some heralded this decision as necessary to preserve freedom from religion, others argued that the decision would result in a "naked public square," that is, a public square stripped of religious speech, one in which a "religion of secularism" (to use words that found their way into the *Schempp* decision) would prevail as the only permitted mode of public discourse.[6]

Religious Rhetoric as a Means of Addressing Cultural Divide

But if language of a doctrinal nature was prohibited by government fiat from being promoted in the public schools, religious rhetoric was still very much in evidence in the public square. The same year the *Schempp* decision was handed down, Martin Luther King, Jr., delivered his "I Have a Dream" speech on government property, before a crowd of 250,000 people, from the steps of the Lincoln Memorial. King's rhetorical technique included quotations from the Bible and lyrics from a religious song, an "old Negro spiritual," to punctuate the conclusion of his address: "Free at last, Free at last; thank God Almighty, we are free at last."[7] Meanwhile, the images of clergy members and religious persons of many faiths marching for civil rights and later to protest the Vietnam war during the turbulent 1960s suggest that religion did not disappear from the public sphere as quickly as some had feared—or as quickly as some others had hoped.

The persistence of religion in American culture, especially as it manifests itself in a particular religious rhetoric, led sociologist Robert Bellah to describe the contours of a curiously American "civil religion." "Behind the civil religion," Bellah observed in 1967,

> at every point lie Biblical archetypes: Exodus, Chosen People, Promised Land, New Jerusalem, Sacrificial Death and Rebirth. But it is also genuinely American and genuinely new. … It is concerned that America be a society as perfectly in accord with the will of God as men can make it, and a light to the nations.[8]

For Bellah, then, American citizens resort to archetypal narratives derived from the Bible in order to construct and comprehend their own culture. In so doing they make an appeal to the will of God, or they call upon God to bless their common work, or they suggest that their actions are the result of prayerful consultation with God.[9] But while God can be called upon conveniently to recommend values that Americans historically have affirmed and continue to share, the importance of the symbol does not lie in a particular belief about who God is, theologically conceived; rather, "God" matters to American civil religion as the symbol for what Americans as a people aspire to be or to become. And this moral objective can be appealed to whether or not one is a "theist."

Thus, during the year of the *Schempp* decision, Bob Dylan's song "With God on Our Side" (*The Times They Are A-Changin'*, 1963) was spinning on turntables across America. The song levels a sustained critique at America's long history of war victories by interrogating the notion that the nation is the recipient of divine favor. Was God on the side of Judas when he betrayed Jesus Christ with a kiss? Dylan asks. Will God intervene on "our" behalf to prevent the next war? Also that same year Dylan's "Blowin' in the Wind" was a nation-wide hit for Peter, Paul, and Mary. It is the model of a kind of song that casts confounding questions into the ether, as it were, like a prayer, a lament, or a "psalm of disorientation" with its suggestions of abandonment and displacement. How many roads? How many deaths? In effect: "How long, oh Lord?"[10] One observes through the construct of "civil religion," then, that religious rhetoric was not banished from the public sphere with the *Schempp* decision. Down in the groove and on the radio—a particularly accessible kind of public space—religion figured prominently during the 1960s and was deployed by partisans on different sides of the social and political divide.

Consider two songs from 1965 that bear the imprint of Dylan's influence. "Eve of Destruction," written by P. F. Sloan, was recorded by former New Christie Minstrels' singer Barry McGuire. The song reached #1 on the *Billboard* charts in September 1965 and stood at #29 for the year.[11] In direct response, "Dawn of Correction," was written by John Medora, David White, and Roy Gilmore, and performed by the Spokesmen; it rose as high as #36 during the summer of 1965. Both songs have in common an appeal to apocalyptic language. Whereas Barry McGuire locates his meditation on the "eve" of apocalypse—as if his song might prophesy or else forestall cataclysm—the Spokesmen suggest that cataclysm has been avoided or superseded and a new age is underway. To put it differently, "Eve of Destruction" takes as its point of reference (by analogy) the penultimate chapters of the Book of Revelation where rage and ruin are about to be unleashed upon the wayward world. "Dawn of Correction," in contrast, looks to Revelation's final chapter and implies a connection between the post-catastrophe New Jerusalem and the freedom-loving civilizations of the western world.

The protagonist in "Eve of Destruction" is caught in a web of contradictions, most of them imposed from outside. He can't vote, but he can kill; war is not part of his personal belief system yet he is an arms-bearer. These contradictions carry over into society at large: the hate that presumably typifies the West's great enemy, Red China, is alive and festering in Selma, Alabama, where, in 1965, protestors were beaten as they endeavored to cross the Edmund Pettus Bridge on "Bloody Sunday." But even this distancing of hatred to some obscure locale in the American South is insufficient as critique. In the final stanza, the Biblical commandment to "love thy neighbor as thyself" is ironically undercut: hatred for the next door neighbor festers at the same time members of the pious household pause to say grace around the dinner table. The resulting critique of American civilization has the sound and feel of a prophetic condemnation.

"Dawn of Correction" does not quite attain to the same high level of religious zeal as "Eve of Destruction." It does paint a picture of western civilization pursuing a contest for world domination, a contest the Spokesmen suggest the West must win. Victory is possible precisely because the threat of atomic annihilation ensures an alternative to mutual destruction, thereby engendering a need for negotiation. Meanwhile, the protests for civil rights are recast not as violent skirmishes, but as evidence that America is an open and free society. In contrast to Barry McGuire's list of negatives, the "Dawn of Correction" partisans point to the worldwide increase in free and independent governments, the work of the Peace Corps, and the constructive efforts of the United Nations as signs of a new and hopeful era.

I mention these two songs because they suggest conflicts and conversations alive in the culture when Creedence Clearwater Revival appeared on the scene in 1968. They represent two poles—both easily accessible on the AM radio band—of a contested conversation about the nature and destiny of America.

While Barry McGuire's take on the cultural situation proved more successful (commercially speaking) in 1965, "Eve of Destruction" was nothing like the last word on the politicized state of affairs in the nation. Within a year, the #1 song in the United States would be an anthem written in support of the Vietnam War effort. Composed by a guitar-toting Staff Sergeant in the Army's Special Forces unit, Barry Sadler's "The Ballad of the Green Beret" praises the role of those heavenly soldiers who descend from the sky on silver wings to help liberate the oppressed masses in foreign lands. The ballad concludes with a young widow receiving the news of her sacrificed Green Beret's fate. He has left her one final request: to offer up their son to military service and, by implication, the war effort. It is not difficult to read into this narrative an apotheosis of the fallen warrior who will undergo resurrection through the redeeming work of his beloved, or perhaps "fortunate," son.

The Myth of America

So far, we have considered the peculiar role that religion has played in certain aspects of American culture. Founded on the principle of separation of church and state, there has been nevertheless a persistent "religious" undertone to American public discourse. Even as Bible reading and prayer were expelled from the public schools of America, biblical language and prayerful tunes persisted on the public airwaves in songs that evoked, addressed, and critiqued contemporary crises and conundrums. I want to suggest now that this recourse to religious rhetoric in song relies upon a certain mythical structure to display its meaning.

R. W. B. Lewis elaborates the kind of myth I have in mind in his book *The American Adam* (1955).[12] Lewis positions at the heart of American literary culture a heroic figure, an innocent, an Adam or Eve in a New World Eden whose story is significantly the story of "the American," or American culture, with its many possibilities and pitfalls. We have already caught a glimpse of this sort of heroic figure in the closing stanza of the "Ballad of the Green Beret." Ready-made for a sequel, a fatherless child is commissioned to undertake the dead man's world-redeeming business. What happens next depends upon the "world view" of the artist involved and her or his "party affiliation." Lewis identifies these as the parties of hope, memory, and irony. Each offers a different narrative trajectory as contribution to an ongoing cultural debate, a debate that, for Lewis, constitutes the culture itself. The importance of Lewis at this juncture is two-fold. First with reference to what has already been said, an underlying religious affiliation animates this heroic figure and the elements that structure her or his story. Second, many of the songs created by CCR are illuminated in relation to this dynamic scheme.

The first of Lewis's interlocutors in the great American cultural debate is represented by the party of hope. The orientation of the hopeful is always toward the future—a future so bright, as suggested by the band Timbuk 3, one would be inclined to wear eye protection ("The Future's So Bright, I Gotta Wear Shades," 1986). There are many representatives of the party of hope in the annals of rock and roll, but the prototype may be Chuck Berry's "Johnny B. Goode" (1958). In 2 minutes and 40 seconds, Johnny is propelled from log cabin poverty in the backwater swamps of Louisiana to fortune and fame on Broadway or some similarly lit-up locale, all on account of his natural ability to play guitar. Johnny is untainted by evil; indeed, his very name is a declaration of his essential goodness. Johnny, as Adam, emerges from the primordial forest to conquer the world beyond—as it were—the gates of Eden.[13]

In contrast to the party of hope, the party of memory is suspicious of the present orientation. A course correction is needed. The way forward should be the way back. To reclaim traditional values is the only way out of the current chaos. This call is sounded in Marvin Gaye's "Mercy Mercy Me (The Ecology)" (1971). Things are not the way they are intended to be. The planet is hurtling toward destruction through pollution, overpopulation, and radiation. The beneficent wind that would escort the hopeful into the future has, for the party of memory, turned poisonous. The Eden that once was has come undone. Marvin Gaye ends his critique of contemporary circumstances with an intimation of a solution. The song concludes with the repeated refrain "My sweet Lord." The title of a George Harrison song from the previous year, these three words may also represent a call for divine intervention.

The broad range of appeal in the party of memory is suggested by another song roughly contemporary to "Mercy Mercy Me." Merle Haggard's "Okie from Muskogee" (1969) depicts a social system in decline, at least from a certain point of view. Marijuana and LSD are consumed in abundance. Gender confusion has caused some men, notably hippies out in San Francisco, to eschew grooming norms and adopt the characteristically feminine practice of wearing long hair. Meanwhile, war resisters burn their draft cards on Main Street and the college campus has become a center for protest and unrest. In contrast to all this decadence, Haggard offers a symbol of rectitude. "Old Glory" still flies proudly over the courthouse in Muskogee, Oklahoma, USA. The values that prevail there are the ones that should provide guidance to the nation through troubled times, or so the song suggests.[14]

Lewis introduces a third party into the debate of American culture. In accord with the party of hope, the party of irony endeavors to move into the future. But in contrast, the party of irony encounters a barrier to progress. This barrier is not, as with the party of memory, so insurmountable that a retreat into the past is the only possible response to it. Nor is this barrier simply the result of the wickedness of others: the perpetrators of environmental destruction in "Mercy Mercy Me," or the ill-behaved youth who come from places other than Muskogee in Haggard's tune. No, for the party of irony a radical confrontation with one's own ways is the necessary prerequisite for progress. The barrier that prevents free movement into the desired future is a problem to be worked through. It has many names including pride, arrogance, and often sin. In rock and roll, the songs of this party tend toward the epic—and, therefore, are more suited for the FM radio band (at least as it was configured in the 1960s and early 1970s). Both Bob Dylan's "With God on Our Side" and the Eagles' "The Last Resort" would fall into this category of national epic.

Among CCR's contemporaries, the song "Monster/Suicide/America" (*Monster*, 1969) by Steppenwolf serves as a particularly pertinent illustration of the party of irony's perspective. "Monster" begins with a rehearsal of the nation's myth of origin. Refugees and victims of religious persecution leave behind the past and come to a new land in search of hope and freedom. Although these settlers prosper in their Edenic environment, they also torture some members of the community and enslave others. Westward expansion connects the Atlantic and Pacific oceans, but it also results in the slaughter of the native peoples. In the midst of these activities, a spirit of America is born and provides guiding light to the people of the nation. Despite wars and various injustices, this spirit remains kind for a time. But eventually "the people" lose sight of the spirit; "she" turns into a monster and this monster turns against the people. Cities become jungles; crime is perpetrated in the name of law and order; and a war of incalculable cost is waged "over there"— that is, in Vietnam. The song draws to a close with a plea or prayer directed to "America": in order to care for the sons and daughters of the nation, in order to secure a common future, the monster that lurks within must be confronted and defeated. The nature of the plea is reminiscent of the Bible's psalms of lament; meanwhile, the casting of the coda in a gospel-like chorus adds urgency and religious weight to the song's message.

A final example, also from the year 1969, shows the complex interplay of voices that constitute the party of irony. Recorded that year by Crosby, Stills, Nash, and Young, Joni Mitchell's song "Woodstock" starts out on the hopeful road to the future, to Yasgur's farm. The song's narrator encounters a "child of God" en route establishing the religious quality of this pilgrimage. It becomes clear, through the conversation that occurs between the sojourners, that a variety of problems hinder their enjoyment of the world as it is. These include air pollution, dehumanization, and a sense of lost identity. At this point, the song seems to reproduce critiques that would be characteristic of the party of memory—particularly when the chorus calls for a venture backwards, a return to "the garden." The third stanza celebrates the festival of song that Woodstock represents and dreams of a new world in which warplanes are transfigured into butterflies. While this image suggests again the party of hope, the final refrain introduces a serpent into the metaphorical garden with a line about being caught in a bargain with the devil. What this devilry means is left tantalizingly open. Perhaps, theologically speaking, the reference is to some ancient fall, or to a Job-like fate that befalls even the good. Or it could be that despite dreams of metamorphosis, there remains this stubborn truth: the "child of God" is a "cog" in a larger war machine that sends planes into Southeast Asian skies with bombs to drop on people of another nation. Whatever the case may be, recourse to religious rhetoric is made to intimate the dimensions of the problem.

CCR and the Contest of American Culture

Which brings us to Creedence Clearwater Revival and the music they made mostly between 1968 and 1970. John Fogerty's songs evoke an atmosphere that is at once magical, bedeviled, nostalgic, and apocalyptic. Myths of origin build upon vaguely biblical imagery to create a curiously conflicted consciousness characteristic of the era during which the songs were produced. The songs offer, at times, a counter to Weber's expectation of cultural disenchantment. They access the rhetoric of American "civil religion" as described by Bellah. And they incorporate ongoing tensions within American culture while contributing to and reconstructing the American myth. This may be their enduring value.

CCR's Songs of Enchantment

Let us consider the Creedence catalogue in relation to five inter-related themes. The first of these is enchantment or the power of imagination. In contrast to sociologist Max Weber's notion of *Entzauberung*, these songs evoke the magical—often drawing upon African-American traditions to do so. Screamin' Jay Hawkins's "I Put a Spell on You," from the first CCR album (1968), is a song of this sort. It stands in a long tradition of songs that invoke spell-binding powers, mojo, gris-gris, hoodoo, and fortune-telling such as Muddy Water's "Hootchie Cootchie Man" or Lieber and Stroller's "Love Potion Number 9." In this particular song, the protagonist boasts that his access to potent words enables him to exercise control over his lover. The social location of the blues singer is pertinent in this regard. The recourse to magic is pursued when one's power in the public sphere is otherwise constrained.[15] While this is may seem a stretch in relation to "I Put a Spell on You," thematically speaking, many of Fogerty's protagonists are located among the least powerful in society. The "magic" musician, Willy, for example, is associated explicitly with the "Poor" Boys who perform songs for random pennies and nickels in "Down on the Corner" (1969).

In "Lookin' Out My Back Door" (1970), the imagination offers a realm of escape or safety as a series of benign apparitions dance on the back lawn. This magical vision arises in contrast to the world against which the front door is barricaded. Reference to "trouble" and "Illinois" may suggest the unrest that occurred during the 1968 Democratic convention in Chicago—an unrest that continues to disturb a sorrow-filled world. But in the sanctuary of the imagination, the bothersome tomorrow is forestalled in a celebration of song. Another magical place is conjured up in "Proud Mary" (1969). Down by the river social distinctions wash away. Even the impoverished, those with "no money," are provided for there. The river upon which "Proud Mary" rolls is a site of transportation. As the paddle wheel turns, the riverboat queen provides shelter between two shores. The river itself, meanwhile, is a symbol of mythical proportions. It is linked to the ancient-most rivers of poetic recollection as conjured up by Langston Hughes, for instance. The river also offers the possibility of rebirth, of "revival" (to use a word significantly associated with John Fogerty and company) that the ritual of baptism presumes to provide.[16]

The Myth of Origin

While the river may suggest to the imagination a place of rebirth, it is also depicted as a birthplace in certain CCR tunes. A second thematic concern contained within the Creedence catalogue is the myth of origin. With reference to the foregoing discussion of R. W. B. Lewis, we see in "Born on the Bayou" (1969) a recollection of Eden-like innocence. The song's protagonist remembers unclothed meanderings among the trees (which may be the same terrain traversed by Johnny B. Goode) in pursuit of hoodoo magic. The pride associated with being born on the bayou is linked to the birth of the nation through a reference to the July 4th holiday. Although national identity provides occasion for celebration, there is also a larger world beyond the bayou that is not entirely kind. This is simply alluded to as a father advises his son to avoid "The Man," whose abuse has caused the father harm.[17] The theme persists into another song of water-born origin, "Green River" (1970). As "home," Green River is a place of consolation and fond memory. In the song's retreat to nostalgic imagination, and perhaps also in actual physical retreat, Green River becomes a safe haven from a "smoldering" world that threatens to overwhelm folks who seek adventure beyond the confines of the familiar.

The "real world," so to speak, is arranged against the American Adam who longs for Eden. No one is born into equality in this post-lapsarian world: some folks are born into privileged circumstances; others are left out. "Fortunate Son" (1969) displays a series of inequities beyond the individual innocent's control. Perhaps the most glaring injustice among these is the State's power to send certain sons off to war. As if that disruption was not enough, the demand for "more" is advanced. And so, the unfortunate son is duty-bound to risk his own life in order to keep others in places of privilege: senators, millionaires, the military elite. Implied among the song's ironic juxtapositions is a prophetic critique of American society during the Vietnam era. Here Fogerty approaches what Robert Bellah called "the central tradition of the American civil religion … the subordination of the nation to ethical principles that transcend it in terms of which it should be judged."[18] For a nation born on the fourth of July, the perpetuation of inequality, the inhibition of liberty, and the sacrifice of happiness, are the secular equivalents of "sin"—or so the song "Fortunate Son" might intimate.

Death Songs

Behind the power to make war abroad and to send unfortunate sons there lurks the malevolent force of death. A third group of songs exposes a deep undercurrent of fear and foreboding in the face of death. This theme may reflect a general sense of helplessness, of being caught between Woodstock and Vietnam, as it were. These songs do not address directly the weekly death count as relayed with grim detachment during the era on the

Huntley-Brinkley Report. And yet those sad reports play on like static in the background of these songs.

"Tombstone Shadow" (1969) relates the tale of a man obsessed with his own death. Good news cannot penetrate the dark shadow that stretches before him, so he ventures to the world of enchantment in an effort to forestall the inevitable. The protagonist engages a gypsy fortune teller in San Bernardino to disclose his fate; only bad news beckons, cryptically wrapped in sayings that involve the number thirteen. "Graveyard Train" (1969) also details an obsession with death. Late one night, in retreat from a lover's quarrel, "Rosie" collides with a bus at the crossroads. She and the passengers from the bus are all killed. Her lover, riddled with guilt, mourns the loss of all who died. He devotes particular grief to Rosie; their argument on that fateful night may have set the whole tragedy into motion. As a consequence, he cannot escape the sense that he is implicated in the deaths of 30 people. So he goes down to the railroad tracks to wait for the "graveyard train" that will take away his life and add one more to the death count: 31, the inverse of 13.

A third song of this sort plays upon another inversion. "Walk on the Water" (1968) evokes a scene from the Gospel according to Matthew (14: 25-33). Jesus, strolling to the other side of the Sea of Galilee, calls out to Peter by name with an invitation to join him. Peter exits the boat and manages a few steps before he begins to sink, at which point Jesus saves him. "Walk on the Water" invokes a similar scenario but in this case the protagonist, after hearing his own name called, is consumed by fear. Instead of joyfully embracing the call to come forth, he races from the riverside and resolves never to leave his home again. Instead of being comforted or encouraged by a familiar vision, only the horror remains.

Hymns

The Book of Psalms is a repository of prayers, laments, cries for mercy, and unanswered questions. Set to music, these lyrics become hymns, which, for lack of a more precise term, is what I would call this fourth category of CCR songs. These hymns interrogate the personal and the prevailing cultural malaise in a meditational mode: they are wonder-filled and desperate. Generally speaking, they do not offer answers. But in the articulation of a question, they at least expose festering wounds to the open air.

"Have You Ever Seen the Rain?" (1970) presents a confused world in which the sun is cold and the rain, hard. This may suggest Bob Dylan's expectation that "a hard rain is gonna fall"—an allusion to atomic warfare in the Cold War era. Fogerty's song is too brief to advance a full-blown apocalyptic vision but it does enunciate uneasiness. A hostile rain might be inferred in relation to another hymn, "Who'll Stop the Rain" (1970). In this song, rain creates a confused environment that inhibits good folk from finding the sun. One could press the homophone to a religious conclusion by insisting this sun quest is also a quest for the "Son," but there is insufficient substantiating evidence in the text to do so. A more resonant homophony might suggest itself as an oppressive "reign." Thus, in the second verse, the protagonist observes a fabled tower rise—a symbol of hierarchy and inevitable doom recalling ancient Babel. He then critiques certain massive government initiatives of both capitalist and communist nations as seductively enslaving: the Five Year Plan and the New Deal are both exercises in controlling the lives of the unfortunate. Powerless to resolve these matters, the protagonist casts his wondering weakness into the prayer-like refrain, "Who'll stop the rain?"

The strategy of question-posing is pursued further in the song "Don't Look Now" (1969)—which is structured along the lines of Bob Dylan's "Blowin' in the Wind." The first and second lines of each verse pose questions concerning society's dependence upon those who labor: the miner, the field hand, the peddler, for example. The third line in each verse raises the matter of dependence to another plane, asking metaphysical questions about the structure of nature, the destiny of unkept promises, or the power of faith. Who, for example, will execute the maneuver Jesus recommends in Mark's Gospel and "say to this mountain, 'May you be lifted up and thrown into the sea'" (Mark 11: 23)? The intervening chorus recalls those who have interceded on behalf of others, as if to say: someone else has starved and prayed on your behalf.

One more example of prayer in the public square appears in "Wrote a Song for Everyone" (1969). The protagonist is, by now, familiar among the cast of CCR characters. He is one of the powerless folk who are acted upon by larger societal forces. The government has him coming and going: from the welfare system, down to war, and off to jail. Where he would have agency is in the crafting of song—perhaps this song (in which case he might acknowledge some indebtedness to the Band's song "The Weight"). The artistic dilemma he faces is his inability to engage his addressee directly. He can compose for humanity in the abstract, but he can't talk to his desired conversation partner. The abiding injustice down the ages appears to have him tongue-tied. The song refers to the ancient Pharaohs: the lies they told, the lives they laid waste. In the face of this paralyzing injustice, without access to answers, the only thing left to do is to get down and pray.

Apocalypse

But prayer is a temporary measure that offers but a modicum of relief in a war-weary world. When things get really hopeless the communal imagination turns apocalyptic. Barry McGuire's "Eve of Destruction" and Steppenwolf's "Monster" have already been mentioned in this regard. In addition, the period of CCR's greatest musical productivity intersects with tragic political assassinations, Hal Lindsay's popular book predicting the imminent end of the world, *The Late Great Planet Earth* (1970), and the massacres at My Lai (1968) and Kent State (1970)—among many other "signs of the times." As already noted, some of CCR's prayerful tunes contain intimations of atomic cataclysm. In addition, CCR also produced several songs of true apocalyptic proportion.

"Sinister Purpose" (1969) begins with portents: the sky turns gray, the earth shakes, and the moon turns to "hate." This transformation is followed by a beckoning: the sinister one invites the addressee to join him. He introduces himself as the reappearance of the "last war" and promises fortune and eternal life to the one who would look into his eyes. According to the Book of Revelation (20: 7-11), as "the end" approaches, the Devil is unleashed upon the land to perform his dreadful deeds. In "Sinister Purpose," "goodness" is an unwanted quality; it must be burned away. A similar conflagration is depicted in another song of apocalypse, "Effigy" (1970). Here a fire spreads out from the palace, the center of political power, and eventually turns the countryside into a vast wasteland. In the end much of the population has also been consumed by fire.

The overwhelming sense of violence that seems to characterize the culture in these songs reaches its zenith in "Run Through the Jungle" (1970). This song unveils a nightmare come true. The protagonist is on the run, hoping to avoid the millions of guns that are aimed at him. "Satan" is mentioned explicitly as the one who gives the firing orders. Indeed, the Devil is "on the loose," exercising his sinister power and enticing the entire nation to self-destruction. The location of this song's activity in "the jungle" links the war in Vietnam to the epidemic of violence on the streets of America. The use of religious rhetoric, meanwhile, underscores the transnational—even transcendent—dimensions of the problem.

The quintessential CCR song of the apocalypse is "Bad Moon Rising" (1970). Part of the song's genius is its jovial rendition. Amid forecasts of natural disaster including earthquakes, floods, and hurricanes, the song jaunts forth in a merry mode. Martin Luther King often repeated variations on his conviction: "the arc of the moral universe is long, but it bends toward justice."[19] For King, this justice was historically inevitable; it would be actualized *in* time. In contrast, the apocalyptic imagination looks beyond the normal course of history to a cataclysmic end of the world: time will cease, justice will at last be executed, and those who have exercised power over others will be held to account for their misdeeds.[20] "Bad Moon Rising" warns about this Judgment Day with specific reference to the law of retribution: "an eye for an eye; a tooth for a tooth" (Exodus 21: 23). The moon that is on the rise in this song anticipates a grand reversal. It is a bad omen for "The Man" and his bedeviled collaborators; but for the simple folk who are memorialized in many of the CCR songs under consideration in this chapter, that moon offers hope for a new earth. Perhaps it is this message, implied beyond the actual words of the text, that accounts for the song's rendition in a major key.

Conclusion

In a speech delivered to the American Society of Newspaper Editors on April 16, 1953, Dwight D. Eisenhower reflected upon the "chance for peace" in an age of militarism:

> Every gun that is made, every warship launched, every rocket fired signifies, in the final sense, a theft from those who hunger and are not fed, those who are cold and are not clothed. ... Under the cloud of threatening war, it is humanity hanging from a cross of iron."[21]

This emblematic statement provides a concise example of religious rhetoric in the public square. Here Eisenhower deplores the escalation in the manufacturing of arms that occurred during the Cold War era over which he presided. He judges the nation's course on the basis of an ethos that transcends mere patriotism—a characteristic appeal, according to Robert Bellah, of American "civil religion." The industry of war, Eisenhower asserts, constitutes a grand theft from society's most vulnerable. Whether consciously or not, he employs a biblical template to his critique: "Then shall the righteous answer him, saying, Lord, when saw we thee hungered, and fed thee? Or thirsty, and gave thee drink? When saw we thee a stranger, and took thee in? Or naked, and clothed thee?" The conclusion to Jesus' parable in Mathew is, "Verily I say unto you, Inasmuch as ye have done it unto one of the least of these my brethren, ye have done it unto me" (Matthew 25: 38-40). This is the level of moral persuasion Eisenhower aspires to but leaves unpreached—except in his image of "humanity hanging from a cross of iron."

CCR inherited both the problems Eisenhower describes and the language he uses to critique these problems. The prevailing "civil religion" provided a mode of public discourse with which to address a repertoire of common concerns in song. I make no claim here for the piety of John Fogerty or his religious orientation to the world. I do insist that there is an underlying religious structure—consisting primarily of elements extracted from the Jewish and Christian traditions—that permeates the public sphere and constitutes the national dialect. John Fogerty's songs reveal him to be particularly fluent in this allusive (and sometimes elusive) rhetoric.

I would like to thank Kevin Kittredge, Catherine Roach, and Frederick Whiting for insight and guidance during the writing of this chapter, a portion of which was presented at the joint annual meeting of the Popular Culture Association and American Culture Association in Boston, MA, on April 13, 2012.

Notes

1. The term "agonizing reappraisal" was advanced by U.S. Secretary of State, John Foster Dulles. In a speech before NATO during the Cold War era, he argued that Western Europe's failure to establish a multi-national army (including West Germany) would result in an "agonizing reappraisal" of American policy toward Western Europe. In the late 1960s, the term was popularized in a 7up commercial featuring a hippie parent who was confused by his children's preference for 7up over cola. Such radical non-conformity was not part of his personal past, the hippie nostalgically and ironically reflects, concluding, "These are times of agonizing reappraisal." See "Dulles Cautions Europe to Ratify Army Treat Soon," *New York Times*, December 15, 1953, 14.

2. Roger Williams, "Mr. Cotton's Letter Examined and Answered" (1644), in *The Bloudy Tenent of Persecution, for Cause of Conscience Discussed*, Elibron Classics Series (London: Adamant Media, 2005), 375.

3. William P. Guthrie, *The Later Thirty Years War: From the Battle of Wittstock to the Treaty of Westphalia* (New York: Greenwood, 2003), 181, 268.

4. Max Weber, "Science as a Vocation" in *From Max Weber: Essays in Sociology* (London: Routledge, 2007), 157.

5. John F. Kennedy, "An Address to the Greater Houston Ministerial Association, September 12, 1960," http://www.npr.org/templates/story/story.php?storyId=16920600 (April 10, 2012). Campaigning for the Republican nomination for President in 2012, would-be nominee Rick Santorum responded viscerally before a crowd in Traverse City, Michigan. Kennedy's 1960 address, he insisted, "makes me throw up." As if to underline the ongoing nature of this debate in American culture, Santorum went on to say, "I don't believe in an America where the separation of church and state is absolute." See "Santorum Makes Case for Religion in Public Sphere," *New York Times*, February 27, 2012, A1.

6. *School District of Abington Township, Pennsylvania V. Schempp* in Henry Steele Commager, ed., *Documents of American History, Volume II* (Englewood Cliffs, NJ: Prentice-Hall, 1973), 678-80. Richard John Neuhaus argues against the notion of a religion-less American republic in his book *The Naked Public Square* (Grand Rapids, MI: Eerdmans, 1984).

7. Martin Luther King, Jr., "I Have a Dream," in James M. Washington, ed., *A Testament of Hope: The Essential Writings of Martin Luther King, Jr.* (New York: Harper and Row, 1986), 217-20. Bible references include Amos 4.24 and Isaiah 40.4: "every valley shall be exalted, every hill and mountain shall be made low."

8. Robert N. Bellah, "Civil Religion in America," *Daedalus* 96, no. 1 (Winter 1967), 18. Bellah's list of archetypes reads like themes from the songbook of Bruce Springsteen.

9. This is the drama that brackets The Doors' magnificent "The Soft Parade" (1969). The song begins with a jaded seminarian intoning that the Lord cannot be petitioned with prayer. It concludes in a riotous frenzy with a choir of petitioners calling out to "the dogs" until the last line of the chant ends the sequence with "calling on the gods."

10. See, for example, Psalms 13, 35, and 94; and Habakkuk 1. For the development of psalms of disorientation, see Walter Brueggemann, *The Message of the Psalms: A Theological Commentary* (Minneapolis, MN: Fortress, 1985), 51–122. From the perspective of a rock-and-roll songster, U2's Bono refers to the lament psalm's "mood of displacement" in *The Book of Psalms with an Introduction by Bono* (Edinburgh: Canongate, 1999), ix. For use of this refrain in American religious and political rhetoric, see the discussion below concerning Martin Luther King's "How Long" speech, in Montgomery, Alabama, on March 25, 1965.

11. This and all subsequent chart statistics were compiled by Music Outfitters, http://www.musicoutfitters.com/topsongs/1965html (and other years) (February 3, 2012).

12. R. W. B. Lewis, *The American Adam: Innocence, Tragedy and Tradition in the Nineteenth Century* (Chicago: University of Chicago Press, 1965).

13. The CCR song "Up Around the Bend" (1970) offers an equal but opposite itinerary characteristic of the party of hope. In that song, the protagonist seeks to leave behind the "sinking ship" of a botched civilization. He calls upon the forces of nature (rising wind and fleet feet) to assist him as he races hopefully toward the forest primeval that waits just ahead.

14. From a British perspective, the pristine virtues of life in Oklahoma are somewhat satirically portrayed in the Kinks' song "Oklahoma, U.S.A." from *Muswell Hillbillies*, 1972.

15. This point is made repeatedly in John Michael Spencer, *Blues and Evil* (Knoxville: University of Tennessee Press, 1993).

16. Langston Hughes, "The Negro Speaks of Rivers," 1921. The river is a recurring metaphor in popular music. Consider, for example, Paul Robeson's version of "Ol' Man River" (1936), Al Green's "Take Me to the River" (1974), Bruce Springsteen's "The River" (1981), or The Call's "In the River" (1987).

17. "The Man" is the oppressor, the one who exercises power over someone else. The protagonist in "Proud Mary" worked for him; the prisoner in CCR's version of Leadbelly's "Midnight Special" endeavors to avoid his wrath.

18. Robert N. Bellah, *Beyond Belief: Essays on Religion in a Post-Traditionalist World* (Berkeley: University of California Press, 1991), 168.

19. Martin Luther King, "How Long" speech, in Montgomery, Alabama, on March 25, 1965, excerpted at http://www.youtube.com/watch?v=TAYITODNvlM (March 1, 2012).

20. See Kenelm Burridge, *New Heaven, New Earth: A Study of Millenarian Activities* (London: Blackwell, 1980).

21. Dwight David Eisenhower, "The Chance for Peace," April 16, 1953, http://www.presidency.ucsb.edu/ws/index.php?pid=9819#axzz1rf3YPqdP (April 12, 2012).

CHAPTER SIX

~

Flying the Flannel: An Americana Salute to Creedence Clearwater Revival

Timothy Gray

To "contain multitudes" has been an American aspiration at least since the time of Walt Whitman, the eminent poet who in 1855's "Song of Myself" made the phrase famous. Many Americans like to think that they benefit from the nation's diversity, and that like other adventurers (think of Tennyson's "Ulysses," a heroic figure cited by Bobby Kennedy on the campaign trail) they are a part of all they've met. But *representing* multitudes, well, that's when things get tricky. Who can purport to speak for every cross section of the national demographic? Nobody. But politicians sure try. And so, in its way, does Americana, a genre of music that emphasizes common roots and homespun values. Unfussy on its surface, Americana purports to be rustic, and sometimes it is, but we should remember that twenty years ago the term caught fire as a radio format conceived by the *Gavin Report*, a music trade journal. Old ideals mixed with slick new marketing strategies: it's the American way.

I don't mean to be cynical. Eventually, music fans who pledge their allegiance to one genre of music or another must plunk down their money, but not at the expense of their deeply held passions. Contemporary strains of Americana treasure aspects of our national past, but not necessarily in a shallow or reactionary way. As Kurt B. Reighley shows in his book *The United States of Americana* (2010), and as *No Depression* magazine has shown in its print (1995–2008) and online versions, aficionados of Americana seek an under-the-radar existence, a simple life that stresses hands-on learning and devotion to time-tested values: aura, authenticity, local color, and neighborly communion (with an ironic acknowledgment that, in today's America, it's the internet enabling friendly connections between far-flung strangers, be they quilting bee participants or front porch banjo pickers). At their most broad-minded, today's creators and purveyors of Americana music challenge arbitrary categories separating rock from folk from soul from country from punk, on down the line. With its "alternative country" wing, especially, Americana has become quietly cutting edge.[1] In this context, Creedence Clearwater Revival, a rock band from the 1960s held in high regard by Generation X musicians, deserves a new hearing. Wearing common work clothes and brandishing re-verb-heavy chords, this band contained multitudes at a time when multitudes of young people resisted containment of any sort. With a voice that came from you and me (as Don McLean might say), CCR were representative of a broad swath of America.

Judging by the artists who've covered their songs, Creedence Clearwater Revival were either a gospel soul act ("Wrote a Song for Everyone," Mavis Staples), an R&B act ("Proud Mary," Ike and Tina Turner), post-punk rock-ers ("Run Through the Jungle," Eight Eyed Spy; "Have You Ever Seen the Rain?" and "Don't Look Now," the Minutemen), or alt-country pioneers ("Effigy," Uncle Tupelo). Add to that list the artists whose songs CCR covered (Ray Charles, Roy Orbison, Wilson Pickett, et al.) and you have an even more delectable mix. A stream of influences courses through CCR's catalog like eighth notes, and this makes them a quintessential roots band. While they dismissed other aspects of 1960s culture, progressive indie kids who came of age in the 1980s located in CCR's music not the tired rewind of "classic rock," but rather the retro appeal of Americana, an imagined com-munity whose flannel flag I'll raise as I salute the band's legacy.

Flannel is versatile apparel. Wearing it, you announce yourself as a grunge rocker, a roots-based rustic, or perhaps both, depending on context and per-sonal preference. A 1993 Gap advertisement reminded consumers that Jack Kerouac wore khakis. Well, in 1969 (the year Kerouac died), on the cover of *Green River* and in concert, John Fogerty wore flannel. If at the time CCR's humble sartorial choices flew in the face of Haight Ashbury or East Village fashion, they'd later become an influence on an array of 1980s bands. In Britain, CCR acolytes Orange Juice wore raccoon caps and button down shirts.[2] Back in America, Mike Watt (of the Minutemen and fIREHOSE) and Jay Farrar (of Uncle Tupelo and Son Volt) flew the Fogerty flannel, as did a number of their post-punk and alt-country brethren.[3] Granted, the Godfather of Grunge, Neil Young, also facilitated the flannel revolution, and assorted longhaired indie outfits like the Meat Puppets and Dinosaur Jr. took their look and sound from him. The soft-focus picture of Young on his

1969 album *Everybody Knows This is Nowhere* (flannel, tree, mountain, dog) is indeed iconic, but remember, Young was just abandoning his Sunset Strip uniform of fringed buckskin when CCR debuted in 1968.

For Fogerty in the 1960s, flannel was more than a fashion statement. Rather, it matched his lyrics, evoking American ideals of rural freedom, summoning mysterious yet vivid images of river waders and choogling trains, flatcar riders and crosstie walkers, hoodoo-chasing hound dogs and Cajun Queens. Flannel also signified hard work. Fogerty may have written about timeless American landscapes, but his songs were forged by daily realities. The pride of El Cerrito, CCR were true working-class heroes, identified by John Lennon (increasingly enamored of that concept) as one of the few bands that mattered. As decades passed, CCR's proletariat credibility inoculated them against anti-hippie venom spewed in punk and post-punk circles, endearing them to DIY practitioners in those communities and the alt-country networks they spawned. Songs such as "Lodi" and "Don't Look Now" were about a common laborer's plight, not rock star excess.

Mike Watt could relate. Jamming "econo" in his flannel shirt and no-frills van, Watt was among the earliest post-punks to salute CCR's style, music, and socio-economic politics. Take the cover of fIREHOSE's major label debut, *Flyin' the Flannel* (1991), which portrayed the front left quadrant of a flannel shirt, slightly billowed. Viewers glimpse a plaid flag flying over an imagined nation of independent rockers (just as, two decades prior, an altered stars and stripes with a field of black, seen flying across the cover of Sly and the Family Stone's defiant masterpiece, *There's a Riot Goin' On* [1971], demanded a new reckoning of black America). Sporting flannel and giving other albums folksy, mashed-together titles like *Fromohio* and *If'n*, fIREHOSE met everyday people on their level, making art music for the masses. Chronicling the Minutemen, Watt's first band, Michael Azerrad set the stakes for Watt's flannel aesthetics: "If you're working class, you don't start a band just to scrape by; you start a band to get rich. So art bands, with their inherently limited commercial prospects, were mainly the province of the affluent. Which makes the Minutemen all the braver."[4] In Watt's gritty hometown of San Pedro, Simon Reynolds reiterated, "dilettante tendencies got inoculated by the heavy-duty work ethic."[5]

A student of rock, Watt suspected that CCR avoided aesthetic over-reaching for the same reasons he did. CCR's salt-of-the-earth worldview was forged in joints they played (first as the Blue Velvets, then as the Golliwogs) from San Jose to Sacramento. They went looking for a pot of gold and found it, but they didn't turn into fey, spoiled hippies. By the 1980s, indie rockers like Camper Van Beethoven were parodying Grace Slick and her jumpsuits.

CCR, by contrast, were regarded by many of the new breed, including Joe Strummer of the Clash, as inviolable holy men. In 1985, while opening for R.E.M. in Atlanta, the Minutemen played an entire set of CCR songs: a very cool choice that nonetheless raised the hackles of R.E.M.'s ambitious tour manager, who threatened to remove the band from future dates. But if that manager didn't want to know, forget him, because then, as now, flannel equaled punk equaled independence. The Minutemen and CCR clearly won on that score, closing a couple of generation gaps in the process, and throwing generic expectations to the (rising) wind. The unexpected result is this: you're just as apt to find CCR mentioned in surveys of post-punk as in studies of classic rock. Greil Marcus has spilled much ink about the Band, CCR's contemporary rival in roots rock matters, but he provides only two references to CCR in *Mystery Train: Images of America in Rock and Roll Music*, maybe the most influential book about rock ever penned. Remember, though, that's a Boomer version of rock's trajectory.[6]

CCR proved inspirational to Gen X kids like me because they didn't brush away the harsh realities of the 1960s with flower petals. Neither were they too preachy, or self-conscious about their relationship with American history; their message was rock and roll, without any frills. Like Chuck Berry's, their music was deceptively simple: it could be jangly and propulsive and still stare down an America in crisis. In the late 1970s, Replacements singer Paul Westerberg listened to his parents' old CCR records and discovered they still packed a punch.[7] Arty New York rockers Sonic Youth were similarly smitten, titling an LP *Bad Moon Rising*, filtering the portentousness of the famous CCR song into nightmarish fables and assorted tales of DIY derring-do. A growing legion of indie kids, including Watt, who got them signed on the SST label, caught Sonic Youth's drift, especially when "Death Valley '69" took the shine off Woodstock Daze. Like the new bands they'd inspired, CCR were hip to the dark side of California, and to the nation at large, but crucially for Gen X tastes, they didn't get bogged down in speechifying. They didn't adopt the gloomy noir posturing of the Doors, the rhetoric of John Lennon, the auteur aspirations of Robbie Robertson, or the crackpot populism of Grand Funk Railroad, and that made their social commentary more believable. In 1969, the year of an emerging Republican majority, it must've been unusually instructive to learn that plainsong laments of the under-30 crowd came from a flannel-clad kid down on the corner, not a Blake-spouting Lizard King or a hirsute millionaire bedding down for peace in the Amsterdam Hilton.

It's true that in "Fortunate Son" and "Don't Look Now" Fogerty indulged in bald political rhetoric, but the songs rocked so hard you barely noticed.

In other songs, he expressed generational disillusionment with American society equivocally and without artifice. As Ellen Willis usefully postulated, "Fogerty's lyrics were both compassionate enough and angry enough to take the curse off their pessimism; his persona in songs like 'Who'll Stop the Rain' and 'Wrote a Song for Everyone' was not the smug liberal secretly happy that he won't have to give up his two cars, but you and me on a bad day."[8] Lest her final phrase kindle smarmy images of sensitive singer-songwriters of the early 1970s, Willis stressed CCR's hard-won victories and harder-edged sound. Just the same, indie rockers of the 1980s and 1990s appreciated CCR's vision because it seemed open to all. Fogerty wasn't Graham Nash or James Taylor. Not for him the airless domestic drama of "Our House" or the Martha's Vineyard preciosity of "Sweet Baby James." An open landscape of vanishing dreams was his preferred territory. Not without honor, 1980s cowpunk bands like the Blasters, Jason and the Scorchers, Green on Red, and the Long Ryders traversed locations Fogerty scouted in advance.

To describe in purely subjective terms CCR's lasting influence on today's alt-country types, I've tried to follow Greil Marcus and devise my own "Real Life Top Ten." Unfortunately, that number proved too limiting. So here's an even dozen, twelve CCR songs that matter, not only because they showcase the multiple influences the band accepted, but also because they speak to a flannel-clad fan's understanding of American independence. In true Gen X fashion, you can consider it a mixed tape, assembled with care and handed from me to you: a communication-through-song of common concerns CCR expressed in their short but influential career (1968–1972). As was true with the tapes I used to share with friends, I hope listeners will find in the list of songs images they can take with them on their own chosen paths, traveling CCR's sonic thoroughfares to territories they've not yet explored.

12. "Someday Never Comes" (Mardi Gras, 1972).

Lyrically, this song presaged Southern rock ballads of experience like Lynyrd Skynyrd's "Simple Man," not to mention the folksy, child-is-father-to-the-man musings of Harry Chapin's "Cat's in the Cradle." Its twiddling guitar fill, meanwhile, harked back to Blues Image's 1970 hit, "Ride Captain Ride." You can parse the song's message the way you can the Beatles' "Long and Winding Road." It doesn't matter when the song was composed, or what it's about; the fact that it's the last single fans heard on the radio made it CCR's lachrymose valediction. Fogerty sounds weary, having traveled his own long road, damaged twice by marital separation (as a son, as a husband) and again by the imminent implosion of his band. But damn if his song isn't beautiful.

I wonder whether, growing up, Jeff Tweedy heard this wistful number on AM radio. Or Joseph Arthur, though he was still in the crib in 1972. Predictably, for an already-winnowed group about to call it quits, "Someday" only hit #25. But listen again and you'll hear pop music in transition, introspection and the calibration of personal limits the dominant keys. "John's finest song," CCR bassist Stu Cook said; "It brought tears to my eyes." It had the same effect on Greil Marcus, who sang its praises in *Creem*.[9]

11. "Have You Ever Seen the Rain?" (Pendulum, 1970).

This is CCR's most perfectly realized car radio single, its bright surface distracting us from melancholy lyrics. It's what country bumpkin Dylan (1969-1974) wished he sounded like, and what Wilco sounds like on a good day. Breaking through the high whine after the chorus, a Hammond organ offers wordless commentary on the ambiguous direction the lyrics mark out: a forked path inviting both idealistic expectation and cynical judgment. If instruments other than CCR's guitars-bass-drums combo should strike you as intrusive, they needn't. The prior year, the band used horns on "Travelin' Band" and Fender Rhodes on "Long as I Can See the Light." Before that, they used Jerry Lee Lewis-style piano on "It Came Out of the Sky." On "Have You Ever Seen the Rain?" the organ disperses storm clouds, even as lyrics send rain down on a sunny day. Accordingly, nearly everybody who heard this #8 hit, even some CCR members, forgot it was about a band of brothers splitting apart.

10. "I Put a Spell on You" (Creedence Clearwater Revival, 1968).

This edges out "I Heard It through the Grapevine" as the band's tastiest psychedelic cover. Covering Screamin' Jay Hawkins was a bold choice in 1968, and with frenetically strummed chords and a hoodoo lead line CCR foreshadowed the spookiness of "Bad Moon Rising." Screamin' John Fogerty! He's as passionate and weird as America (or the 1960s, for that matter). Other songs on CCR's debut album aimed for Paul Butterfield-style blues interpretations, but this track summoned something more undecipherable and unmatchable. As with the best artifacts of Americana, aura meant everything; basically, the song assumed the power of Hawkins's 1956 spell because of Fogerty's wise decision not to try to break it. Bootleg footage from Woodstock captures CCR's blistering live version.

9. "*Green River*" (Green River, 1969).

Where does this idyllic stream run, you may wonder, on the map (there's a Green River in Wyoming, another in Washington State) or in the mind? Here's something that might mean anything: in the 1980s, a Seattle-area psychopath known as the Green River Killer vied with the CCR song as the nominal influence for Green River, a feeder band for flannel grunge gods Mudhoney and Pearl Jam.[10] As Leslie Fielder and Leo Marx hinted in their early 1960s studies, behind most sunny versions of pastoral there exist violent impulses and sounds ready to break loose.[11] "Bad Moon Rising" gets all the press, but CCR tapped this incongruity constantly. As an All-Americana boy, I love two things about "Green River." The first is the placid cover of *Green River*, released around the time of Woodstock. It portrays a sun-dappled nowhere: the kind American pastoral fantasy feeds on (you'd never catch the Velvet Underground cavorting in such a "meadow," Ben Edmonds griped in *Fusion*, to no real purpose).[12] We find here the chosen destination of anyone from Rip Van Winkle to Huck Finn to a back-to-the-land hippie; it's a place to remember all we don't know. John Fogerty stands proudly in the foreground. Flannel, denim, leather, and guitar: all that's needed to emerge from the woods self-sufficient and happy, but not too deluded, or blind to the killers in our midst. Second, I love that when Fogerty thrice yells "well" ("waaaiiilll!") he's taking refuge in the ineffable rather than offering watertight reasons for escape. Such forestalling appears in literary works by William Faulkner, Cormac McCarthy, and assorted Southern Gothic writers. Tormented characters say "well …" when prompted to account for suspicious actions or attitudes. To excessively rational folks, it might seem ridiculous, but to say "well" is actually sublime. If you're born to move, explanations get in the way.

8. "*Effigy*" (Willy and the Poor Boys, 1969).

"Who is burnin'?" The question begged asking in December 1969. My Lai was by this point public knowledge; the Manson Family had been found out; the bombing of Cambodia was being planned. The gripping paranoia of this song, the last track on CCR's final album of the 1960s, portrays the holocaust that ensued after the bad moon rose and hippie idealism was sent scurrying. The Silent Majority was no longer silent. Nixon and Agnew reigned. Altamont left Woodstock Nation fractured. The blissful trip CCR offered in "Green River" had gone awry. Dire prophecies like "Sinister Purpose" and "Bad Moon Rising," portentous as they are, can't hold a candle to the flames torching America's fiefdom in "Effigy." When Uncle Tupelo covered this lost classic in 1993 for the compilation album *No Alternative*, it was my first exposure to Fogerty's stinging diatribe. Flexing some muscle, the heartland punks came down heavy on the bass notes, amplifying them, tapping the song's menace, making us feel the pain of America's broken promises. It's as good as first wave alt-country got. Besides Jay Farrar and Jeff Tweedy, we have Fogerty to thank for that.

7. *"Who'll Stop the Rain"* (Cosmo's Factory, 1970).

It rained a lot in the jungles of Vietnam, and also in Max Yasgur's pasture in Bethel, New York, one fine weekend in August 1969. Given the abstract nature of the lyrics, this song describes both locales. In-country soldiers and anti-war activists alike loved "Who'll Stop the Rain," so much so that Fogerty played it by request at a Welcome Home concert for veterans in 1987.[13] Woodstock references color the final verse, and for me this context is just as important. On *Green River's* "Wrote a Song for Everyone," Fogerty saluted Woody Guthrie's folk populism, but he also shared the failures he'd suffered trying to put Guthrie's message into play. With its reflection on how pop communalism overwhelms impressionable American youth, "Who'll Stop the Rain" broadens that conversation. In 1970, listeners got hung on Joni Mitchell's stardust words when Crosby Steals the Cash (thanks, Tom Waits, for the epithet)[14] took her Woodstock anthem to #11. But as many know, Mitchell never made it to the famous encampment; she composed "Woodstock" in a New York City hotel. It's a great song. For Fogerty, though, it's harder to get caught up in the fable when rain's pouring in your ears. In recent years, alt-country troubadours Jeff Tweedy and Dan Bern have penned revealing songs about their relationships with audiences ("Standing O," "Black Tornado"). Fogerty did the same years ago, with far greater stakes. Essentially, "Who'll Stop the Rain" forced smug, callow youth, convinced Woodstock *meant something* (and it did), to consider what their massive mud bath actually meant. As long as this song plays, the rain keeps falling down, and the music festival's promise of spiritual rebirth in nature's garden receives an uncertain baptism.

6. *"Ramble Tamble"* (Cosmo's Factory, 1970).

"Ramble Tamble" proved that rockabilly rave-ups and psychedelic workouts could co-exist, even reinforce one another, in the same song. Often, in the middle of today's alt-country shows, there's an extended jam in which the lead guitarist shows off some chops and the band works a groove instead of trying to prove something lyrically. Stage lights switch to blue and the twang turns edgier so as to find favor with urban hipsters. To my ears that jam always sounds like the middle section of "Ramble Tamble," a song that may have served the same purpose in the hippie ballrooms of San Francisco. As much as I appreciate Fogerty's lyrics and adore his voice, it's a relief when he steps away and lets his guitar emote. The final minutes of "I Heard It through the Grapevine" (also on *Cosmo's Factory*) also attest to that dynamic. For other high points in matters of the jam, consider a pair of instrumentals, "Broken Spoke Shuffle" and "Glory Be," unreleased backing tracks appended to the *Green River* reissue. The latter is as deliriously danceable as any Velvet Underground workout, bolstering Willis's assertion that CCR was "*the* white American dance band."[15] "Ramble Tamble" goes for trance more than dance, its *Deliverance*-style twang modulated and pumped through amplifiers. But you can still spin to your heart's delight.

5. "Cotton Fields" (Willy and the Poor Boys, 1969).

For my pilgrimage through Americana, I've thrown away the maps and taken Fogerty as my guide. So who cares that Texarkana sits more than a mile away from Louisiana? "Cotton Fields" sounds like an old folk song, and it is, having been performed decades earlier by Lead Belly. Nowadays, though, you're more likely to hear the CCR version on Americana stations. It's a great sing-along, as perfect for today's urban hayseeds as it was for the down-on-the-corner gang depicted on *Willy and the Poor Boys*. It's true that cotton fields provide an agricultural link between California and the Mississippi Delta. But this song's connection lies in the acoustic strumming, as simple as the fieldwork is hard. Poor Boy or not, once invited, you can't help but join in.

4. "Fortunate Son" (Willy and the Poor Boys, 1969).

What's the opposite of a fortunate son? A baby punk swaddled in flannel! Indignation without pretense or self-righteousness: that's the message alt-country types take from this song. On Son Volt's *Okemah and the Melody of Riot*, Jay Farrar can grandstand against the Iraq War all he wants, knowing "Fortunate Son," like trusty army buddy, provides him cover. George W. Bush was clearly more fortunate than Farrar, a bookseller's kid from southern Illinois, and Farrar must have realized in turn that he couldn't match Fogerty's proletariat credibility. But songs are powerful medicine, counter-acting history whenever it returns to bite us. Even without a draft, Bush the Second preyed on working-class kids to fight delusional battles against worldwide evil. Thus it was that Farrar, resistant, emboldened, and fortified by his knowledge of rock history, set aside his acoustic guitar, reassembled his band, and plugged in, loudly venting fury at American inequality, just as Fogerty did thirty-five years earlier in his upside-down national anthem. "Fortunate Son" sent senators' sons scurrying in 1969, and in 2004 it made an equally apt soundtrack for Michael Moore, who in *Fahrenheit 911* tracked down bellicose congressmen and asked why their children weren't serving in the military. Like Farrar and Moore, those who love CCR's most political song join the fortunate ones it excoriates in one important sense: we were all born to wave the flag. It's just that some of us appreciate the way flannel clashes with stars and stripes.

3. "Lodi" (Green River, 1969).

If my number two selection references a mythical American dwelling place that becomes real, this song honors a real place that has become mythical. There's a Lodi, California, and unlike the members of CCR, I've never been there. But then we've all been stuck in Lodi, facing dashed dreams and humdrum condescension. We all know the tune. Just a year before this single was released (as the B side of "Bad Moon Rising"), CCR were, as the lyrics indicate, a hard-luck quartet playing one-night stands for drunken barflies. Indeed, two months before their debut album came out, Tom Fogerty said, the band had exactly two dollars in their checking account.[16] That would change, but even after playing Woodstock, the Oakland Coliseum, and the Royal Albert Hall, CCR never forgot their roadhouse roots. In "Lodi," beer joints don't lie; they just shuffle reality a bit. If a downcast Fogerty is "you and me on a bad day," as Willis claims, then the rock star is just a frustrated American worker, like the rest of us.[17] Listening to "Lodi," we in turn become rockers shuffling past our cubicles to hit the stage at nine. Sorry, Madison Avenue, but Budweiser commercials have never said it so well.

2. "Up Around the Bend" (Cosmo's Factory, 1970).

If misery lights ever hit my rearview, I want the siren to sound like the opening of "Up Around the Bend," so I know I'll not be summoned to traffic court but transported to an America offering crystal days and good conversation. "Up Around the Bend" is the ultimate Americana anthem. It has a Huck-and-Jim spirit of adventure at its pastoral core. Leslie Fielder should've listened up! All that's missing is mention of a raft. The titular bend could be in a river or on a highway. It doesn't much matter, so long as urban neon fades to wood. Lyrically, "Up Around the Bend" proves a counterweight to "Lodi." You're invited by a chorus of rockers to dispense with whatever crap workaday life dishes out. Leave the sinking ship behind, get while the getting's good, light out for the territories ahead of the rest, and keep on chooglin'! Across our society's real and perceived divides of class, race, geography, etc., there's a utopian experience to which all Americans can lay claim. This song may just be it, even as it directs us up yonder.

1. *"Born on the Bayou"* (Bayou Country, 1969).

In a vast array of song and literature, to be born in the USA is to be reborn with whatever identity, heritage, persona, or hometown you wish. Ask Bob Dylan. Fictional origins are our birthright, made more plausible on the Fourth of July, mentioned by Fogerty here, and a hot topic for Marcus in writings on "the old, weird America."[18] CCR's unique sound adds to the mystery. In "Born on the Bayou," Fogerty takes a basic blues chord, an E7, and makes it spookier by isolating its treble notes in a hypnotic pattern. Then the rhythm section kicks in. Ten seconds into the song—before the lyrics about freight trains, hound dogs, and hoodoo—you're entranced, transported. It's too bad CCR refused to grant release of their Woodstock performance, because "Born on the Bayou," their traditional opener, is a swampy masterpiece. For me, it's as worthy of historical preservation as are the medleys by Sly and the Family Stone, Janis Joplin, and The Who, the acts that followed CCR that magical Saturday night. Today, I wonder what would happen if Woodstock-era CCR got in a time machine and hit Austin City Limits. How many roots rockers would lay down their guitars and kneel down in fealty? And if that's a fantasy, so is the song. Upon its release, Fogerty hadn't yet choogled down to New Orleans, but you sure couldn't tell by listening to him. The accent and down-home images are by this point part of an assumed identity, open to any American. To understand this, pull up Woodstock footage on YouTube and imagine yourself present at the opening of CCR's set, in the wee hours of the night, when our national character seemed free and limitless. It wouldn't stay that way; it couldn't. CCR were like both nations they represented, America and Woodstock. Millions agreed on them and came together in their name, but they couldn't agree with themselves. They'd fall apart someday. For the moment, though, it's okay. Generational rivalries dissolve. This scrappy band can take on all comers. So go back, get born again, and hope someday never comes.

Notes

1. Championed by *No Depression* magazine and known not only by its abbreviated version, alt-country, but also by such colorful epithets as "y'allternative" and "twangcore," this synthesizing genre emerged in the late 1980s as a punk rock antidote to Nashville gloss. It gained momentum in the early 1990s with bands like Uncle Tupelo, the Jayhawks, the Bottle Rockets, and Whiskeytown. For an academic (and unnecessarily sour) overview of the alt-country movement, see Pamela Fox and Barbara Ching, eds., *Old Roots, New Routes: The Cultural Politics of Alt.Country Music* (Ann Arbor: University of Michigan Press, 2008).

2. Simon Reynolds, *Totally Wired: Postpunk Interviews and Overviews* (New York: Soft Skull, 2010), 312.

3. "Alternative Country (whatever that is)" was the subtitle of *No Depression* (1995–2008), the deflective parenthetical suggesting that the new genre's blend of punk insouciance and traditional country sounds was more accidental than it was deliberate or studied. Of course, this belies the fact that many of today's alt-country stars are musical historians whose style and performance betray strict allegiances to boundary-breaking forebears. Again, CCR looms large. Sid Griffin, front man of the Long Ryders and the writer of books about Bob Dylan and Gram Parsons, clearly got down the Prince Valiant hairstyle John Fogerty pioneered, even if, in terms of clothing, he tended toward the frontier dandy look (vests, jackets) made popular by another 1960s band, Quicksilver Messenger Service. But then the Long Ryders would sometimes sport the bandanna neckerchiefs Fogerty wore, and we should recall that for CCR's late night Woodstock performance Fogerty wore a fringed leather vest, the kind Griffin favored, so differences are minimal.

4. Michael Azerrad, *Our Band Could Be Your Life: Scenes from the American Indie Underground 1981–1991* (Boston: Back Bay, 2002), 62.

5. Reynolds, 388.

6. Marcus would later write brief liner notes to CCR's greatest hits collection, *Chronicle*, but his references to the band in his voluminous output of rock criticism are surprisingly few.

7. Jim Walsh, *The Replacements: All Over but the Shouting* (Minneapolis: Voyageur, 2007), 48–49.

8. Ellen Willis, "Creedence Clearwater Revival," in *The Rolling Stone Illustrated History of Rock and Roll*, ed. Anthony DeCurtis, James Henke, and Holly George-Warren (New York: Random House, 1992), 449.

9. Hank Bordowitz, *Bad Moon Rising: The Unauthorized History of Creedence Clearwater Revival* (Chicago: Chicago Review Press/A Cappella Books, 2007), 136, 138.

10. Azerrad, 416.

11. See Leslie A. Fiedler, *Love and Death in the American Novel* (New York: Criterion, 1960); Leo Marx, *The Machine in the Garden: Technology and the American Ideal in America* (New York: Oxford University Press, 1964).

12. Ben Edmonds, "The Velvet Underground," *All Yesterday's Parties: The Velvet Underground in Print 1966–1971*, ed. Clinton Heylin (Cambridge, MA: Da Capo, 2006) 218.

13. Bordowitz, 85, 224.

14. Barney Hoskyns, *Lowside of the Road: A Life of Tom Waits* (New York: Broadway, 2009), 180.

15. Willis, 449.

16. Bordowitz, 32.

17. Willis, 449.

18. See, especially, *Invisible Republic: Bob Dylan's Basement Tapes* (New York: Henry Holt, 1997), since re-titled *The Old, Weird America: The World of Bob Dylan's Basement Tapes*.

~

CHAPTER SEVEN

The 1969 Creedence Clearwater Revival Recording Contract and How It Shaped the Future of the Group and Its Members

Hank Bordowitz

By 1969, the record business had been around, in some way, shape, or form for nearly 80 years. For an octogenarian, it had never been healthier. A study commissioned by John Wiley of Columbia Records said that the business had grown 250 percent in the decade between 1955 and 1965. It predicted the record business would double in size again within the next decade. "The end of the upward trend is not yet in sight," added Wiley. "Our future has never held more promise."[1]

With the passing of rock and roll into just rock, the day of the music business robber barons had begun to fade. The previous decade saw musicians with massive hit records living in poverty, contracted to virtual slavery as recording artists. As Etta James once said,

> I ... started my show business life living in a private hotel where you could cook. Other entertainers were there, like Curtis Mayfield. Everybody lived in this one hotel. I was the one who had the kitchen. We used to put all our money together to eat. At that time, we would get two cents, three cents, five cents for bottles and, at the end of the day, we would get our money together and we'd get some food and cook it. I remember us putting together and not having much, just enough to get some corn meal. And I learned that whenever you get hungry—I've told my kids this—if you've got enough money, you get some yellow corn meal and you get some sugar. You can always get some sugar somewhere, even if you have to walk into a McDonald's someplace, and steal some of the sugar. Take sugar and cornmeal and fry it. Boy, is that good. Then,

if you've got enough money, you get a little syrup. I remember we ate that for two days.[2]

James recorded for Chess Records at the time, and had enormous cross-over hits like "At Last" that continued to make money for *someone*, but certainly not for James (except, perhaps when she would perform in concert). That such famous and popular musicians could be living in relative poverty on Chicago's South Side spoke to both legalities within the music business and race relations of the times, but only in terms of the degree they were exploited. James further recalled,

I remember going to Chess records and Leonard Chess had a check on his desk. He said, "I want you with Chess Records. You will be really good. I'll get you out of the deal with Modern."[3]... He picked up this check and said, "Let me show you what kind of royalties my artists make." He lifted this check up to me and it was for ninety some thousand dollars, and it was made out to Chuck Berry and Allan Freed. I was about to faint, there were so many zeros there. And he said, "This is just for six months payment for 'Maybelline.'" I had one hit record, "All I Do Is Cry," and then I had "Stop the Wedding," and then I had, "My Dearest.". . . They were going in layers. So, it was about a year later, when it would be time for me to receive some royalties, I went down there. I was rubbing my hands together. I knew I was going to look down there and see a nice fat figure. I saw that it was written in red. And I said, "$14,000! All right!" And Leonard said, "Hold it, hold it. Don't get all bent out of shape." And I was kind of confused, like what is he saying that for. And he says, "Look Etta, don't worry about what that says. What do you need?" Now, I'm really confused. Here's what I need, in big red numbers. I said, "Wait a minute. You're saying I don't have this coming?" "Hell no, you don't have this coming," he said. "You owe me this. Just tell me what you need." I received a check for $10,000. I took that $10,000 straight to Los Angeles and put $8,000 down on a house.[4]

She passed on in that house in 2012. Fellow Chess recording artist and rock-and-roll pioneer Elias "Bo Diddley" McDaniels's feelings about Chess were more succinct: "They made me a mean dude."[5]

In part, due to the low maintenance paid to the artists, in part due to the giddy advent of youth culture, the music business would continue to live up to Wiley's predictions until the very late 1970s and early 1980s, when it would experience its first major dip since prior to World War II. The advent of rock had been a boom time for all aspects of the music business—people lined up around the block to get into the Fillmore Ballrooms on both coasts, musical instruments sold well, and perhaps half a million people gathered in the exurbs of New York City and Albany to see several dozen bands over the course of three days (and a bit) at the Woodstock Music and Art Fair. In many ways, it was a legendary time for both music and the business that thrived off the music.

One of the bands at Woodstock was Creedence Clearwater Revival. People sometimes forget that as their leader, John Fogerty refused to let the producers use their music on the records and their images on the screen—he was not happy with the band's performance or the circumstances of that performance. They followed fellow Bay Area denizens the Grateful Dead and took the stage at 3 a.m. Fogerty said, "Wow, we get to follow the band that put half a million people to sleep. . . I look out past the floodlights and I see about five rows of bodies just intertwined—they're all asleep. ... It was sort of like a painting of a Dante scene."[6] Stu Cook added, "I'm still amazed by the number of people who don't even know we were one of the headliners at Woodstock."[7]

The late '60s were also the latter days of the Wild West as far as the legalities of the music business were concerned, at least in terms of issues between recording companies and artists.[8] Some attorneys at the time had started to learn the basics of the music business, but to most attorneys not affiliated with the entertainment industry in general and the music business specifically, the nature of the "statutory rates" or "controlled copyrights," the determination of gross and net sales, how a non-compete clause could destroy a career, just what the heck music publishing actually involved, and what ASCAP, BMI, and SESAC actually *did* were mysteries. Still, more and more artists had the foresight, or heeded warnings from folks like James and Mc-Daniel who had been there before, to find and hire lawyers literate in these issues. These attorneys were generally either practitioners of intellectual property law or refugees from drawing up music business documents for the record, publishing, and management companies. However, there continued to be many artists who were just happy to have a contract proffered them. This latter was pretty much the case for CCR, who were overjoyed to find that they did not have to go to Los Angeles to explore making records since they had a record company (with hits!) just across the bay.

Creedence Clearwater Revival actually had a quasi-entertainment attorney in their camp; the law firm Stu Cook's father worked for was counsel to the Oakland Raiders. However, even Herman Cook, Esq., was unprepared for the document Fantasy President Saul Zaentz extended to the band in 1967, and so he was unable to save his son and friends from years of grief.

Fantasy, like Chess, was an "independent" record company. This meant they had to count on other companies for the distribution of their product, as opposed to the "major" record companies that had their own distribution networks. Fantasy had a long history of putting out phenomenal jazz records by artists like Dave Brubeck and John Coltrane, spoken word albums by Alan Ginsberg and Lawrence Ferlinghetti, and comedy albums featuring Lenny Bruce. While cutting edge and in keeping with the tastes of the Weiss Brothers (owners of the company from when it made plastic novelties), these were not powerhouse sellers, albeit slow and steady catalog albums. What Fantasy was not used to was having their records become huge hits. They had a fair sized hit in 1962 with Vince Guaraldi's "Cast Your Fate to the Wind." In a PBS program about the song (the same program that made CCR aware of the record company in their backyard), it shows everyone who is not pressing copies of the single loading boxes of the single into trucks, including Guaraldi. At one point the artist wipes his face with a handkerchief and says, "As you can see, we're not ready for success."[9]

While not as onerous as the rarely read Chess contracts (which were often—as in the James story—ameliorated by Leonard's genuine fondness for his artists), the Fantasy boilerplate contract contained many clauses that would help the company recover the money they spent on small press runs, such marketing as they were able to do, and the notorious financial practices of the independent record distributors. For example, most recording contracts continue to contain a passage like, "Article 4.1—Any recordings made by the Artists or any of them during the term hereof and all reproductions made therefrom and performances embodied therein and the copyrights and/ or copyright renewal rights therein and thereto are and shall be entirely the property of Galaxy free and clear."[10] Very few artists had and have the forethought and leverage to retain their masters. These, the actual recordings of the songs, generally become the property of the record company.

Stu Cook, Doug Clifford, and the Fogerty brothers, John and Tom, initially signed to Fantasy as the Blue Velvets in 1964. When former head of sales, Saul Zaentz bought the company in 1967, he gave the band a new contract. The company offered CCR the 1969 contract—or more correctly Creedence demanded it—because over the course of the previous year they had become the number one American band, and in the next year, with the dissolution of the Beatles, they would become the world's most popular band, if just for a year.[11]

After comparing notes with bands on other labels, they realized that they were getting a pittance with the 10.5 percent royalty in the contract.[12] While Zaentz would not raise their royalty rate (although it would slide as high as 12 percent in two years), he had a plan. The contract would no longer be with Creedence Clearwater Revival. It would be with a Bahamian company *owned* by Creedence Clearwater Revival, but not subject to US taxes.[13] This way, Zaentz told them, they would receive 35 percent more than they had before, which made their royalty more like 13%, and it would slide up to the 15 percent that most of their successful contemporaries were earning. Thus, as a corporate entity, Creedence Clearwater Revival became "King David Distributors Limited, a Bahamian corporation."[14]

Despite the changes, much of the contract remained boilerplate. Fantasy retained the right to buy the Artists out of the contract if they wanted to cut them loose by paying $100 to $400 per contracted master based on the minimum number of masters required in the contract.[15] They also allowed Fantasy to reduce the "statutory mechanical royalty" rate 2/3 on all singles, 5/6 for original songs on albums, and 2/3 of 5/6 (5/9 if my math is correct) for recordings and new arrangements of compositions that were out of copyright, still a pretty common practice. The contract actually didn't require the 10 percent breakage allowance, built into the boilerplate of contracts even to-day, over 65 years after the last glass and lacquer disc of recorded music left a factory. However, the 100 percent was based on the net sales rather than the gross sales.[16] In the movie business, percentages of the net are referred to as "monkey points," because you have to be a monkey to take them. A clever accountant can theoretically, using such clauses as section 3.4 which allows the company to maintain a reserve account of 25 percent against returns, make it so a project never achieves a net.[17]

The contract also gave the group 1/2 of that rate on cassettes, which slid up to 2/3 on music released after 1970. This rate also applied to "any device utilizing a new medium of sound and/or sight and sound reproduction."[18] Even more than the previous boilerplate, this would come back to haunt them when CDs became the prevailing medium for sound recordings.

The new contract revised several aspects of the previous contract, reflecting the band's learning curve over the previous two years. For one thing, John Fogerty hated being on compilation albums. The main culprit in that arena was a company called K-Tel that licensed the original recordings of six-month old hits and put them together on one album.[19] You might find songs like "Dizzy" by Tommy Roe, Henry Mancini's "Love Theme from *Romeo and Juliet*," "Sugar Sugar" by the Archies, Simon and Garfunkel's "Bridge Over Troubled Water," and "Ain't No Mountain High Enough" by Diana Ross, all of whom prevented CCR from ever having a #1 single, compiled on one of the company's mail-order packages. Thus, one of the things that Fogerty negotiated into the new agreement was clause 4.3, which rendered Fantasy unable to "without prior written consent of King produce or release records comprised of masters recorded by Artists hereunder with other masters."[20]

More importantly, Fogerty also finally realized what he had given away in Article VII of the contract. This was a lot more delicate. Article VII is sub-headed "Musical Compositions." Within that article, the band originally agreed to assign their music to "any publishing companies designated by Galaxy with statutory fees applying unless otherwise agreed to."[21]

To understand just how important these fourteen words are, you need to understand the vast riches (even today) generated by a hit song. Briefly, a song theoretically makes performance royalties, which are distributed by ASCAP, BMI, and SESAC, the music business performing rights agencies, every time it gets played on the radio, every time someone performs it for money, every time it gets played on TV. Every time a song gets recorded or pressed onto a medium of musical delivery it gets mechanical royalties at a statutory rate set up by the U.S. Office of Copyright or the fraction thereof agreed to in the contract. When a film or television show uses a piece of music, they need to negotiate synchronization rights. This can be worth hundreds of thousands of dollars to the songwriter and publisher, and even something for the Band. When Microsoft used the Rolling Stone's "Start Me Up" to introduce Windows 95 those many years ago, they reportedly paid the Stones a fee that has been estimated at $8 to $15 million for the privilege. The owner of two key songs of the winter solstice season told me that those two songs, with all these streams of revenue, made roughly $4 million *every year.*

Now, "Proud Mary" alone has been covered on one "medium of sound and/or sight and sound reproduction" or another by well over 500 artists, including performers ranging from Elvis Presley to New York Yankee Nick Swisher.[22] This is not to mention the thousands of performances by bar bands around the world. All performances of "Proud Mary" by Ike and Tina Turner, Elvis, or even Swisher, all airplay, all live performances, any time it went over the public address system of a ballpark, theoretically meant money for both Fogerty as the songwriter and Fantasy (actually their Jondora Music Publishing subsidiary) as the publisher.

So as much as Fantasy was making via selling actual Creedence recordings, it didn't hold a candle to the money they were raking in as the publishers of Fogerty's songs. It is postulated that somewhere in the world at any given time, someone is broadcasting or playing a Creedence Clearwater Revival song. The amount of Performance Royalties paid to the songwriter and the publisher for music that earned sizable amounts of airplay, cover versions, and other legal performances of this music is phenomenal. Beyond that, the contract allowed Jondora to keep the publisher's half of the Mechanical Royalties, a nice little kickback. This is where much of the funding for the movie *One Flew Over the Cuckoo's Nest* came from.[23] It was the predominant source of funds for the Saul Zaentz Center that occupies the better part of a square block in Berkeley, California. Fogerty and his bandmates had signed a contract that assigned the songs to Jondora, and Fantasy was loathe to lose this income. Fogerty hated the fact that he had been "duped" out of his publishing through his own ignorance and impatience to sign a recording contract. So negotiations ensued.

Eventually, they decided to split Article VII into two sections. Until midnight on December 31, 1970, about 18 months after they signed the contract, the then current situation would remain in place. Starting with the New Year in 1971, songs written by the band "could be assigned by Artists or their respective successors in interest to a publishing company or companies of their choice."[24]

If signing away his publishing angered Fogerty, another series of agreements would prove far more onerous. A recording contract, by its legal nature, is a personal services contract. Indeed, most recording contracts *specify* this, as it says on the second page of the CCR contract:

> 1.1 *Grant of Exclusive Rights*. King hereby agrees to furnish Galaxy the exclusive *personal services* as performers of each Artist in connection with the production of phonograph records and/or sight and sound recordings during the period commencing on the date hereof and ending December 31, 1974 or such later date as any suspensions or extensions of this Agreement may require. (second italics author's)

The date is important, as it is seven years after the initial contract was signed. In many states, including California where the CCR contract was signed, there is a strict limitation on personal services contracts. "[The] California State Labor Code has a '7 Year Rule' (as referred to in the music industry) stating that personal service contracts which last more than seven years cannot be specifically enforced," write attorneys Ira Scott Meyerowitz and Jon Jekielek.[25] "Many record companies may define the contract's term as, say, a two-year initial period plus three one-year option periods to protect themselves against California's seven-year rule." This rule was instituted in the 1930s to allow stars caught up in the Hollywood "studio system" the ability to renegotiate their contracts or go out as free agents after seven years.[26] This statute—California Labor Code Section 2855—should have prevented Fantasy from holding CCR and it members for more than seven years.

Fantasy finessed this in several moves within the contract. On the second page of the contract, in section 1.2, *Number of Recordings*, reads:

> King agrees to cause Artists to record for Galaxy a minimum number ... of masters ... embodying performances by the Artists ... in each year of the term

hereof ... and such additional number of masters not to exceed ten (10) as Galaxy may elect upon written notice to King no later than three (3) months from the end of each year in which such election is made by Galaxy, and such additional number of masters as required under Article XI. ... All material shall be subject to Galaxy's approval as commercially satisfactory.[27]

While a cursory explanation of what Fantasy meant by a "master" is included in this paragraph, to get the "official" definition of how the contract views a master, you have to turn to page 24, under article XIV, section (b):

"Master" means an original recording whether sound only or sight and sound and embodying the performance of the Artists delivered to Galaxy by King and accepted as commercially satisfactory for the production of records. ... If the selection performed has a playing time of five (5) minutes thirty (30) seconds or less, it shall be deemed to be one master. If the selection has a playing time in excess of five (5) minutes thirty (30) seconds, but less than ten (10) minutes and thirty (30) seconds it shall be deemed to be two (2) masters ... and so forth.[28]

Article XI, section 11.1 establishes the *Minimum Number of Masters* that the band had to record for Fantasy (and the advance royalty per master) (Table 7.1). Doing the math we discover that the contract called for the band to record 120 masters, plus the 10 additional masters called for in section 1.2, for a grand total of 180 masters owed.

Which brings us back to Article V, Section 5.1, a paragraph called *Failure to Perform*:

Should there be a failure to perform on the part of King under this Agreement and should such failure to perform not be corrected to the satisfaction of Galaxy, Galaxy in addition to all other rights and remedies available to it, shall have the absolute right in its sole discretion to extend the then current year and/or the term of this agreement until such failure to perform is corrected.[30]

Table 7.1.

Period	Minimum Number of Masters to Be Recorded	Advance Royalty Per Master
Date of Agreement to Dec. 31, 1969	12	$100.00
Jan. 1, 1970 to Dec. 31, 1970	12	$100.00
Jan. 1, 1971 to Dec. 31, 1971	24	$200.00
Jan. 1, 1972 to Dec. 31, 1972	24	$200.00
Jan. 1, 1973 to Dec. 31, 1973	24	$400.00
Jan. 1, 1974 to Dec. 31, 1974	24	$400.00[29]

While this would seem to fly in the face of the seven-year statute, it was tough to fight for several reasons. The film industry honored the statute to the degree that "contract players," once the lifeblood of the business, have become a quaint anachronism. Contracts are doled out by the project, and one of the "below the line" expenses is what the talent gets paid. However, the music business has not challenged this law, so, as attorney Stan Soocher says, "There's not a lot of case law."[31]

It's not the sort of issue that anyone wants to set a legal precedent on and lose. *The Harvard Law Review* notes that the California statute left "record companies wary of the possibility that a section 2855" ruling favorable to the artists, granting them free agency, might irrevocably change the way they do business. This led the industry to "renegotiate dissatisfied artists' contracts, often providing more generous terms and large advances."[32]

Indeed, the closest court case dealing with what Creedence had signed, in terms of their personal services, was litigated several years after the group broke up, when Olivia Newton-John fought an injunction that prevented her from recording for any company besides MCA. Nor would this ruling have helped Fogerty regarding the "Seven Year Statute." While the court had "grave doubts that defendant's failure to perform her obligations under the contract could extend the term of the contract beyond its specified five year maximum," they would not rule on the statute, per se.[33]

"According to the original contract between CCR and Fantasy, it seems that they contracted for the members of the band to remain obligated under the terms of the contract, should the band break up," noted music business attorney Jeffery Jacobson points out.[34]

> Under Article 10(g), if the group disbanded, a new agreement could be entered into by each member for a term not less than the remaining time left on this agreement, but the agreement could be extended if there were masters that still needed to be provided (Article 5). Since Fantasy released the other members of CCR from their contracts, it seems that Fogerty entered into a solo artist agreement that branched off of and incorporated the terms of this contract. Therefore, a new contract would have been entered into and triggered a new time period, and avoided the "seven year statute," California Civil Code §2855.[35]

Or, as John Fogerty described it about a decade after he was finally cut loose from that provision of the contract, "I owed so much product. ... I felt like I was chained in a dungeon."[36]

Over the course of nearly five decades, the members of CCR continue to feel the legal ramifications of this agreement because the terms of contracts continued to be binding as regards the band's output from that time, even after the parties to that contract have moved on. Some of the repercussions from this contract were mind boggling. The personal services issue, combined with the betrayal John felt from Zaentz's not negotiating in good faith, and the "loss" of his publishing ultimately caused severe writer's block. After two post-Creedence albums that were released and one that was not, John became a rock-and-roll recluse. He did not put out any music, nor perform for a paying audience, for over a decade. He wouldn't play any of his CCR songs for payment for just shy of two decades.

In 1975, David Geffen bought John out of his indentured servitude to Fantasy, at least in North America. He was still recording for Fantasy everywhere else in the world. "I think [Fantasy] proposed a number that Asylum wasn't ready to pay," noted John's brother Bob—who has served as his aide-de-camp for 40+ years.[37]

John's first, eponymous album for Asylum met with mixed criticism and lukewarm sales. His next record for Asylum, *Hoodoo* never came out commercially (though, because of press advances, you can find it pretty easily as a bootleg). John spent the next decade "working on a solo LP," said Tom. "Nobody gets to hear it. He gets about halfway through it, then he scraps the whole thing and starts over."[38]

While his indentured servitude to Fantasy, and their subsequent ownership of the non-American rights to his music was part of the reason for his creative paralysis and withdrawal from the public eye, there was more to it. He (and the rest of the band members) suffered from the upshot of the tax-dodge at the heart of the contract rewrite.

When Asylum Records President Joe Smith told John that he was not going to put *Hoodoo* out, he suggested John take some time off. This reduced his sources of income to his performance royalties, so he decided to take some of his King David Distributors money out of the Bahamas. He sent his attorney down to the Islands to make the withdrawal. When his attorney got there, he found the door to the bank chained. A look in the window revealed nothing but a few trash cans and shredders. All the money had disappeared. "Rumors are that it's either the Mafia or the CIA," Tom Fogerty said, "or the officers of the bank offed with it. We got left holding the bag. The *Wall Street Journal* printed a couple of stories on it, and it was on *60 Minutes* twice."[39]

Whoever took it (as far as can be determined, no one ever found out), the band's nest egg, some $6 million, had disappeared. First John and then the rest of the group sued and, by 1980, the members of CCR were together again, in a lawsuit against the people that had fiduciary responsibility toward the band—the law firm in which Stu's father had been a partner (specifically, attorney Barry Engle, who oversaw the account), the Chicago based law-firm that promoted the Bahamian bank in America, and the group's accountants. The two attorneys settled with the band, but the accountants did not. So the band was often together in Bay Area law offices getting deposed. The case didn't get settled for over ten years, with a federal appeals court finding the accountants liable.

By the time the case finally got settled, John had done a bold and perhaps foolish thing: he decided that the royalties he actually did receive from Fantasy for the CCR recordings, the worldwide, non-America sales of all his music, and his share of the mechanical royalties for his songs owned by Jondora, now that they were not getting sent to the Bahamas, really didn't amount to much. Fantasy owed him much of the foreign royalties he accrued for his more recent music. He told Zaentz (who by this time was far more involved with his film production business than the record business) that he could keep those royalties, and anything else they owed him from then on if he no longer had to release his music on Fantasy worldwide, trading his past for his future. For the first time in his professional career, he was no longer financially beholden to Fantasy.

Even as John abrogated his fiscal rights to masters and the royalties, that money became a major issue for the rest of the band. On August 17, 1982, Phillips introduced a new medium for sound recording, the digital compact disc, and by the middle of the decade, it had all but replaced the vinyl record.[40] People rushed to record stores to replace their popping, skipping vinyl LPs with this new medium. Historically, the recorded sound industry makes a large percentage of their money selling through the catalog. Some people discover older music and want to own it. Some people wear out music in an older medium and want to replace it with a shiny new medium. Certain people have to have the latest technology and purchase music they might already own in a new format for their new technology.

As previously mentioned, under the terms of their contract, the greater portion of the music recorded by Creedence earned a ½ royalty tape rate, somewhere between 5 and 6 percent of the net profit earned by Fantasy, as per Article II, section (b). This is because, per section (c) of the same Article, that rate also covered new technology—which included the CD and the download. So, as the vinyl record sailed off into the sea of dead media (to rise from the dead some years later), the royalties the band earned on their catalog began to shrink considerably from when the LP reigned. They needed to renegotiate.

One of the things John insisted on in the 1969 contract was article 4.3 about not combining masters without the group's permission. By 1988, Cook and Clifford had negotiated an override on this clause for the trio masters (i.e., music made after Tom Fogerty left the group). When Tom signed on, there was the majority needed for all the masters. In exchange, the band got a significant increase in their royalties for CDs. John did not participate in these, and was further outraged when his songs started turning up on compilation albums.

Of course, the biggest issue for John was the music publishing. John's music fueled the company in a way Vince Guaraldi, Lenny Bruce, or John Coltrane could not. They were selling millions of albums worldwide and continue to sell perhaps a million catalog items a year. Their songs are featured in films and other media. As the majority of the band regularly out-voted John on contractual issues, he became angrier. While Fantasy retained the rights to his masters and his publishing, the songwriter's share of his songs continued to belong to him. However, for two decades he would not play any of his CCR songs, would not give Fantasy the satisfaction of collecting more royalties based on his work. Eventually it took no one less than Bob Dylan to break this self-enforced moratorium. During an after-hours jam session, Dylan requested that they play "Proud Mary." John demurred. Dylan scowled at him and said, "If you don't start playing it, people are going to think that it was a Tina Turner song." So by the time CCR was inducted into the Rock and Roll Hall of Fame, he had been playing his CCR heritage for over half a decade.

Still, the anger rankled. John remained upset at the rest of the band members, so much so that he nearly did not visit his dying brother, Tom, in 1990. He certainly did not grant his dying brother his wish to play together one last time. Indeed, at the Hall of Fame ceremony inducting CCR, John refused to play with Cook and Clifford. This led them to form their own version of Creedence. While they had the majority needed to call the group Creedence Clearwater Revival, they decided, instead, to call it Creedence Clearwater Revisited. Even that name caused John to get a legal injunction against his former bandmates—for several months, early in their new career, they were known as Cosmo's Factory, after one of the band's most successful albums and Doug's long-standing nickname. Ironically, they have now been playing together as Creedence Clearwater Revisited for over a decade, over twice as long as the original CCR existed.

Toward the end of November, 2004, Concord Records bought Fantasy's musical assets from Zaentz. In 2005, Fogerty re-signed with the Zaentz-less, under-new-management Fantasy Records. To celebrate, the new owners gave him the back royalties he gave up in the early '80s, about a quarter century's worth. They were not prepared, however, to give him back his publishing: "...we can't do that, because we just paid a lot of money for (it)," said one of the company's new owners, Glen Barros.[41] The publisher's half of the songwriter royalties from the CCR catalog was still one of the company's biggest assets, and certainly one of the key points in purchasing the company.

When teaching about the music business, I find it useful to go through an actual recording contract or two. Creedence Clearwater Revival's 1969 contract works as a cautionary document for any artist or manager who might be too anxious to sign a contract with a record company. In the four-and-a-half decades since the group signed it, this document has served as a catalyst to destroy a friendship that predated high school. Because of the contract, two brothers didn't talk to each other for many years. It caused one of the most prolific, exciting songwriters of the rock era to become a veritable hermit, going decades between album releases. In an era where bands that went through hurtful, seemingly irreparable splits reunite successfully, the upshot of this agreement makes John Fogerty, Stu Cook, and Doug Clifford the least likely to join that fray. While it has never been challenged in court, it has caused three musicians to spend years in litigation over other matters related to it. It pays to remember that artists could have to live with the terms of their contracts for the rest of their lives.

Notes

1. George Rood, "Holiday Expands Recording Sales," *New York Times*, Dec. 19, 1965, F12.

2. Etta James, interview by author, 1988.

3. The LA based company with which James had her earliest hits, like "Roll with Me Henry."

4. James.

5. Elias McDaniel, "Bo Diddley," interview by author, 1996.

6. James Henke, "John Fogerty," *Rolling Stone*, November 5, 1987, 151.

7. Stu Cook, e-mail message to author, 1996.

8. The Wild West in music business legalities between the recording companies and *fans* would evolve sometime later.

9. *Anatomy of a Hit*, directed by Richard Moore (1963; Ralph Gleason/KQED), Television.

10. "Recording Contract," June 5, 1969, 8. CCR's recordings were and are re-leased via Fantasy, but they were actually signed to Fantasy's Galaxy affiliate.

11. "Despite their continued inability to land a number 1 single, they were the world's number-1 singles and album band. Despite their problems with royalties, they were the number-1 band monetarily, too." Hank Bordowitz, *Bad Moon Rising: The Unauthorized History of Creedence Clearwater Revival* (Chicago: Chicago Review Press/A Cappella Books, 2007), 105.

12. "Recording Contract," 18.

13. Ibid., 1.

14. Ibid., 1.

15. Ibid., 14–15, 18.

16. Ibid., 3.

17. Ibid., 7.

18. Ibid., 4.

19. Larry Jaffee, "K-Tel's Place in the Music Industry: Where Have All the One-Hit Wonders Gone?" *Popular Music and Society* 10, no. 4 (1986): 43–50, http://www.rocksbackpages.com/article.html?ArticleID=19219.

20. The new corporation, King David Distributors was known as "King" in the contract. "Recording Contract," June 5, 1969, 9.

21. Ibid., 13.

22. "Proud Mary,"*All Music Guide*, http://www.allmusic.com/search/track/Proud+Mary/order:default-asc (October 28, 2011).

23. See Bordowitz, 159. Zaentz also produced *Amadeus*, *The Unbearable Lightness of Being*, *The Mosquito Coast*, and *The English Patient*, among others.

24. "Recording Contract," 13.

25. Jon Jekielek and Ira Scott Meyerowitz, "Unreasonable Duration of Recording Agreement," February 18, 2009, http://mjlawfirm.com/entertainment-law/unreasonable-duration-of-recording-agreements/ (October 25, 2011).

26. Ivan Hoffman, "The Price of Popcorn, the Personal Services Contract," 2006, http://www.ivanhoffman.com/personal.html (October 25, 2011).

27. "Recording Contract," 13, 2–3.

28. Ibid., 24–25.

29. Ibid., 18.

30. Ibid., 9.

31. Stan Soocher, interview by author, November 3, 2011.

32. "California Labor Code Section 2855 and Recording Artists' Contracts," *Harvard Law Review* 116, no. 8 (June 2003): 2632.

33. MCA Records, Inc, Plaintiff and Respondent, v. Olivia Newton-John, Defendant and Appellant, Civ. No. 54177, March 2, 1979, Court of Appeal of California, Second Appellate District, Division Two (Lexis-Nexis).

34. Jeffery Jacobson, e-mail message to author, November 24, 2011.

35. Ibid.

36. Joel Selvin, "John Fogerty on Threshold of Big Comeback," *San Francisco Chronicle*, Jan. 6, 1985, 17.

37. Bob Fogerty, interview by author, 1997.

38. Tom Fogerty, interview by author, 1981.

39. Ibid.

40. Rob Beschizza, "Compact Disc Is 25 Years Old," *Wired.com*, August 18, 2007, http://www.wired.com/gadgetlab/2007/08/compact-disk-is/.

41. Anthony DeCurtis, "John Fogerty Is Closer to Peace with a Label," *New York Times*, Nov. 1, 2005, E1.

PART III

"CENTERFIELD"

～

CHAPTER EIGHT

America as Patron and Muse: The Creation of the Blue Ridge Rangers

Lawrence Pitilli

Story #1

I have long been a fan of bumper stickers. I have always felt that their inscriptions reflect the pulse and issues of the day in a most terse and perspicacious manner. One such sticker that has recently caught my attention states that DISSIDENCE DOES NOT MEAN UNPATRIOTIC. This prompted the question, "What does it mean to be patriotic?" This, in turn, led to "What does it mean to be an American?" which led to "What is America?" which led to ... Well, you get the picture. And so, being a curious individual and a huge fan of all things rock and country, I once again found that all roads and questions lead to music.

Story #2

Somewhere in the late fall of 1988, I was given a cassette of *The Blue Ridge Rangers*. I was told that this was a long ago side project of "that guy from Creedence." Eight bars into "Blue Ridge Mountain Blues" and I'm totally gone—love at first hearing. And, yes, the love affair continues to this day.

Story #3

I am presently disappointed that my officially paid-for (on a monthly basis) Napster subscription does not provide me, as of this date, with the listening delights of the aforementioned side project album. However, I do possess a CD of this album as well as the original cassette, so all is well. Curious, I have delved into the history of this classic album and have tied it together with some of my probing from Story #1. And, thus, we begin.

Genesis

In 1972, during the last surviving days of Creedence Clearwater Revival, the band was touring with Tony Joe White of "Polk Salad Annie" fame. After many of the concerts, there would be informal jam sessions in the hotel rooms. In the middle of one of these sessions, John Fogerty was playing a version of Hank Williams's "Jambalaya" when Mr. White turned to him and said, "You oughta record that. Man, that's exciting!"[1] That one statement pronounced the origin of Mr. Fogerty's one-man band solo recording project known as the Blue Ridge Rangers. This album has been by no means a commercial success. Yet it has created not only a cult following amongst discophiles but also yielded a recent follow-up album entitled *The Blue Ridge Rangers Rides Again.*

The original album is much more than just a band leader wanting to assert himself in the arena of self-produced solo efforts. John Fogerty's hugely successful band, Creedence Clearwater Revival, had just broken up. He was estranged from his brother and fellow bandmate Tom Fogerty, and he owed his label, Fantasy, eighty master tapes. To make matters worse, he was suffering from writer's block. So, was this album a mere first response to a contractual obligation? Hardly. The genesis of this album is found in one man's love of America and Americana in the purist sense. The album is composed solely of country and gospel classics. It can be argued that country and gospel music, along with the cowboy-western, jazz, and the spelling bee share that singularly defined space reserved for those forms of expression and invention endogenous to America only. Nevertheless, the songs on this album serve as a reflection of a support system for and a source of inspiration to a unique American artist during a most critical time in his artistic and personal life.

The Blue Ridge Rangers of 1973 embodied one man's individual interpretation of American culture both in its choice of music and embrace of such heralded ideals of ingenuity, individualism, and a pioneering spirit. John Fogerty once stated, "I'm just made differently. Man, I just love being an American, I love my country."[2] Let's now see how this album sings those praises.

Custom Made in the USA

In an article posted in the *Freedom Daily*, Richard M. Ebeling poses the question, "What makes someone an American as opposed to, say, an Englishman, or a Frenchman, or a German, or an Italian?"[3] In *Letters from an American Farmer*, J. Hector St. John Crèvecoeur asks, "What then is the American, this new man? He is either an European, or the descendant of an European, hence that strange mixture of blood, which you will find in no other country. I could point out to you a family whose grandfather was an Englishman, whose wife was Dutch, whose son married a French woman, and whose present four sons have now four wives of different nations. He is an American, who leaving behind him all his ancient prejudices and manners, receives new ones from the new mode of life he has embraced, the new government he obeys, and the new rank he holds."[4] As one may perceive, the answers to these questions lie in race, multi-generational ancestry, linguistics, and even genetics. The United States, however, has as its citizenry people of many different racial, religious, and ethnic backgrounds who have emigrated from all parts of the globe. Thus, for an individual to be defined as an American, they must acquire citizenship within the parameters of the legal system, the law of the land. The law of the land is found in the Constitution, and its purpose is to secure and protect the fundamental liberties of its citizens. Thus, we can say that to be an American is to share a belief system that allows us to speak the language of our choice, observe or not observe any religion, hold forth with any traditions that we choose, and pursue and embrace any profession or vocation which we regard as our calling. It is these last two tenets of tradition and profession that invoke John Fogerty's love of America. In a 2007 interview, Mr. Fogerty states that "I come from a generation that came of age in the '60s, so that intense pride comes out a little differently in me than it does in, say, John Wayne. ... But it happened to me during the Nixon time, especially pre-Watergate, that as I watched Nixon for the first time in my life I felt shame. I had to analyze myself. What is this emotion? I realized that my government was separate from my country. It was the first time I ever felt ashamed of the government, not the country. I felt that the population as a whole, of which I am one member, I was proud of that. I was proud of our history, all the things that have led us to where we are and what we stood for and stand for still—I hope."[5]

It is this love of America, this custom made self-defining American individualism, which perhaps fueled Mr. Fogerty's initiative in choosing songs so deeply steeped in his country's musical roots. It also took quite the individualist to make a record so diametrically opposite of one's commercial persona. Although the country rock genre was steadily developing with the likes of the Eagles and Poco, country music in the '70s belonged to the traditional Nashville establishment—hardly a rock-and-roll crowd. Moreover, a genre switch could hasten the commercial destruction of his career by alienating

Creedence fans. Yet the album was not a disaster in any sense of the word. Perhaps this had more to do with John Fogerty's purity of spirit in choosing and performing those songs. Perhaps this spirit was not unlike the purity of spirit of the Founding Fathers in composing a document which would allow freedom of expression regardless of race, religion, ethnicity, and even musical tastes and commercial allegiances. Perhaps Crèvecoeur eloquently captured Fogerty's American spirit when he stated that "The American is a new man, who acts upon new principles; he must therefore entertain new ideas, and form new opinions. From involuntary idleness, servile dependence, penury, and useless labour, he has passed to toils of a very different nature, rewarded by ample subsistence. This is an American."[6]

Whose Patriotic Songs Are These Anyway?

Patriotic songs, regardless of any one country's association, embrace, evoke, and, in a sense, eulogize a nation's history and the traditions of its people. They can also serve as a focal point for a nation's identity. Many patriotic songs have found their origins in wartime, the "Star Spangled Banner" serving as a quintessential example of such. A large number of American patriotic songs have been written during four main wars—the American Revolution, the War of 1812, the American Civil War, and the Spanish-American War. World War I later produced such classics as "Over There" by George M. Cohan and Irving Berlin's "God Bless America."[7] This latter song is regarded by some as the unofficial national anthem. Interestingly enough, Woody Guthrie wrote "This Land Is Your Land" as a protest response to Berlin's song stating that it was unrealistic and complacent. However, in the last few decades, there has been a proliferation of newly composed patriotic songs. These songs can either stir up national pride, console us in times of loss, or wink at us, knowing that we are part, at times, of a huge commercial complex known as the American Dream.[8] Some examples of this neo-genre are as follows: Toby Keith's "Courtesy of the Red, White and Blue," written after the 9/11 tragedy; Billy Ray Cyrus's "Some Gave All," which eulogizes the mortally wounded in combat; Chuck Berry's swaggering testimonial to the American Dream in "Back in the U.S.A."; Johnny Horton's "The Battle of New Orleans"; and, perhaps most famously of all, Lee Greenwood's "God Bless the USA."

However, if we consider that a patriotic song can embrace, with some latitude and musical appreciation, songs outside the wartime context, then we can begin to understand the patriotic value of the Blue Ridge Rangers' repertoire. History and tradition certainly play vital roles in restructuring one's definition of the patriotic song, and here is where America as muse asserts itself. Fogarty chose three gospel songs, "Working on a Building," "Have Thine Own Way, Lord," and "Somewhere Listening (For My Name)," as representative samples of the gospel genre. It can be asserted that gospel and musical tradition are almost synonymous and possibly symbiotic concepts which serve as testimonials to the American musical spirit. In fact, a good part of the American culture is rooted in the Protestant religion and its adherence to the Bible. Adelaide A. Pollard's composition of "Have Thine Own Way, Lord" is an example of this congruence. She was a Bible teacher and hymn writer who worked as a missionary in Africa. At a very trying time in her life, she was inspired to write the aforementioned gospel song. In fact, the lyrics are based on a story told in Jeremiah 18:3.[9]

When it comes to evoking and eulogizing traditional American country-music artists, surely the likes of George Jones ("She Thinks I Still Care"), Hank Snow ("You're the Reason"), Hank Williams ("Jambalaya"), Merle Haggard ("California Blues"), and Hank Locklin ("Please Help Me, I'm Falling") serve as abundant inspiration in constructing a song list for an album. It may be worthwhile to note, at this point, that simplicity of musical and lyrical composition in country and gospel music go hand in hand with simplicity in arrangement. Fogerty was, in fact, the one-man Blue Ridge Rangers band. Thus, we hear basic rhythm and bass guitar, drums, lead voice, and some lead guitar riffs and backing vocals. Once again, the performance credits stand as John Fogerty. Also, it is important to note that the keys in which these songs are played, as well as the original keys of standard patriotic songs, bear a simple key signature. But consider "The Star-Spangled Banner." The original sheet music is in the simple key of C—no sharps, no flats. It is mostly arranged in the key of G—one sharp which is F sharp in its key signature—to accommodate most vocalists due to its octave and a half range. If we consider the musical simplicity of the Blue Ridge Rangers song list in order to draw a similarity of those songs to the standard patriotic, country, and gospel songs, we must then consider the keys in which the Rangers' songs are sung.

Six of the twelve songs are placed in the key of G which, as previously stated, has F sharp in its key signature. These songs include "Blue Ridge Mountain Blues," "Somewhere Listening," "Jambalaya," "California Blues," "Working on a Building," and "Please Help Me, I'm Falling." The gospel hymn "Have Thine Own Way, Lord" is sung in the most simple key of C. The remaining five songs are played in the keys of F sharp, D, and B and are listed as follows: "You're the Reason," "Hearts of Stone," and "Today I Started Loving You Again" (key of F sharp); "She Thinks I Still Care" (key of D); and "I Ain't Never" (key of B). With the exception of "Have Thine

Own way, Lord," all of the remaining eleven songs bear a commonality in terms of key signature and a specific note that is played. This note is F sharp, and as previously stated, the key of G has F sharp in its key signature. However, the F sharp note is placed significantly in the remaining keys of F sharp, D, and B. In the key of F sharp, the note F sharp is placed in the tonic position, that is, the first note in the F sharp major chord. In the key of D, the F sharp note lies in the third position of the D major chord. In the key of B, the F sharp note takes the fifth position in the B major chord.

Thus, I find it most curious that Mr. Fogerty chose these specific keys in which to play, sing, and arrange. Remember, he was the one man band in this project. Also, it is very easy to play a guitar in the keys of G, C, and D. However, the keys of F sharp and B, with their complicated key signatures, pose the simple question, "Why?" Did it make that much of a difference to play these songs in those keys which have key signatures consisting of six and five sharps respectively? If you raise each one of these keys a mere half step, they become the popular aforementioned keys of G and C. It just might be that Fogerty, being the skilled musician that he was (and still remains), felt that those individual keys would enhance certain dynamics in his vocal and instrumental performance. Then again, why not simply lower each of these keys a half step so that F sharp now becomes F and B becomes B flat (or A sharp depending on one's perspective)? I would like to believe that the answer lies in some kind of musical collective consciousness where certain notes have, in a sense, a life of their own. Perhaps this life is based on history and tradition with, in this case, the genesis of life lying in the key constructions of the early American patriotic songs. Hence, we recognize the commonality of key signature choices of both the Rangers' playlist and the traditional patriotic songs. We may also speculate that there is some form of spiritual chemistry in these keys that lie beyond the threshold of consciousness. This perspective has been explored through the works of Rudolf Steiner (1861–1925) of the Anthroposophical Movement and the German poet Christian Schubart (1739–1791) whereby tonal awareness is starkly correlated with human consciousness. Musical keys are a combination of various tones based on specific pitches. Steiner states that tones have the power and ability to draw man's soul qualities or deep emotions, if you will, out of the realm of the physical body. When this occurs, one "feels the beat," one's "soul is filled" and we, through soulful and physical identification, get "lost in the music" and "become one with the music." Steiner believed that the physical world, which surely includes our physical bodies, lies upon the foundation of tone since the physical world is regarded as a vibratory realm. Thus, tonality and the physical body share the same realm.[10] Christian Schubart compiled a list of major and minor keys and the qualities and emotions which each provokes.[11] For instance, relative to the specific aforementioned keys, the key of C represents pure innocence; G represents discontent and uneasiness; D is victorious and rejoicing; F sharp surmounting difficulty; and B is associated with wild passion. All of these qualities and emotions may perhaps be related to the lyrical content of the BRR songs as well as Fogerty's inner turmoil at the time. On the other hand, it just might have well been that Fogerty found the keys of G and C to be too commonplace and redundant and, thus, posed a personal challenge for himself.[12] If this be the case, then we can always recall ZZ Top's Billy Gibbons's famous line, "Always play it in the key of G demolished," which speaks volumes about the sometimes erratic and creative mindset of musicians.[13] So, where does the truth lie? In all of the above? None of the above? Somewhere in between? Who knows? At the very least, it may just provoke a whole new set of questions and speculations.

Writer's Block! It's a Good Thing—or—Necessity Is the Mother of Convention

So, it's 1972 and you're John Fogerty, lead singer, guitarist, and primary songwriter of an internationally renowned band as in CCR. The problems are a) your band is dismantling itself; b) you have become estranged from one of your bandmates who just happens to be your brother; and c) you have writer's block not to mention that you are contractually obligated to your label, Fantasy, for eighty master tapes! What to do? Well, a) you need to continue making a living; b) just know it happens in the best of families; and c) ah, there's definitely a problem here. There are a host of reasons for writer's block. First, for consideration, is that you are much too self-critical and filled with the fear that "Oh, my God, I'll never write again!" This could possibly be valid if your expectations are too high. Perhaps the source of this problematic area is found in the obligations of the commercial music world. Maybe you've been writing songs that you "should" have been writing as opposed to writing songs that you "wanted" to be writing. Then there's stress. That could kill any muse. Just look at the stressful situations surrounding John Fogerty in 1972. And finally, just for good measure, the well possibly went dry.[14]

Solutions? Any number of self-help articles on curing writer's block will provide you with many a practical and creative approach to the problem.[15] However, whichever way you look at the problem, it all comes down to either Door #1: do something different, or Door #2: when in doubt—substitute. I would say that Mr. Fogerty went through Door #2 back in 1972. The obvious interpretation is that he selected time honored country and gospel songs steeped in tradition and convention as his creatively chosen song substitutes. Yes, these songs were a far cry from the rock-and-roll genre of CCR. However, in paying homage to the progenitors of rock and roll, he remarked that "The early rock guys all seemed kind of country: Elvis, Carl Perkins, Jerry Lee … ."[16] We could also consider that creativity has much to do with courage in being vulnerable. Mr. Fogerty, in referring to the Blue Ridge Rangers' album, stated, "I thought making that record was the most loving, coolest thing I could do. I was baring my soul."[17] And bare his soul he did. Just listen to that album's playlist and you'll find songs of heartbreak, yearning, and pure devotion to a Higher Being. And if you have any doubt about this artist's willingness to be vulnerable, give a good listen to "Please Help Me, I'm Falling." Talk about working without a net.

If we are to step further through Door #2, then we must connect these "substitutions" with John Fogerty's individual interpretation and embodiment of the American socio-political way. So, let us divide some songs into two categories at this point: God/ country and remembrances (both fond and not so fond). The first category can immediately be represented by "Somewhere Listening." The singer is making a plea for inspiration from God. Suffice it to say that God and country go hand in hand in the American mindset and culture as well as in Fogerty's personal vision. In "Have Thine Own Way, Lord" a very weary soul is calling out once again to a Higher Being in a time of need. "Working on a Building" proclaims the work ethic as a religiously inspired activity. The Rangers album could very well be that building. And, so, we have both God and country as patron and muse in the form of spiritual support and inspiration. The second category, which reflects memory function positively and negatively, is first represented by "Blue Ridge Mountain Blues." This is a fervent paean to remembrances long ago in the form of a great geographical icon. Lastly, we have "California Blues," a song which evokes feelings of love, loss, and insecurity about the future. The lyrics tell us that someone wasn't treated right, they're weary from this mistreatment, and they're sure going to leave. I'll go out on a Psychology 101 limb here saying that Fantasy Records is the subconscious provocateur of these feelings.

As a final thought regarding the issue of writer's block and passing through doors, one can speculate in the realm of the alternative universe theme. Therefore, we now have the big "what if," and that is: what if Fogerty realized that writing is only half of the game and performance the remaining half? He wouldn't have been able to write songs at that time that held up to the classics that he was recording. So, what does he do? He overcompensates by creating himself in the form of a group persona, the Blue Ridge Rangers, starring himself as the lead singer. Look, Elvis wasn't a songwriter, yet he is as synonymous with America as the cowboy western, jazz, and the spelling bee, and his contribution no less great. So perhaps we can now say that BRR wasn't necessarily a cure for writer's block but rather an opportunity to set his performance talents free. Isn't this one of the American culture's great ideals—the ability to change your mind, change your direction, and be free to do so? So, at second glance, John Fogerty also went through Door #1 in that he certainly did something different. Yes, writer's block, it's a good thing.

Lastly, it would be very easy to say that this album is nothing but "filler" in that it filled a portion of a record contract's obligation. One could speculate that it simply filled time in a person's life or that it filled space on a record. If we take the "filler" approach then we would be discarding the almost Herculean effort it took to, first and foremost, be a one-man band. John Fogerty not only sang lead on these songs but also served as the backup vocalists. If that weren't enough, he coordinated his musical efforts by playing lead, rhythm, and bass guitars and being the band's drummer. Next, take a look at his musical predecessors. Try competing with the likes of country music's Holy Trinity of Hank Williams, George Jones, and Merle Haggard. That is, in a word, courageous. And if that isn't enough pressure, think about this: you're riding on the heels of a huge 1970 hit album which was a one-man band effort containing all original songs. And who was this one-man band? It just happened to have been a former Beatle in the name of Paul McCartney. Filler? I don't think so.

Epilogue

It's 2009 and the Blue Ridge Rangers Part II has arrived in the form of *The Blue Ridge Rangers Rides Again*. Among its many components are masterpieces provided by such legendary writers as John Prine and Phil Everly. Yet, the big question looms in the air: What happened between the two Rangers projects? What was John Fogerty doing? There was, for one, much resurfacing going on—some of it successful, some not so successful. There was, however, the creation of a standard for the neo-American songbook entitled "Centerfield," one of Mr. Fogerty's great solo career efforts. Regarding the new Rangers' album, the production is, for lack of a better word, slicker as it doesn't have that "let's start a band" feel to it. At this point, though, we'll reserve commentary on the post 1973 John Fogerty musical season for another day. Perhaps that overview will begin with Story #4.

Notes

1. Barry Mazor, "John Fogerty Twangs Again," *Wall Street Journal*, Sept. 29, 2009. http://online.wsj.com/article/SB100014240529702034401045744028405402 53868.html.

2. Joshua Klein. "Interviews: John Fogerty." *Pitchfork*, November 27, 2007, pitch fork.com/features/interviews John Fogerty.

3. Richard M. Ebeling, "What Makes an American?" *The Future of Freedom Foundation: Freedom Daily*, May 2001, www.fff.org/freedom.

4. J. Hector Crèvecoeur, "What Is an American?" *Letters from an American Farmer*, 1782, xroads.virginia.edu/letters from an American farmer.

5. Klein.

6. Crèvecoeur.

7. See Mitford M. Matthews, ed., *A Dictionary of Americanisms* (Chicago: University of Chicago Press, 1951).

8. See Robert Fontenot, "Top 10 Patriotic Oldies," *About.com*, http://oldies .about.com/od/buyersguides/tp/patrioticoldies.htm (May 21, 2011).

9. For additional information, see Cliff Barrows, Donald Hustad, and William Franklin Graham, *Crusader Hymns and Hymn Stories: Crusade Hymn Stories* (Minneapolis, MN: Billy Graham Evangelistic Association, 1967).

10. Rudolph Steiner, *The Inner Nature of Music and the Experience of Tone: Selected Lectures from the Work of Rudolph Steiner* (London: Rudolph Steiner Press, 1983).

11. Rita Steblin, *A History of Key Characteristics in the 18th and Early 19th Centuries* (Ann Arbor, MI: UMI Research Press, 1983).

12. See "Affective Key Characteristics," http://www.wmich.edu/mus-theo/courses/ keys.html (March 1, 2012).

13. "Stargazer in a Puddle," *Bones* (season 2, episode 21, May 16, 2007). TV.

14. For a discussion of what may cause writer's block, see Ana Parker Goodwin, "Seven Reasons for Writer's Block," *Bitterroot Mountain*, Oct. 26, 2009, www.bitter rootmountainllc.com.

15. For example, see Ginny Wiehardt, "Top 10 Tips for Overcoming Writer's Block," *About.com: Fiction Writing*, http://fictionwriting.about.com/o/writingroad block/tp/block.htm. (December 4, 2011).

16. Peter Cooper, "John Fogerty Considers Long Career, Nashville's Influence," *The Tennessean* Nov. 19, 2009, http://blogs.tennessean.com/tunein/2009/11/19/john -fogerty-considers-long-career-nashvilles-influence/.

17. Ibid.

∼

CHAPTER NINE

The 1980s Comeback of John Fogerty

Thomas M. Kitts

"Where Has John Fogerty Gone?" asked Dave Marsh from the pages of *Musician, Player, and Listener* in April 1981.[1] Ironically, the music of Fogerty's former band, Creedence Clearwater Revival, seemed to be everywhere. That previous November, Fantasy had released *The Concert*, a live CCR set said to have been recorded at London's Royal Albert Hall, but actually recorded at the Oakland Coliseum in January 1970. *The Concert*, which would turn platinum (sales of over one million copies), was just another in a long line of Fantasy's releases, re-releases, and repackagings of CCR's music since the band's break-up in 1972.[2]

In addition to the Fantasy releases, CCR's songs were heard regularly in films: *Who'll Stop the Rain* (1978, "Hey Tonight," "Proud Mary," and, of course, "Who'll Stop the Rain"), *An American Werewolf in London* (1981, "Bad Moon Rising"), *Twilight Zone—The Movie* (1983, "Midnight Special"), and *The Big Chill* (1983, "Bad Moon Rising"), among others. Many performers—Dave Edmunds, Emmylou Harris, the Minutemen, and Alabama, to name a few—paid homage to CCR on albums or in concert. Bruce Springsteen began to perform "Who'll Stop the Rain" in response to Ronald Reagan's election to the presidency and John Lennon's death. (Inexplicably, Springsteen omitted his powerful rendition from *Live 1975/85*). In a 1982 interview, Joe Strummer praised Fogerty for some ten minutes and wondered about his absence before returning to the music of the Clash, and, in her *Rolling Stone* 4½ of 5 stars review of *The Concert*, Debra Rae Cohen pined "for another dose of the original."[3] Clearly, as the Reagan era began, rock listeners were anxious to hear from the driving force of CCR.

But Fogerty, who had not released any new music since 1975 and who had not toured since his CCR days, was not ready to break his silence. His immediate post-CCR years had not been very satisfying, either commercially or artistically. He had released two albums on which he played all instruments and sang all vocals. *Blue Ridge Rangers*, in 1973, was an album of country covers which peaked at #47 on the *Billboard* pop chart, and *John Fogerty* (1975), known as "the Shep album" because Fogerty sits with his dog on the cover, peaked at #78. In 1976, Fogerty submitted *Hoodoo* to Elektra/Asylum, which rejected the album. After a few hours of dejection, Fogerty felt relieved. He hadn't much liked the Shep album, despite some fine moments ("Almost Saturday Night," "The Wall," "Dream/Song," and "Rockin' All over the World," which served as the theme song for Live Aid in 1985), but, he said, "*Hoodoo* [was] even worse.[4].... A lot of that album was just gibberish. I even put a Scottish drum corps instrumental track on there because I couldn't think of anything else to do."[5] The rejection, he said, was delivered to him "very gently ... it felt more like freedom."[6] As the 1980s began to progress, more and more rock listeners wondered about the "great lost American rock and roller of the Sixties."[7] For several years, there had been no new music, no live performances, and no interviews: "Nothing is worse than a has-been rock 'n' roll singer telling you his problems," he later explained.[8]

As the 1970s turned into the '80s, Fogerty was living with his wife Martha and their three teenagers in El Cerrito, not far from his former high school. He practiced relentlessly in his tiny studio, "obsessed," he said, to improve his musicianship on keyboards, bass, saxophone, drums, and guitar.[9] "I wanted to become a *good* guitar player, not just sort of a rock guitar player, but really play. Use *all* my fingers [*laughs*]."[10]After dinner, he brought an instrument or two into the TV room, "where my family could see I was actually alive."[11] Fogerty had become a musical recluse, communicating with his record label, Elektra/Asylum, only through a post office box and recording by himself but releasing nothing: "I've learned to talk to the machines."[12] Although he had little interaction with other musicians, he performed two impromptu sets with former CCR members: first, at his twentieth high school reunion in October 1980, and then again at his brother Tom's wedding in September 1982. Each set featured covers and CCR originals and lasted over an hour. John enjoyed both performances, calling the one at his former high school, "very sincere and honest."[13] The other members hoped the performances would spur a CCR tour, but John would have none of it: "It's humiliating to feed off the past."[14]

Disappointed in his creative output since his days with CCR, mired in an oppressive contract with Fantasy which called for 180 masters or some 10 albums of material, and entangled in all kinds of legalities with his former label, Fogerty lost his ability to concentrate. "I owed [Fantasy] so much product," he said. "I couldn't even brush my teeth. I couldn't focus. The pressure was there all the time. I felt like I was chained in a dungeon."[15] Reports indicated that Fogerty had suffered from an ulcer, writer's block, depression, insomnia, and more. Fogerty compared himself to both a "blind man in a fog"[16] and to Jack Torrance (the Jack Nicholson character in *The Shining*) who sat at his typewriter for months typing the same sentence over and over.[17] An especially crippling blow came shortly after *Hoodoo's* rejection when Fogerty sent his attorney to the Bahamas to withdraw some of the $6 million that belonged to him and his former bandmates only to discover that the bank had collapsed and that the money had disappeared. (As Bordowitz reports elsewhere in this collection, the Bahamian tax scheme was devised by Saul Zaentz, president of Fantasy, so the label could avoid paying CCR a higher royalty rate while, in effect, giving CCR the income a higher rate would have generated.) By 1980, to recoup the missing money, the former CCR members were deeply involved in a lawsuit against the group's accountants. Fogerty found few moments of peace. He always seemed to be punching walls and knocking over lamps, or as his daughter Laurie succinctly put it, "Dad was always mad."[18]

Good News and *Centerfield*

In June 1983, John Fogerty emerged from seclusion to announce that he and his former bandmates had won their multimillion dollar lawsuit against their former accountants and financial advisors in the Bahamian debacle. "I feel more relieved than anything," he said at his press conference. Fogerty, who was awarded $4.1 million, continued, "I haven't been able to focus on what I want to say. ... But I feel the next album is finally on the way."[19] Although appeals would keep the case in litigation for several more years, Fogerty, almost immediately after the settlement, did indeed begin to compose the songs that would appear on *Centerfield*. It was in May while on a fishing trip, just prior to the press conference, that he started to write "I Saw It on T.V." "When I finally got out of the boat, I said to myself, 'I got it. I can do this now.' It was the first time that switch had gone on in maybe nine years. ... It hit me like a ton of bricks. It meant, 'Here we go! It's back. You can work.' Apart from children being born or getting married, that was one of the bigger moments in my life."[20]

By the following year, Fogerty had six songs completed and recorded, with himself on all instruments and vocals for his new label, Warner Brothers (who received Fogerty's contract from Elektra in an internal transfer within the Warner Communications conglomerate). On September 10, 1984, he arrived at Warner headquarters in Burbank with a tape of six new recordings: "I Saw It on T.V." "I Can't Help Myself," "The Old Man down the Road," "Rock and Roll Girls," "Searchlight," and "Zanz Kant Danz." Mo Ostin, president of Warner Bros. Records, and Lenny Waronker, eventual successor to Ostin, organized a listening party for Warner Bros. executives and staff. The response was ecstatic. Fogerty was back. He returned home that night and left a note for his family on the refrigerator, "The monkey is off my back" and drew a dancing chimpanzee.[21] Within a few short weeks, Fogerty had completed *Centerfield.*

Released in January 1985, *Centerfield* received mostly glowing reviews. In *Rolling Stone,* Kurt Loder gave it four out of five stars and called *Centerfield* "a near-seamless extension of the Creedence sound and a record that's likely to convert a whole new generation of true believers," although Loder finds Fogerty's "one-man band brilliance … slightly alienating."[22] In *Time,* Jay Cocks disagreed with Loder and wrote that Fogerty is "less a one-man band than a single-engine soul train." With *Centerfield,* Cocks continues, Fogerty "fetches up, even at its fiercest moments, a feeling of exuberance and release. … Fogerty is rounding third and heading for home. But this time he'll make it standing up."[23] In *Melody Maker,* Allan Jones pronounced that with *Centerfield* "we are in the presence of greatness," and in the *Saturday Review,* John Swenson declared that Fogerty "balances personal and moral concerns deftly in some of his strongest songwriting ever."[24] Clearly, *Centerfield* surpassed everyone's expectations. By March 23, the album shot to #1 on the *Billboard* pop chart, just a couple of weeks shy of baseball's opening day and ahead of Phil Collins's *No Jacket Required,* Bruce Springsteen's *Born in the USA,* Wham!'s *Make It Big,* Tina Turner's *Private Dancer,* and Madonna's *Like a Virgin.*

As part of the album's promotion, Fogerty filmed a Showtime special, for which he assembled an all-star band to perform live before an invited audience of 200 friends, fellow musicians, and Warner Bros. staff. The band included old friends Booker T. Jones on keyboards and Donald "Duck" Dunn on bass from Booker T. and the MGs, Steve Douglas on saxophone of the Wrecking Crew, Albert Lee on guitar, Prairie Prince on drums of the Tubes and Journey, and four backup singers. Fogerty performed three sets of mostly rhythm-and-blues standards that he grew up with, including "Let's Go, Let's Go, Let's Go" (by Hank Ballard and the Midnighters), "Mannish Boy"

(Muddy Waters), "My Pretty Baby" (Medallions) which segues into "Leave My Woman Alone" (Ray Charles), and the gospel "Mary Don't You Weep" (the Swan Silvertones), all of which made it onto the broadcast and can be found on YouTube, and "Who's Making Love" (Johnny Taylor), "Long Tall Sally" (Little Richard), "Blue Suede Shoes" (Carl Perkins), and "Honky Tonk Women" (Rolling Stones), among others, which did not make the broadcast cut. Surprisingly, Fogerty played only two *Centerfield* tracks that night with only "Rock and Roll Girls" airing, although his performance of "The Old Man down the Road" was, according to Michael Goldberg, "one of those classic rock & roll moments."[25] Fogerty played no CCR songs. The show also featured clips of Fogerty with George Thorogood chatting at a spring training game and Fogerty performing the zydeco international hit "My Toot Toot" with Rockin' Sidney at a crawdad fest, a performance released first as the B-side to "Change in the Weather" (November 1986) and then as a bonus track on the 25th anniversary edition of *Centerfield*. In attendance at the taping of the show was *Newsweek*'s Jim Miller, who said he witnessed "one of the most astonishing resurrections in rock-and-roll history," a sentiment echoed by Goldberg who said the show marked "one of the most amazing rock & roll resuscitations in recent years" and said at moments the show was "chilling" and "like being in rock & roll heaven."[26] The Showtime special was Fogerty's first professional live set and first time he recorded with a band since 1972.

Fogerty was exhilarated by the success of the album and the attention it brought him. "*Centerfield* knocked me off my feet. It came in a big whoosh. The acceptance. It was very joyful and tearful for me for a couple of months."[27] As could be expected, the album had a strong CCR connection, as Fogerty works through genres that CCR explored: swamp rock, rockabilly, New Orleans funk, Memphis rhythm and blues, and rock and roll. But *Centerfield* isn't as dark or shadowy as many CCR albums, like *Bayou Country*, *Green River*, or *Willy and the Poor Boys*. Throughout his career, Fogerty, at his darkest and most effective, manifests a jeremiad vision—perhaps second only to Bob Dylan in the pantheon of rock-and-roll Jeremiahs. On *Centerfield* there is more sunlight and, at times, pure joy and innocence as in the pastoral of the title track and "Rock and Roll Girls."

A Rock-and-Roll Jeremiah

Yet Fogerty's jeremiad vision informs *Centerfield*, rearing its head at times more visibly than others. By definition, a jeremiad, named after the Biblical prophet Jeremiah and his *Book of Jeremiah* and *Book of Lamentations*, bitterly denounces a society fallen into wickedness and warns of imminent destruction brought about by God's wrath. Fogerty's jeremiads, like Dylan's, are at least on the surface more secular, especially as compared to the Puritan jeremiads of seventeenth-century America, but no less invective. Like the American Puritans, Fogerty howls with disappointment and rage at an America gone wrong, responding to a series of crises: the Vietnam War in the 1960s, Reaganomics in the 1980s, the George W. Bush presidency and the Iraq War in the 2000s, rampant consumerism and political corruption always.

Consumed with anxiety and dread, Fogerty warns of the impending apocalypse with a vague mysticism but with concrete fire-and-brimstone images of thunder, lightning, hurricanes, bad moons, dark nights, floods, etc. Consider the consistency of Fogerty's prophet-like persona: "Walking (later "Walk") on the Water" (single with the Golliwogs, 1966, *Bayou Country*, 1969), "Bad Moon Rising" (*Green River*, 1969), "Who'll Stop the Rain" (*Cosmo's Factory*, 1970), "The Wall" (*John Fogerty*, 1975), "Change in the Weather" (*Eye of the Zombie*, 1986; *Blue Ridge Riders Ride Again*, 2009), "Walking in a Hurricane" (*Blue Moon Swamp*, 1997), "Premonition" (*Premonition*, 1998), much of *Déjà Vu (All Over Again)* (2004), and "Long Dark Night" (*Revival*, 2007), among many others. Even CCR's eleven-minute version of "I Heard It through the Grapevine" evinces a threatening personal darkness unlike any of the Motown versions (Smokey Robinson & the Miracles, Gladys Knight & the Pips, Marvin Gaye, for example). Much like T. S. Eliot who began writing "The Love Song of J. Alfred Prufrock" while an undergraduate at Harvard, Fogerty never sounded young.

But part of Fogerty's jeremiad vision and, for that matter, the Puritan jeremiads, includes hope and a way out of despair, as Sacvan Bercovitch notes.[28] In the Puritan jeremiads hope might come in the salvation of an afterlife or an America eventually becoming, as John Winthrop wrote in 1630, the "City upon a Hill," or a community built on justice and mercy. In this new city, Winthrop wrote, citizens will "delight in each other, make others' conditions our own, rejoice together, mourn together, labor and suffer together," a community that will serve as a beacon of light, a paradigm for the world, so others will strive to recreate their communities "like that of New England."[29] Rarely does Fogerty find hope in the afterlife, although "Sail Away" from *Eye of the Zombie* is a notable exception, or in a future utopian vision of life on earth (perhaps "Lookin' Out My Back Door"). For Fogerty, relief, not quite salvation, comes in several forms: an imaginative past often set in lush landscapes far removed from cities ("Born on the Bayou," "Green River"); in simple people who dwell by a river and remain uncorrupted by the greed of consumerist culture ("Proud Mary," "Where the River Flows" from *John Fogerty*, and "Bring It Down to Jelly Roll," *Blue Moon Swamp*); in music (suggested by his hibernation in his private studio in the late 1970s and early 1980s and by the many covers he has recorded, especially on the Blue Ridge Rangers albums); and in love, apparent in his later work, specifically after his marriage to Julie Kramer in 1991 ("Joy of My Life," *Blue Moon Swamp*; "I Will Walk with You" about his daughter on *Déjà Vu*).

The Songs of *Centerfield*

Fogerty's jeremiad vision on *Centerfield* is not as consistently dark as it is on, say, *Green River*; neither is it as national as in "Fortunate Son" or "Who'll Stop the Rain." Rather, the album is more personal and, overall, seemingly more hopeful as in the occasional CCR song, like "Up Around the Bend" (1970, where you can find a smile and song) and "Hey Tonight" (1970, where all will hear the song and Jody will get religion). This personal hopefulness, which resulted from Fogerty's having recently survived lawsuits and writer's block, are consistent with the mid-1980s' zeitgeist and led, at least in part, to the album's huge success. However, the jeremiad vision, while not always dark, informs all of *Centerfield*. The album's nine songs can be neatly divided into three groups of three songs each. There are the invectives with varying tones of condemnation: severe ("Mr. Greed," "Vanz Kant Danz"), and despairing and resigned ("I Saw It on T.V."); the songs of quest for truth and transcendence which can be as frightening as Jeremiah's verses ("The Old Man down the Road," "Searchlight," "I Can't Help Myself"),[30] and the songs of hope, in which life is at least relieved of stress and in which corruption is absent ("Rock and Roll Girls," "Centerfield," "Big Train [from Memphis]").

Quests for Truth and Transcendence

"The Old Man down the Road," the opening track and first single (peaked at #10), typifies Fogerty's signature swamp rock style. The song develops from a strong but thin guitar riff which creates a mesmerizing effect, at once ominous and compelling, with guitar phrases overdubbed over and underneath this organizing riff. After the second verse and chorus at the 1:26 mark comes the first of Fogerty's classic economic guitar breaks, followed immediately by another at 1:40, with both reprised for the last minute of the song. Fogerty's unique vocal phrasings—his pronunciation of *road* ("ROW-d")and non-standard constructions like "he take," "he bring" and "he make"—further contribute to the song's swampy backwoods mystique and suspense. We are back in Fogerty's bayou, a world of hoodoo and revelation. Like other figures in Fogerty as far back as 1966's "Walking on the Water," the old man in the title possesses secrets and magical powers, and is able to control thunder, lightning, strong men, dogs, and the river. He casts terrifying shadows across windows and induces people to jump, hide, and run. He at once attracts and frightens the singer, who observes him from a safe distance and who is afraid of his wisdom and revelations. Throughout the song, Fogerty connects the old man with mysterious ancient and recent truth-sayers. Like the priestesses of Delphi, he speaks in riddles; like Bo Diddley, he is associated with rattle-snake hide (his suitcase, Diddley's house in "Who Do You Love"), and like many of Fogerty's own creations, he is comfortable among barking hound dogs, thunder, lightning, and swampy guitar riffs—see, for example, "Born on the Bayou," "Green River," and "Sinister Purpose." The song ends with the singer-quester paralyzed with fear, locked, as it were, in hypnotic guitar riffs.

The second of the quest songs, "Searchlight," opens side two of the original 33 1/3 album. With its slow, swaying Stax rhythm and its horn charts, the track reveals a singer "runnin' blind," restless and lost in his quest to understand his inner demons. The fat bass line and heavy drums, reminiscent of the work of Stu Cook and Doug Clifford in CCR, suggest the singer's dark, suicidal state as he ends up on a sea shore with no direction and perhaps "lost for all eternity," until, in the song's final line, a vision of hope, a smiling face, looks back at him. The third of the quest songs, "I Can't Help Myself," could be Fogerty's 1984 state-of-self address. The steady rocker, almost rockabilly (despite the digital drums which intrude throughout the album), reveals an artist perhaps nervous and ready to bust loose, "chomping at the bit," who can't help but create and release his work. The song suggests Fogerty's antici-pation and nervousness at his comeback attempt and the inevitable resulting question: Is the music still relevant and moving?

The Invectives

Of the three songs of condemnation "Mr. Greed" rants about an unspecific soulless "devil of consumption," almost certainly Saul Zaentz, Chairman of Fantasy Records, who indeed took it as a personal attack. While Fogerty's voice is passionate—so much so that in concert, for vocal preservation, he often played the song as an instrumental—and there is a piercingly effec-tive guitar solo, the song is a derivative hard rocker with unoriginal images of a corporate monster feeding off the poor and with uninventive questions directed at his conscience ("Did you do your mama proud?"). However, the usually perceptive John Swenson did call "Mr. Greed" "frighteningly angry" and "as powerful a political statement as he's ever made."[31] Far more effective is the second song about Zaentz, the album's closing track, originally entitled "Zanz Kant Danz"—at least on the first 600,000 pressings. When Zaentz threatened to sue for character defamation, which he eventually did, Warner pressured Fogerty to change the title and do some overdubbing to transform the song into "Zanz Kant Danz" on additional pressings. The relentless assault on Zaentz locks into a quasi-reggae beat that, as Kurt Loder writes, with "its Judgment Day horns, suggests a familiarity with old Burning Spear sides—and a sense of personal vengeance that seems near Biblical in its relentless intensity."[32] Despite its bitterness, which inspires the track's occasional pig grunts, and despite an almost one-minute disco-like digital-drum break and synthesized sounds, the song works, empowered by the firm beat, the light chant of the chorus, the lead vocal rising above the mix, and the high-register guitar leads.

As Fogerty was writing and recording *Centerfield*, Zaentz's latest film production *Amadeus* was generating favorable pre-release buzz. What especially galled Fogerty was that Zaentz's film career was bankrolled by CCR's success and the publishing royalties to Fogerty's songs—which Zaentz owned at the time. In 1980, Zaentz had created The Saul Zaentz Film Center (now Zaentz Media Center) in Berkeley, California, a well-used state-of-the-art editing and sound-mixing studio. A little over a week after Fogerty presented the first tracks from *Centerfield* to Warner executives, *Amadeus* was released to rave reviews. The film would go on to earn Zaentz his second of three Best Picture Academy Awards—first winning with *One Flew over the Cuckoo's Nest* (1975) and, later, with *The English Patient* (1996). Besides *Centerfield's* lyrical attacks, what may have further angered Zaentz is the video for "Zanz Kant Danz," which gained MTV play and gathered attention in *Billboard* as perhaps the first music video to use claymation.[33]Somewhat ironically, *Centerfield's* success increased Zaentz's CCR earnings as the album sparked renewed interest in the band. A year after *Centerfield's* release, *The Concert* (released in 1980) went gold and *Chronicle* (1976) turned platinum, and, for 1987, CCR held the top selling indie catalogue.[34]

Although we may see "Mr. Greed" and "Vanz Kant Danz" as satires on corporate leaders and consumerist cultures, the obviously personal nature of the attacks gives the songs a narrowness with relatively slight national implications compared to the more far-reaching "I Saw It on T.V." The first song Fogerty wrote in nine years, "I Saw It on T.V." can be considered a companion piece to "Who'll Stop the Rain," which Fogerty signals at the end of the track with guitar runs lifted from "Rain." If "Rain" questions the "clouds of mystery" and "the confusion on the ground," "T.V." identifies the source for that confusion and for the American "fable," which T.V. wraps in "golden chains" with images edited and manipulated to limit American consciousness. In the first verse of "T.V.," Fogerty references a powerful President Eisenhower in his black limousine, an emblem of power against the threatening Soviet empire, and then follows with a reference to Hooterville and Doodyville, before wondering "which cartoon was real." Fogerty goes on to cite Davey Crockett, baseball, Kennedy's assassination, the Beatles, the moon landing, and the Vietnam War with the ironic chorus in which the singer echoes what might be considered an American maxim: "I know it's true ... 'Cause I saw it on T.V." He brings the song to conclusion with a forceful image of resignation and hopelessness as he describes an immobile old man, a "prisoner" on his porch, who lost his only son in Vietnam. Embittered about the death of his son and the realization that the "light" he saw in the American fable was nothing more than "a burglar's torch," the man is "chained" in his despair while the manipulators of the fable are "rich and free." The stunning entrance of the tingling electric guitar riff from "Rain" brings the song to a compelling and resonating conclusion.

The slow ballad rhythm of "T.V." conveys the hopelessness and the lack of fight left in the singer and the old man on the porch while also looking forward to Fogerty's "Déjà Vu (All Over Again)," another song about the manipulation of the media to shape American consciousness and political perspectives. Asked in 1987 about his favorite songs, Fogerty responded, "And also 'Who'll Stop the Rain,' just because lyrically it deals with things with a lot of pathos. And 'I Saw It on T.V.' It hits that same vein with a kind of endless and fatalistic point of view. I hate to dwell on that, but some things just don't seem to change."[35] "T.V.," one of the strongest tracks on *Centerfield*, is as Joel Selvin notes, "one of the centerpieces" of the album.[36]

Songs of Hope and Transcendence

The more hopeful songs of *Centerfield* are joyful escapes from realities, any reality: mundane everyday problems, personal complications, national political quandaries and deceptions, lawsuits, etc. In "Rock and Roll Girls," for example, the singer escapes from a world of endless struggle (introduced in the opening line's image of riding a bronco in a rodeo) and into a "sweet" world, a place "out of time" and filled with music, love, and girls. Lyrically similar to his other road songs, "Rock and Roll Girls" has a breezy melody and an old-time, rock-and-roll rhythm and soft sax solo. However, Fogerty's craftsmanship and quest for perfection as an instrumentalist and as a producer might have stripped the song of some needed rawness and seeming spontaneity, the kind we hear in "Travelin' Band," "Up Around the Bend," and even "Rockin' All over the World."

"Big Train (From Memphis)" is another song about escaping the present, but this time into the "sweet" past of Sun Studios, where Sam Phillips recorded Elvis, Jerry Lee Lewis, Carl Perkins, and Johnny Cash. Fogerty celebrates the Sun sound through this rockabilly ballad complete with echoey vocals, a guitar intro and solo not unlike Scotty Moore's on Elvis's "Mystery Train," and a pumping bass line recalling Bill Black's contribution to the same record. The train of Fogerty's title is both figurative (suggesting Presley and the force of his "roar") and literal, as the singer recalls playing on train tracks and dreaming of escape—train imagery is associated with escape throughout the blues and rock and roll. While "Big Train" celebrates Sun and the dream it planted in not only the young singer but also the world, the song also laments the passing of the Sun sound, which is "gone, gone, gone"—suggesting the end of the dream and the passing of "rock's original, unaffected power," as Kurt Loder puts it.[37]

If "Big Train" is in some ways ambiguous, "Centerfield" is an absolute paean to spring, renewal, and baseball. "Spring training, and spring in general, because of baseball, is my favorite time," says Fogerty. "I think to say, 'Well, on opening day, everybody's in first place'—y'know, that sort of describes how it all is. You're hopeful: 'Okay, it doesn't matter whatever happened last year, this year's a new year and we got a clean slate, look at all this cool stuff that's gonna happen!' And you get to feel that way through spring training, at least, 'til you start playing *real* games."[38] But the escape for Fogerty, like a nine-inning game or the spring, is always only temporary, "a moment in the sun," as he sings on "Centerfield," or only as long as a train ride, a walk, or the duration of a song. "Centerfield," like the album's following track "I Can't Help Myself," reveals Fogerty's state of mind in 1984-1985. Free of lawsuit distractions, Fogerty had a renewed and energetic imagination which made him both excited and anxious, but, once again, "ready to play." The "new grass" of the baseball field is every bit reflective of his renewal and as lush and inspiring for him as his imaginative bayous.

At the album's release, Fogerty was especially nervous about this track. By his own definition a "superfan" of baseball, he called it "just a kind of pop song" and worried about listeners' reactions.[39] He aptly explained over two decades later: "Rock 'n' roll has some built-in political stances whereby things are considered lame, to put it mildly. You're really swimming against the stream to write a sports song. I knew the possibility that it would be considered lame was looming."[40] Fogerty retreated to childhood for his point of view in "Centerfield," stating that his perspective was that of an "eight-year old boy saying thank you to baseball for all the joy and inspiration it has given me."⁴¹The song recreates the innocent exuberance of the baseball experience for a boy who believes in the absolute integrity and purity of the game. The track features drums which mimic the rhythmic handclaps of fans, a stadium-sounding organ which underscores verses and riffs, the knock of a ball jumping off a bat, and a player anxious for the coach to insert him in centerfield; there are also references to baseball immortals like Willie Mays, Joe DiMaggio, and Ty Cobb, to baseball mythology with Ernest Lawrence Thayer's "Casey at the Bat" (1888), and to Chuck Berry's brown-eyed handsome man, who is introduced with a guitar riff borrowed from Berry and who, here, as in Berry's song, is rounding third and heading home. The upbeat melody, the sprightly intro which recurs throughout the song, and the excitedly optimistic singer, all create a joyful romp.

On July 25, 2010, Fogerty performed "Centerfield" in Cooperstown, NY, at the induction ceremonies of the National Baseball Hall of Fame, which further honored the song with a display of "Slugger," Fogerty's bat-shaped guitar. In the showcase with "Slugger" were three versions of original lyrics to the song, a *Centerfield* CD, and a vinyl copy of the original release. On that day, which saw the induction of player Andre Dawson, manager Whitey Herzog, and umpire Doug Harvey, Fogerty told the audience that it was an "amazing feeling" for him to be so honored by baseball and "that eight-year old boy [or the narrative voice of 'Centerfield'] is saying that it doesn't get any better than this." He then explained how "Slugger," which plays only one song and was designed for Fogerty in 1986 by Kubicki Guitars, had to be restored after a recent Nashville flood decimated his warehoused guitars. He hoped "Slugger" would "give inspiration to some other folks."⁴²

The Aftermath of *Centerfield*

After the success of *Centerfield*, Fogerty was anxious to tour, but he did not feel as if he had enough material. It had been ten years since his Shep album, which he hadn't liked much, and the Blue Ridge Rangers songs, even older, didn't quite blend with the new material. Furthermore, he had vowed never to play CCR songs again since every time he performed for payment meant more money to Zaentz, who owned Fogerty's publisher Jondora, a subsidiary of Fantasy. In short, Fogerty needed another album. He entered the studio enthusiastically but under great stress. Much had happened since the release of *Centerfield*, and not all positive. There were increased hostilities with his former bandmates, which Fogerty exacerbated by choosing to communicate with them through attorneys and short letters and which they exacerbated by publically stating their friendship with Zaentz and their disappointment with *Centerfield*. In the *San Francisco Chronicle*, Fogerty's brother Tom said that he trusted Zaentz "to the max" and called *Centerfield* a "mediocre copy of something that was once and still is great."[43] In the *Los Angeles Times*, Stu Cook also reaffirmed his friendship with Zaentz and stated that he was "not impressed" by Fogerty's album, cuttingly adding that "if he was going to copy an old Creedence tune [with 'Old Man down the Road'], he should have picked 'Proud Mary' instead of 'Run through the Jungle.' If we weren't good enough to play in his band, and this is what he's come up with by playing all the instruments himself, I am glad I didn't play on this album."[44] Nor did Doug Clifford hold back: "I expected it to be a little more contemporary. It sounds really stiff. I guess you can't expect much growing if you haven't worked with anyone else in 10 years."[45]

By the time of *Centerfield*'s release, Fogerty's marriage to Martha had collapsed. After their divorce in 1986, Fogerty moved to Los Angeles and took an office in the basement of Warner Bros. Suddenly "the notorious puritan of rock" began to live like a star: "I was living the life of a rock 'n' roll party animal. ... I spent a lot of time going to bars and looking for cocktail waitresses. I did everything I thought I should to feel like a rock star."[46]

Perhaps what most outraged and depressed Fogerty, however, were the lawsuits that Zaentz leveled against him as a result of "Mr. Greed," "Zanz Kant Danz," "The Old Man down the Road," and Fogerty's statements in interviews. Zaentz was not satisfied that Fogerty had changed *Zanz* to *Vanz*. "It's defamatory," said Norman Rudman, the attorney for Zaentz and Fantasy. "It's slanderous or libelous, depending only on the medium that's been used to perpetrate it. When you call somebody a thief or say that somebody stole your money or acted like a slave driver, you've gone beyond the bounds of saying merely unfavorable things about people and gone into the kinds of statements that are just plain, irreducible defamations."[47] Zaentz contended that as a result of Fogerty's songs and statements that potential signees lost faith in Fantasy, whose image, he claimed was also hurt with the record-buying public. In the summer of 1985, Zaentz sued Fogerty for $144 million in damages. Fogerty responded, "All I did was write a song about a pig."[48] Eventually, the case was settled out of court with Fogerty's issuing a public apology to Zaentz along with a large check for an undisclosed amount.

The other case Zaentz brought against Fogerty was for copyright infringement, claiming that Fogerty plagiarized himself by basing "The Old Man down the Road" on CCR's "Run through the Jungle," for which Jondora owned the copyright. The case went to court for a two-week trial in the fall of 1988. Stressed by the case and entering the court in a cast, Fogerty had punched a chair and broke his right hand in two places: "I thought I

124 ⌒ Thomas M. Kitts

was restraining myself, but in moments of passion you don't always do that well."[49] Nonetheless, Fogerty spent an entire day on the witness stand with an electric guitar and small amp to demonstrate his style by performing intros and fragments from songs old and new. The jury took less than three hours to find him not guilty. One juror said, "Creative people have got to have rights to create without being harassed by too many business-people types."[50] For his defense, Fogerty spent over $400,000 and Warner Bros. an additional $600,000—more than the song earned. But Fogerty felt an obliga-tion: "What's at stake is whether a person can continue to use his own style as he grows and goes on through life. ... I can feel Lennon, Dylan, Bruce Springsteen and Leiber and Stoller standing behind me going, 'Johnny, don't blow this.'"[51] After the victory, Fogerty and Warner Bros. sued Zaentz to recoup their legal expenses. Denied initially and again on appeal, Fogerty's case eventually came before the U.S. Supreme Court in December 1993. In a landmark decision concerning intellectual property law, the court decided in Fogerty's favor, awarding him $1.35 million in legal expenses.[52]

Despite his very satisfying resurgence with *Centerfield*, Fogerty was in the midst of all kinds of conflicts when he began writing and then recording his next album, *Eye of the Zombie*. He had just divorced and moved to Los An-geles; his ongoing war with Zaentz had escalated, and he was at increasing odds with his former bandmates and brother. For the new album, he was, as Bordowitz states, "in a dark frame of mind."[53]

The Full-Fledged Jeremiah Returns

Just as crises, like Indian wars or doctrinal controversies, triggered the jer-emiad vision of the seventeenth-century American Puritan, so was Fogerty's jeremiad imagination galvanized by national or personal problems. In 1986, Fogerty made an album while consumed with venomous personal and legal disputes—all of which inform *Eye of the Zombie*.

Fogerty sets the tone for the album and for Jeremiah to descend to earth or at least ascend to the pulpit with the eerie "Goin' Back Home," the church-worthy opening track, which features wordless choir-like vocals with soprano *oohs* and bass *uhms*, accompanied by Fogerty's synthesized keyboard and effectively piercing guitar solo just past the two-minute mark. The Jeremiah-like minister then enters with his rousing fire-and-brimstone warning on "Eye of the Zombie," the album's second track and first of two failed singles, peaking at a dismal #81. In typical jeremiad imagery of shad-ows, darkness, fire, mass confusion, terror, and helplessness, the angry rocker announces "the moment of truth" and the imminent "dance of the zombie."

The zombie, Fogerty's apocalyptic agent, is indestructible and hideous, ready to bring destruction upon the world. Lyrically, "Eye of the Zombie" recalls William Butler Yeats's "The Second Coming," an apocalyptic metaphor for World War I with its images of anarchy, a "blood-dimmed tide," a "revelation at hand," and a "rough beast" with "lion body and the head of a man" and "a gaze blank and pitiless as the sun"—not unlike Fogerty's "beast" with "leopard feet," "flashing hideous teeth," and "evil … zombie eyes"—featured on the album's cover.

Various songs on *Zombie* identify why, presumably, the apocalypse is at hand. The following track, "Headlines," a mediocre rocker or what Anthony DeCurtis called a "refried boogie riff posing as a song," rants about the continued violence in the world, which everyday is "screamin'" from the newspapers, radio, and television.[54] The only way the Jeremiah-singer can respond is to escape to the temple "up on the mountain" where he can find sanctuary for himself and others. But the weakest track on the album is the diatribe "Violence Is Golden," a too heavy-handed attack on arms dealers, which invites comparison to Dylan's "Masters of War." Fogerty, however, lacks Dylan's direct confrontation of the arms dealer and his striking conclusion in which the singer stands with satisfaction over the grave of the merchant confident that even Jesus could not forgive his sins. Instead of this gripping confrontation, Fogerty substitutes predictable scenes with commonplace imagery (the merchant's justification that he has a wife and child and payments on his Jaguar), inane food images ("plate of shrapnel," "grenade salad"), and guitar fills and sound effects right out of Jimi Hendrix's Woodstock performance of "The Star-Spangled Banner." Fogerty, at the time, seemed pleased with the song: "I'd been playing with 'Violence Is Golden' for nearly 20 years—I had written it in this little notebook I keep—and it finally all came together. It didn't belong on a happy album; it belonged here! But it was maybe too much of a bad thing. There was no counterbalance."[55] And then somewhat defensively, if ineffectively so, "I mean, the song was out and being played for a couple of months, then Iranscam hits, you know, and it was right there in the verses of the song."[56]

Elsewhere, as in the catchy "Soda Pop," Fogerty attacks an obsessed consumerist culture in which all can be commodified and greedy pop stars who, with profit-driven motives, privilege commerce over art: "I have an idea for a song called 'Piece of the Rock.' Before a baby is born, its mother and father would be given a choice of one of three companies: an insurance company, a gas company or a soda-pop company. And just before birth, they choose one of those three companies, and it gives them a million dollars for the child, to take care of the kid forever. In return, the company emblazons its logo on the kid's forehead, so that wherever he goes in life, you know, when people look at him, they will see the company logo."[57]

"Change in the Weather," a classic Fogerty swamp rocker and Fogerty jeremiad, choogles along with what DeCurtis calls a "mesmerizing groove and atmosphere."[58] The lyrics reveal all the signs of a Fogerty apocalypse: a jungle-like world, a panicking populace, impending storms, hurricanes, floods, earthquakes, fires, and a demon ready to strike. Not even the river, like that in "Green River" or "Proud Mary," provides comfort. Neil Stubenhaus's firm bass line, high in the mix, supports the sturdiness of the vision and frightened back-up singers enhance the bleakness. For the last approximately 2:30 minutes, Fogerty commandeers the track with a spirited guitar workout not dissimilar to what could be heard on "Suzie Q." Fogerty re-recorded "Change in the Weather," the high point of Zombie, in a more countrified version for Blue Ridge Rangers Rides Again (2008).

Another highlight is "Knockin' on Your Door," about a singer who waits in the rain trying to work up the courage to ask his beloved to reconcile. The soulful Otis Redding-like track, complete with hummable brass section, could have been produced at Stax studios in the 1960s and, with a much earlier release and a little trimming, been a hit single. Another track steeped in Stax flavoring but a bit less effective, "Wasn't That a Woman," concerns a singer who falls in love at first sight and futilely pursues the woman in all his "sweet agony." Light in tone, the song fades with playful banter about a "fine woman" with "skinny legs and all."

In the final song, "Sail Away," a world-weary Jeremiah is anxious to leave earthly pain behind. If "Eye of the Zombie" is Fogerty's "Second Coming," "Sail Away" is his "Sailing to Byzantium." Yeats's exhausted speaker wants to rid himself of his deteriorating body and pass "into the artifice of eternity," just as Fogerty's is eager to rid himself of earthly "chains" and take "the silent ship" into "the light up in the sky" where he can behold new "wonders" and "beauty." "Sail Away" brings the album to a quiet but disturbing conclusion. Again, as in Yeats, the singer resigns himself to his and earth's limitations and failures, which in "Sail Away" suggest that the warning of the Jeremiah-minister has gone unheeded. The only hope for either Yeats's speaker or Fogerty's singer is in a rewarding afterlife, which both long for and seem confident of attaining. "Sail Away," in its death wish, recalls "Flyin' Away," the concluding track on John Fogerty in which the singer seeks the "light" above. However, given the consistently dark vision of Zombie, "Sail Away" is charged with more significance as Fogerty's soothing voice (rare especially in pre-Blue Moon Swamp songs) and the dreamy synthesizer suggest a resigned contentedness at having tried but failed to bring about at least some reform.

It is a very Puritan vision of life. Given the pervasiveness of human violence, greed, selfishness, and failed love, it seems Fogerty, at least on *Zombie*, finds hope only in the afterlife.

The Reviews

Unlike the overwhelmingly positive reviews that greeted *Centerfield*, *Zombie*'s reviews tended to be mixed. Gene Santoro in *Down Beat* praises Fogerty for his unique vision and intelligence while making "a terrific rock & roll record" and Scott Isler in *Musician* states that *Zombie*, while not "a musical grand slam," did mark Fogerty as "one of the most promising players in the majors."[59] In *Creem*, however, Robert Christgau rates the album a mediocre "B," stating that the album holds "an undeniable modicum of interest" before reminding us that "the '60s are over," and in the same issue, Craig Zeller complains that the album is "overloaded with excess baggage, belabored social commentary, and a batch of unimaginative songs sadly lacking in spirit."[60] In *Rolling Stone*, Anthony De-Curtis concludes that "Fogerty's flesh-and-blood people [in his previous songs] have become zombies and caricatures, and his hooks don't cut as cleanly as they used to."[61] The album peaked at a disappointing #26, although Fogerty did earn a Grammy nomination for Best Rock Male Vocalist for "Eye of the Zombie," losing to Robert Palmer for "Addicted to Love."

As the negative reviews point out, there are several reasons for the relative failure of *Zombie*. For one, Fogerty tried too hard to sound contemporary. Although he has always been interested in sound effects (just listen to "Suzie Q") and while *Centerfield* made sporadic and not always effective use of modern recording techniques like digital drums, Fogerty overindulges himself with high tech on *Zombie* in an effort to sound contemporary—a poor strategy, especially given his roots music fan base. Fogerty explained his turn to technology: "While it was nice that I was received well on *Centerfield*, I kept hearing roots and roots rock 'n' roll and I don't wanna be typecast in that role. I love old records and all that sort of thing, but I'm not stuck there. ... I don't like to carry that mantle around. I'd much rather be thought of as aware and making use of whatever's out there to create the best possible songs."[62] Then, "It meant tracking from noon to seven at night and coming back to my little cubbyhole in the basement [at Warners] and working with digital sampling synths, a Macintosh computer and a pile of manuals six feet high ... until the next morning. I know all three shifts of the [high tech] maintenance people at Warner Bros. on a first-name basis."[63] As Craig Zeller wrote in *Creem*, for Fogerty, apparently, "... being in the '80s means getting microchips, computers, synthesizers, and digital samplers in the studio."[64]

In addition to the intrusive high-tech sonics, most songs on *Zombie* are just too long and in need of editing. After the opening instrumental at 3:25, none of the remaining eight songs is shorter than 4:13. None has the quick in-and-out decisiveness and energy of Fogerty's great singles, like "Green River" (2:34), "Bad Moon Rising" (2:19), or "The Old Man down the Road" (3:32). On *Centerfield*, six of nine tracks are below 4:13 and two clock in at slightly above ("I Saw It on T.V." at 4:19 and "Searchlight" at 4:29).

But, more than anything else, its seems, *Zombie* was out of touch with the national mood. As Fogerty admitted, the album "was pretty hard hitting and even ugly at the time. And maybe totally out of whack with the background of the social awareness of the country. And it kind of fell on deaf ears. ... *Zombie* would have been a lead-pipe cinch in 1969"[65]—well, maybe. At the time of the album's release on October 1, 1986, the country was relatively content with life and politics. President Reagan had won reelection by a landslide in 1984, gaining almost 60% of the popular vote, and in a Gallup poll at the time of the album's release, Reagan had an approval rating of 63% with less than 30% disapproving.[66] The timing was decidedly off for such an album as *Zombie*, especially with an intended prime audience of increasingly contented baby boomers.

But *Eye of the Zombie* has much to recommend it. In many ways with its strong soul and funk feel, it is Fogerty's Stax/Memphis album. Explaining how CCR was different from other Bay area bands, he said, "Our musical love was soul music—Stax and all that. We tended to play a lot of shorter, upbeat numbers because we considered ourselves a dance band."[67] He once called Booker T. & the MGs "the best rock and roll band of all time, bar none," and frequently praised Stax musicians like guitarist Steve Cropper, bassist Duck Dunn, and drummer Al Jackson—"'Proud Mary' was sort of me doing Steve Cropper."[68] While Fogerty played most of the instruments on *Zombie*, he employed, for all tracks, bassist Neil Stubenhaus and drummer John Robinson, a forceful rhythm section who helped forge the album's Stax feel. Consider, for instance, the album's bass lines, especially, for example, on "Headlines"; the brass charts on "Knockin' on Your Door" and "Wasn't That a Woman"; the soulfulness of "Soda Pop"; the obviously African-American background vocals on several tracks (for which Fogerty brought in vocalists); and the funky Cropper-like rhythm guitar on "Wasn't That A Woman" and "Soda Pop." The Stax sound works well on *Zombie* with Fogerty's always strong vocals, powerful lead guitar work, and the album's unified, albeit dark, vision. Despite its obvious flaws, *Zombie* has long been undervalued and neglected.

Fogerty Tours

Just prior to the album's release, Fogerty began touring. He chose to open the tour, appropriately enough, in Memphis on August 28, 1986, his first public concert since 1972 or in 14 years. "I wanted to start here because this city is sort of the center of my musical roots and orientation," he explained.[69] The tour extended well into the fall, with time off for the plagiarism trial, and into the following year. Fogerty performed songs from *Centerfield*, *Eye of the Zombie*, covers of rhythm and blues hits, gospel songs, but no CCR songs. "I'm still proud of them, but I don't own them," he said at the time. "They're all owned by Fantasy, and I've been fighting with them since 1970. We're going to be in court yet again after this first month of the tour. When I hear 'Proud Mary' on the radio, I just think of a lawsuit, and I don't want to keep reminding myself of all that pain."[70] As the tour went on, Fogerty had to contend with chants for Creedence songs. In Pittsburgh, he was shaken to the extent that he had to walk to the side of the stage to collect his thoughts. "I know they're doing it because they love those songs," he explained afterwards. "But it wasn't their fight. There are certain principles at stake that I simply won't subvert. And it won't change."[71]

On July 4, 1987, however, Fogerty ended his CCR boycott at a benefit for Vietnam veterans at the Capital Center, outside Washington, D.C. After playing the opening notes to "The Old Man down the Road," Fogerty launched into "Born on the Bayou" to a frenzied crowd, continuing with several CCR hits: "Who'll Stop the Rain," "Up Around the Bend," "Bad Moon Rising," "Fortunate Son," and "Proud Mary." Fogerty called the performance "the high point of my life," explaining that "I always had wanted to [play CCR songs], I was looking for an excuse—you know, 'Lord help me get out of this.' I wanted to play these things, but my own ethics wouldn't let me do it."[72] He pointed to several reasons for his change of heart: a conversation with Duane Eddy who had similar problems and put his bitterness aside; the New York Giants Super Bowl victory in 1987 and the controversy or "fuck the fans" attitude, as Fogerty termed it, concerning the location of the parade (New York City or New Jersey, where the Giants play their home games); and, most especially, a conversation with Bob Dylan. After an impromptu stage appearance on February 19, 1987 with Dylan and George Harrison at a Taj Mahal concert at the Palomino, a Los Angeles club, Dylan told Fogerty, "Hey, John, if you don't do these tunes, the world's going to remember 'Proud Mary' as Tina Turner's song."[73] Fogerty has been playing CCR songs ever since.

Postscript

As the 1980s closed, Fogerty seemed wracked by extremes. He was still in litigation to recover legal expenses from his defense of Zaentz's plagiarism suit and his problems with his bandmates were still unresolved: "My relationship with them," he said, "is like a divorce that never heals and the combatants just keep fighting."[74] Most tragically, he never reconciled with his brother Tom, who died in 1990 from pneumonia as a result of the AIDs virus contracted through a blood transfusion for one of his back surgeries. John visited his brother before his death and even spoke at his funeral, but it was only, in John's words, as "the dutiful, polite relative."[75]

A turning point for Fogerty occurred in 1987 when he began a romantic relationship with Julie Kramer, whom he met in Indiana while touring in support of Zombie. On one visit to Julie he heard Duke Tumatoe and the Power Trio, a popular regional band. In 1989, Fogerty produced their rousing live album, I Love my Job, which remains their most popular recording. In 1991, Fogerty married Julie, who has become an integral part of Fogerty's career decision-making and who, with their children, has inspired several songs, including "Joy of My Life," "Honey Do," and "I Will Walk with You."

For Fogerty, the 1980s were traumatic, just as much as the 1970s had been for him. However, as the decade drew to a close, he seemed destined for stability, but a stability that could not be achieved without his wife Julie and that was still several years away. More lawsuits had to be resolved and others filed and resolved. It would only be at about the time of Blue Moon Swamp (1997) that the roller coaster life of John Fogerty would begin to show signs of balance.

Notes

1. Dave Marsh, "Where Has John Fogerty Gone?" Musician, Player, and Listener, April 1981, 12.

2. Almost immediately on the heels of CCR's demise and in time for the 1972 holiday season came Creedence Gold (multiplatinum, sales over two million), then More Creedence Gold (July 1973, gold or sales over one million), Live in Europe (December 1973), The Golliwogs (1975, a collection of recordings under the band's pre-CCR moniker), Chronicle (1976, multiplatinum), and following The Concert, Chooglin' (1982) Chronicle 2 (1986), and on and on. In 2001, Fantasy released a six-CD box set, which includes the recordings of the Golliwogs and all CCR albums. But Fantasy wasn't done. Bad Moon Rising: The Best of Creedence Clearwater Revival was released in 2003, Creedence Clearwater Revival Covers the Classics in 2009, among others, and for the Australian market, The Ultimate Collection in 2012.

3. Robert Hilburn, "Fogerty's Nightmare Is Over," Los Angeles Times, January 6, 1985, 54; Debra Rae Cohen, "Creedence Clearwater's Revival's Rock & Roll: It's a Gift," Rolling Stone, June 11, 1981, 55.

4. Joel Selvin, "John Fogerty on Threshold of Big Comeback," San Francisco Chronicle, January 6, 1985, 17.

5. Hilburn, 55.

6. Sam Sutherland, "Rock Recluse Fogerty Returns," *Billboard*, February 2, 1985, 66.

7. Marsh, 12

8. Hilburn, 54.

9. Ibid.

10. Dan Forte, "John Fogerty Returns," *Guitar Player*, April 1985, 74.

11. Jay Cocks, "Music High Tide on the Green River," *Time*, January 28, 1985, 78.

12. Forte, 60.

13. Hank Bordowitz, *Bad Moon Rising: The Unauthorized History of Creedence Clearwater Revival* (Chicago: Chicago Review Press/A Cappella Books, 2007), 196.

14. Hilburn, 54.

15. Selvin, 17.

16. Ibid.

17. Hilburn, 54.

18. Cocks, 78.

19. "Creedence's Fogerty to Revive Career," *Rolling Stone*, July 7, 1983, 41.

20. Bordowitz, 196.

21. Ibid., 199.

22. Kurt Loder, "Fogerty Still Hits with Power," *Rolling Stone*, January 31, 1985, 48.

23. Cocks, 78.

24. Allan Jones, "Centre Points," *Melody Maker*, February 2, 1985, qtd.in Bordowitz 201; John Swenson, Rev. of *Centerfield*, *Saturday Review*, March/April 1985, 70.

25. Michael Goldberg, "Fogerty Returns to the Stage," *Rolling Stone*, March 14, 1985, 62.

26. Jim Miller, "Another Clearwater Revival," *Newsweek*, February 18, 1985, 89; Goldberg 12, 62.

27. Michael Goldberg, "On the Road Again," *Rolling Stone*, October 9, 1986, 26.

28. Sacvan Bercovitch writes, "And Jeremiah asserts the fulfillment of the promise as the very telos of history. The exile, he announces unequivocally, will end; eventually, Israel will return to a second paradise, a Canaan abounding in blessings beyond anything they had or imagined. ... As he envisions it, the restoration is sometimes a reward for performance, sometimes a gift. Israel's redemption, it would seem, will come by miracle." *The American Jeremiad* (Madison: University of Wisconsin Press, 1978), 31.

29. John Winthrop, "A Model of Christian Charity," 1630, *Religious Freedom Page*, http://religiousfreedom.lib.virginia.edu/sacred/charity.html (May 24, 2012).

30. In Jeremiah 5:1, God challenges Jeremiah: "Run ye to and fro through the streets of Jerusalem, and see now, and know, and seek in the broad places thereof, if ye can find a man, if there be *any* that executeth judgment, that seeketh the truth; and I will pardon it." Jeremiah's search, like Fogerty's, is futile. In verse 6, the prophet envisions a time when "a lion out of the forest shall slay [transgressors], and a wolf of the evenings shall spoil them, a leopard shall watch over their cities; and every one that goeth out thence shall be torn in pieces."

31. Swenson, 70

32. Loder, 48.

132 ～ Thomas M. Kitts

33. Jim McCullaugh, "Claymation Creator Molds Fogerty Clip," *Billboard*, July 13, 1985, in *Billboard Archives*, http://www.billboard.com/archive#/achive (November 18, 2011).

34. "Creedence & Run-DMC Top NARM Best Sellers at Independent Confab," *Variety*, November 4, 1987: 71. Fantasy was not considered a major label.

35. James Henke, "John Fogerty," *Rolling Stone*, November 5, 1987, 151.

36. Selvin, 17.

37. Loder, 48.

38. "John Fogerty Revisiting Creedence Hits on New Duets Set," *KHITS96 Classic Hits*, April 4, 2012, http://www.k-hits.com/musicnews/Story.aspx?ID=1681428.

39. Henke, 151.

40. Clark Collis, "John Fogerty Talks about Being Honored by the Baseball Hall of Fame—and Having George W. Bush as a Fan," *Music Mix*, May 2010, http://music-mix.ew.com/2010/05/25/john-fogerty-centerfield-baseball (May 19, 2011).

41. "Fogerty Performs Centerfield, 7/25/10." *MLB.com*, "Baseball Video Highlights & Clips," http://mlb.mlb.com/video/play.jsp?content_id=10264413.

42. "Fogerty Performs."

43. See Bordowitz, 206.

44. Jon Matsumoto, "Where Did the Rest of Creedence Go?" *Los Angeles Times*, January 6, 1985, 55.

45. Ibid.

46. Bordowitz, 210, 211.

47. Michael Goldberg, "John Fogerty alters album: 'Zanz' becomes 'Vanz,'" *Rolling Stone*, March 28, 1985, 34.

48. Ibid.

49. Dennis McDougal, "The Trials of John Fogerty Singer, Executive Locked in Decade-Old Legal Feud," *Los Angeles Times*, November 15, 1988, 1.

50. Robin Tolleson, "John Fogerty Wins Lawsuit," *Billboard*, January 19, 1988, 71.

51. Michael Goldberg, "Fogerty wins unusual self-plagiarism suit," *Rolling Stone*, January 12, 1989, 15.

52. Fogerty v. Fantasy, Inc. (92-1750), 510 U.S. 517 (1994).

53. Bordowitz, 214.

54. Anthony DeCurtis, "Fogerty eyes the apocalypse" *Rolling Stone*, November 20, 1986, 125.

55. Scott Isler, "Fogerty vs. Fogerty," *Musician*, February 1989, 97.

56. Henke, 148.

57. Ibid., 151.

58. DeCurtis, 125.

59. Santoro and Isler, qtd. in Bordowitz, 220.

60. Robert Christgau, "Christgau Consumer Guide," *Creem*, February 1987, 21; Craig Zeller, Rev. of *Eye of the Zombie*, *Creem*, February 1987: 16.

61. DeCurtis, 125.

62. Bordowitz, 213.

63. Ibid.

64. Zeller, 15.

65. Henke, 148.

66. "Job Performance Ratings for President Reagan," Roper Center: Public Opinion Archives, http://webapps.ropercenter.uconn.edu/CFIDE/roper/presidential/webroot/presidential_rating_detail.cfm?allRate=True&presidentName=Reagan (May 2, 2011).

67. Henke, 147.

68. Forte, 66, 67.

69. Robert Palmer, "Pop: Show by Fogerty in Memphis," *New York Times*, March 30, 1986, Sec. 1, 9.

70. Ibid.

71. Daniel Brogan, "Getting Past John Fogerty," *Creem*, January 1987, 7.

72. Henke, 151.

73. Ibid.

74. Neil Strauss, "The Pop Life: A Lurking Album Is Freed," *New York Times*, May 21, 1997, C13.

75. "The Fortunate Son Returns," *San Francisco Chronicle*, May 11, 1997, 38.3.

~

CHAPTER TEN

Multimodal Fogerty: Scoring and Scaffolding the Music of CCR to a Vietnam War Literature Unit

William C. Sewell and Christian Z. Goering

Using popular music in K-16 classrooms is a subject well-covered in the scholarship of the past forty years, beginning with Steven Carter's 1969 article about using the Beatles to teach composition. Music makes sense; it is an early part of a child's development and the associations with prematurely learning the alphabet vis-à-vis the aid of a song offers an insight to the connections between music and learning. From that point forward, music offers ways into new concepts and curriculum for students throughout their education, perhaps only limited by the creativity with which each teacher approaches the classroom and curriculum. Whether it is a U.S. history professor teaching the 1950s through the caveat of Elvis Presley and Chuck Berry or a 5th grade social studies teacher helping her students learn the states and capitals through a song, music and learning fit well together and hold potential for the classroom. But music is a driving force in the larger sense of meaning-making and can be heard as a dominant force in advertising campaigns, a backdrop to presidential campaigns, and a general soundtrack to the ebb and flow of one's life, a ubiquitous force.

As former high school English teachers, we each found countless ways of teaching the various language arts through music. Now we primarily prepare teachers and continue a quest to share and advocate approaches that include music in pedagogy. Being engrossed in this approach and longtime admirers of John Fogerty, it was natural for us to find new ways—through multimodal teaching and learning—to not only provide teachers and students with learning strategies that introduced Fogerty into the classroom but also to further his place in the educational curriculum and consciousness, something currently not the case.

Why the music of a cultural icon like Fogerty isn't as prevalent in the curriculum as other, less popular or profound artists is a bit of a mystery. Clearly, there is lyrical complexity and sophistication in the music. Some of the songs of Creedence Clearwater Revival are still played often on the radio and in movies. The popular stories about copyright and royalty lawsuits of those songs have circulated in the news of the past twenty years. Fogerty continues to produce and tour in support of music that is widely appealing and important, yet, searches of the internet, several lesson plan sites, and leading educational databases returned only one result, a single lesson plan posted on VH1 in the early 2000s. Since the heyday of CCR coincided with the Vietnam War, we selected that period of Fogerty's music on which to focus our multimodal instructional sequence.

Contextual Factors

In the past few decades, teachers have appropriated the literature of the Vietnam War as a means for teaching the era. Not only do we find a wealth of richly told war narratives, but we also find our students easily identifying with the protagonists, young soldiers "at war with an unseen enemy" in a "faraway place where bad things happened to Americans who regrettably did bad things in turn."[1] The problem, however, when engaging adolescents in the study of the war, is students have low schema, or background, into the complex socio-political situations surrounding the war's inception and conclusion. History teachers wishing to delve into the topic find themselves limited by a host of equally important topics necessary to cover by the end of the school year; often they only provide a cursory introduction. Furthermore, when English teachers attempt to take up the important literature of the time period, we meet a certain resistance based in ignorance.

To further mire instruction, the knowledge-base our students had, if any, was often constructed by popular culture texts like *Forrest Gump*, or to a lesser extent, *Platoon* or *Good Morning Vietnam*. While the sum of all movies concerning the Vietnam War might certainly build a valid understanding of the event, our students had not seen a large percentage of those films and would, rather, fall back to clichéd sayings and quotations from Gump. The "coda" of war films has shifted fundamentally since 9-11 as exhibited in the 2002 film *We Were Soldiers* which repurposes the Vietnam War narrative for an unending "War on Terror" where as Young observed,

> The victims of massacres in Vietnam, it turns out, were white men. My Lai dis-
> appears; there are no burning villages but instead well-armed, uniformed Viet-

namese regulars; napalm strikes burn Americans and Vietnamese alike—the B-52 sorties crucial to the battle are never shown; the American commander is everywhere in the midst of the battle, barely protected and always in danger; and the Vietnamese commander gives his orders from the safety of a clean, well-kept, underground tunnel complex. Americans die in great numbers but are still victorious over the far more numerous Vietnamese and a soldier's last words express gratitude that he has sacrificed his life for his country.[2]

What we needed was a way for students to access the real story, to fill the gaps and misunderstandings they had, to discover the non-Hollywood iteration of it. In sum, students need a way to see and hear the coda of an era which still resonates in American cultural and political memory. Our answer: utilize the music of John Fogerty and Creedence Clearwater Revival in a thematic literature unit as a bridge to the past.

Rock and Roll Hall of Fame Inductee John Fogerty's place in popular culture of the past, present, and future is fully confirmed: "U2, Def Leppard and Bruce Springsteen have all acknowledged a debt to Creedence, covering Fogerty's songs in concert and, in U2's case, on record. Feedback-guitar heroes Sonic Youth even named one of their albums, *Bad Moon Rising*, after a Fogerty composition."[3] As the intertextual landscape of American music is intertwined, so must be the textual experiences of high school students. In her discussion of intertextuality, Kristeva observed, "Conceived as crossed threshold between languages and cultures, intertextuality exposes the self either to an essential work. ... Intertextuality is a way of placing us, readers, not only in front of a more or less complicated and interwoven structure (the first meaning of texture), but also within an on-going process of signifying."[4]

Hence, in order to implement a unit utilizing multimodal intertextuality, it is imperative to make multiple connections between the reader and the text throughout each stage of the reading process: pre-reading, during, and post-reading. In this essay, we offer a practical example of how Fogerty/CCR's music can be used effectively in a classroom situation, explain the value of those songs, and discuss the implications of multimodal and intertextual approaches to teaching about these poignant topics.

"Multimodal Fogerty": An Intertextual Vietnam War Literature Unit Plan Developing Pre-Reading Activities

The American Literature of the Vietnam War unit plan modeled here draws upon the Scaffolded Reading Experience (SRE) strategy which divides literature units into three phases (pre-reading, during reading, and post-reading activities) in order to help students manage knowledge development.[5] Pre-reading activities significantly enhance reading comprehension because they can create interest, build and activate background, model reading strategies, observe text structure, and introduce new terms and concepts to students.[6] Typically, teachers spend only one or two days for pre-reading activities. "Given the limited working memory of human beings, skilled reading simply cannot take place until lower level skills such as decoding, lexical access, and parsing become automatic."[7] Consequently, for students with low or faulty schema, it would be beneficial to utilize one or more extended activities rather than a quickly executed mini-lesson; that is, teachers should consider chunking the literature unit plan into more manageable "mini-units." Some teachers may find that a single pre-reading activity may not suffice if students have a particularly low background knowledge in a subject area.[8] The number of mini-units will also vary based upon the demands of the curriculum; however progressive and thorough inquiry will help students strengthen their nets by providing sufficient background in order to master assigned readings.

The music of CCR "scores" the SRE in that each section contains a signature song which helps to explicate the sectional themes. For pre-reading, we chose "Fortunate Son" to highlight class implications of the Vietnam era. In writing the song, Fogerty noted:

> It was written, of course, during the Nixon era, and well, let's say I was very nonsupportive of Mr. Nixon. There just seemed to be this trickle down to the off-spring of people like him. I remember you would hear about Tricia Nixon and David Eisenhower. ... You got the impression that these people got preferential treatment, and the whole idea of being born wealthy or being born powerful seemed to really be coming to the fore in the late-Sixties confrontation of cultures.[9]

Our pre-reading activities begin with a schema-forming assignment which catalogues students' prior knowledge of the Vietnam War. We guide our students through pre-reading through the use of five questions:

1. Who were the key players of the war?
2. How did the U.S. get involved in Vietnam?
3. Why was the war controversial?
4. How did the war divide people based upon class and race?
5. Would you fight in Vietnam?

"Fortunate Son" provides the starting "text" for pre-reading as it provides foundational themes for the unit and is an excellent vehicle to incite student interest in the unit. According to Fogerty, the song critiques America's preferential treatment of the elite class (in particular David Eisenhower) who received preferential treatment and avoided going to Vietnam by earning a variety of medical and educational deferments.[10] At the time it was written, U.S. ground forces in Vietnam surged to an all-time high of over 500,000 soldiers. While the "unfortunate sons" found themselves waging a war they did not understand, David Eisenhower, a grandson of former President Dwight D. Eisenhower, escaped overseas deployment by serving in the Naval Reserves. During the 2000 U.S. presidential election, the song picked up renewed interest when George W. Bush's Vietnam service record in the Texas Air National Guard was heavily scrutinized in Hatfield's biography of Bush, *Fortunate Son* (1999).

Next, we discuss the other non-visual points of communication with the song: the music. The driving rhythm, arrangement, and vocal approach of the song support the meaning of the lyrics—this is a protest song. From the introduction before any lyrics are uttered, Fogerty's guitar is flippant, taking on the characteristic of someone standing up to the government specifically or status quo, generally speaking, as it twangs for the audience's attention. He uses his voice differently in "Fortunate Son," almost as if he were addressing a crowd on the Washington Mall through a megaphone. A simple arrangement of lead guitar, rhythm guitar, bass, and drums drives home a cadence further communicating a frustrated perspective, one that builds on the social class divisions in the context of war and delivers the message of protest.

Since we emphasize the multimodality of a text, our introduction utilizes YouTube videos which incorporates stills and video from the war with the song. One such example is "Vietnam War footage—Fortunate Son CCR," which highlights a number of iconic images and can be used to help students visualize song imagery.[11] Another key factor is the fact that the enemy is unseen in the video and it helps us expand on the theme of the divisiveness of the war: not only were we fighting abroad, but we were also fighting at home.

Although Wikipedia is sometimes disparaged as "non-scholarly," it is actually an appropriate resource for generating pre-reading activities. Using the entry as their textbook, students can learn more about the Vietnam War and John Fogerty. Rather than giving them a handout, students were expected to read the web site and take careful notes in order to find answers to the first four questions. As a quick check for comprehension, we shared our notes together in class, although with more advanced students, the notes would serve as an excellent study guide for a quiz over the reading.

In addition to the creation of new learning, multimodal intertextuality may be utilized to scaffold new learners who are not yet capable of making connections by providing tools for organizing new learning so students can better make sense of their knowledge and retrieve it for later use. For example, in either printed or computerized formats, graphic organizers (GO) help students visualize connections made by rendering information into summarized text and or symbols. GOs are excellent tools for helping student synthesize new information and may be utilized as a pre-reading tool or even summative assessment.[12]

Through multimodal intertextuality, teachers weave numerous connections between students' prior knowledge of material with new material in order to build a solid foundation to guide students through literature units. GOs provide a concrete and visual reference of connections made. As they may be shared during class activities, students have an opportunity to revise their learning in order to correct errors or enrich thinking.

In terms of how the pre-reading activity enhanced student performance, students felt comfortable with the reading material since many of them had used Wikipedia before the project; hence, they read the articles pertaining to the Vietnam War. The poster presentation fostered a deeper interaction with readings as they each were accountable for learned information and had to explain conceptual knowledge. Finally, since their projects were oral, feedback was immediate so inaccuracies in course concepts could be adjusted during the presentations.

Once students have developed background information on the Vietnam War, it is helpful to have students read or view Martin Luther King, Jr.'s "A Time to Break Silence," delivered April 4, 1967 one year and one day before his assassination. The five guiding questions recorded on the GO may help students navigate the text as we can see King's interpretation of the facts, in particular, how the war divided the nation based upon race. An extension of this activity is to observe the media's reaction to King's speech, which was not met favorably by magazines such as *Time* and newspapers such as the *Washington Post*.[13] King's speech serves as a segue for the summative activity for the pre-reading phase: a "Fortunate Son" debate where students deliberate whether or not they would volunteer for Vietnam. Utilizing their notes and GOs, students articulate three reasons for their decision in a roundtable debating the pros and cons of the war. The advantage of this assignment is that it synthesizes learning in a public way so students can see various opinions. Evaluation may be based upon the three justifications and their roundtable participation.

During Reading Activities

Most during-reading activities include silent reading, reading to students, guided reading, oral reading by students, and modifying the text.[14] When considering multimodal instructional approaches, however, teachers might consider extending instruction beyond merely reading and listening to plays so a variety of codes such as sounds, gestures, and images are incorporated into the learning process.

To this end, we introduced the primary text through the song "Bad Moon Rising," which like "Fortunate Son," has a number of YouTube adaptions such as "Bad Moon Rising CCR Vietnam History Video," which can help students visualize texts multimodally.[15] Our decision to use this song is based upon two factors. The song emphasizes first-person narration, which fits appropriately with first-person narratives such as *The Things They Carried* (1990), and the music contradicts the lyrics. The song, according to Fogerty, "was about the apocalypse that was going to be visited upon us."[16] Thus, the song captures the novel's protagonist, both in terms of his voice (first-person narration) as well as destructive conflagration which will kill dear friends and forever maim his soul.

What might be most compelling about this song is that its lyrics and music are an apparent mismatch. With apocalyptic lyrics that signal the end of the world, the music's up-tempo rhythm, vocal styling, and guitar work signal the opposite. From the first chords of the song, Fogerty sings like he's celebrating a victory rather than facing total defeat. And even though the lyrics could be about Vietnam and the impending doom from the war, no direct lyrical connections exist. Rather, we infer that the popularity of CCR's stance with "Fortunate Son" may have bled over to "Bad Moon Rising" and caused that song to become another anthem of the anti-war movement. Having students analyze the music and then make connections to the lyrics allows them to gain perspective on the paradoxical nature of "Bad Moon Rising," as a composition and ultimately, to the Vietnam War era itself.

We chose Tim O'Brien's *The Things They Carried* for multiple reasons. Most importantly, the novel has been recognized as an important work of literature, a finalist for the Pulitzer Prize and the National Book Critics Circle Award, and winner of the French *Prix du Meilleur Livre Étranger*. The titular story, "The Things They Carried," was selected in the 1987 volume of *The Best American Short Stories* as well as *The Best American Short Stories of the Century* and further canonized in school owned literature collections. Furthermore, the text has a number of multimodal extensions; teachers may utilize several internet videos featuring O'Brien as well as student-generated tributes to his novel.

We employed a number of traditional summative activities in order to measure reading compression such as reading quizzes and class discussion. To incorporate multimodal strategies, we "tooned it up" during the reading. Throughout the novel, students were assigned to draw various single-page cartoons, or "toons." Some days, students were assigned toons which depicted their interpretations of key scenes. On other occasions, students created toons which taught important vocabulary terms. Finally, to help students keep track of main characters, they "tooned" or created renderings of what they believed the main characters would look like. As each set of toons were completed, we discuss them with the rest of the class. This helped students focus on visualizing the play and it helped correct misunderstandings as we could discuss the play as we could address plot, theme, and characters through their observations of the drawings.

By the end of the novel, students had a collection of toons which served as visual archives of their learning. Research demonstrates a high correlation between creating visual images and mastery and retention of learned material.[17] "This provides an opportunity," argued Elliott, "for students to elaborate and encode the information in a personally meaningful way."[18] For the most part, students enjoyed the activity and by placing the drawings on the walls around the room, we could have a visual reminder of key scenes of the play.

Post-Reading Activities

When speaking about "Have You Ever Seen the Rain?" Fogerty observed a singular meaning: "That song is really about the impending breakup of Creedence. The imagery is, you can have a bright, beautiful, sunny day and it can be raining at the same time. The band was breaking up. I was reacting: 'Geez, this is all getting serious right at the time when we should be having a sunny day.'"[19] Within the larger context of the U.S. involvement in Vietnam, this song serves a multiplicity of interpretations worth investigating alongside students. Rain, for example, could mean the rain of goods and supplies delivered to the troops from ammunition to beer to sparklers. It could mean a rain of tears for fallen comrades, or the gore and blood of Ted Lavender's head when he was shot outside of Than Khe. (Lavender is a character in *The Things They Carried*.) It could mean the rain of bombs from B-52s or bullets from AK-47s. It could mean many things to many students, and it is for this reason, we chose to have students conclude the unit. This ambiguity serves as a runway from which the students' own connections can take flight.

Musically, "Have You Ever Seen the Rain?" furthers the lyrical meaning with musical walk-downs that provide a sense of falling or failing to the song. If we are to believe Fogerty's words as published in *Rolling Stone* than the musical composition here extends the lyrics, leaving a sense of hopelessness towards the end of the band. While the lyrics could be viewed as contradictory, like the idea of it raining when the sun is shining, the music here carries the more poignant, accurate message of decline. Fogerty's vocals could best be described as ambivalent, somewhere caught between a protest song voice of "Fortunate Son" or the uplifting styles used in "Bad Moon Rising."

As we have observed in this essay, YouTube has provided an excellent template for assessments in that students could choose a multimedia project called Toons which synthesizes their learning of *The Things They Carried*. Students are given the option of choosing a CCR song or another similar song to narrate a slide show that communicates key components of the novel such as plot, characters, and themes. By scanning their toons, students can draw during-reading activities into their summative activity. The benefit of such projects is that they are utilizing multimodality and presenting their information to the whole class so students may again gauge the accuracy of their learning as well as add to their knowledge base by adding peer perceptions with their own.

Should teachers wish to employ print assessments, a highly suitable activity is the multigenre essay as originated by Romano which would communicate answers to the five guiding questions as well as content knowledge of *The Things They Carried* in a variety of student-generated texts which range from poetry, postcards, letters, and even death certificates. In her study of the multigenre essay, Painter observed that the activity is highly suitable for varied student abilities and provides the time and flexibility to work with students individually or in groups.[20] As she observed, "In addition, it was clear that when students presented their final products to one another, all students had constructed their own knowledge about historical events and that they had independently demonstrated technology and research skills they had learned throughout their elementary school years."[21] Essentially applying the framework of the multigenre essay to the modalities with which students are so familiar is our preferred method; the essay itself should not be overlooked as a key building block for larger projects, however, as it can encourage creative and critical thinking.

Discussion

John Fogerty and CCR can help ground students in a study of the Vietnam War era of American literature and history; taking up these songs in the context of multimodal composition has clear educational benefits for students and is grounded in solid theory and practical literature. An unintended benefit of the project is that students produce multimodal projects, something that they often choose to share on venues like Facebook and YouTube, thus furthering the messages of Fogerty and potentially expanding his reach into the realm of education.

Whatever the text, a primary teaching challenge lies in managing content with students' ability to read assignment material. Reading may be "seen as an active process of constructing meaning by connecting old knowledge with newly encountered information in text."[22] Thus, a cause for students' difficulty engaging in highly complex texts is their poor background knowledge of the material, an issue we've faced when attempting to teach literature about the Vietnam War. For instance, students who read *The Diary of Anne Frank* in their eighth-grade language arts courses may not have sufficient prior knowledge in order to understand the Jewish plight in Nazi-held European countries. Students reading *To Kill a Mockingbird* in their ninth-grade classes may not have sufficient prior knowledge of life in a 1950s "Jim Crow" South to fully grasp Atticus Finch's heroism. For both texts, it is equally important to comprehend race, religion, and gender relations in order to fully appreciate the novels' significance. As the literature of the Vietnam War has multiple narratives which have been shaped by war "hawks" and "doves" and since then shaped by the events of 9-11, it is critical to create a centering mechanism to help students organize their learning.

Kristin Fontichiaro observed that, "New learning builds on existing prior knowledge."[23] Hence, it is important to create "intentional learning activities that can give that strong foundation and level the playing field for all learners."[24] In order to create new and refine prior knowledge, one centering mechanism is the drawing upon students' more frequently used processes for learning about the world around them: electronic media. In fact, studies demonstrated an increased learning efficiency "when information is processed through multiple sensory input stimuli (i.e. verbal and non-verbal)."[25] This "multimodal literacy instruction" is the practice of knowledge construction through images, sounds, and animated movements.[26]

Knowledge construction through print or electronic media, of course, does not occur in isolation. "Any text," according to Barthes's theory of intertextuality, "is a new tissue of past citations. Bits of code, formulae, rhythmic models, fragments of social languages, etc., pass into the text and are redistributed within it, for there is always language before and around the text."[27] Through multimodal intertextuality, teachers may weave numerous connections between students' prior knowledge of material with new material in order to build a solid foundation or the scaffold to guide them through literature units.

It was 1969 when Steven Carter shared one of the first accounts of using music to teach English. His project was an attempt, through using the Beatles lyrics, to get the attention of his college composition students and ultimately lead them to "better writing skills through the common rhetorical elements of voice, tone, structure, continuity," an experience he reported as "vast and rewarding" for his students.[28] Since a host of researchers and teachers have shared practical accounts of teaching writing, reading, and other intricacies of language, for example, shared practical advice on how song lyrics can act as "literary texts," ultimately "rich in imagery and metaphor," and provide a student friendly manner of, "teach[ing] irony, tone, diction, point of view … theme, plot, motif, and character development."[29] As the authors point out, music lyrics provide their urban high school students pathways to content and curriculum that are a natural part of any English classroom. With rural eighth grade students, Roger Caswell explained an approach to specifically teaching *The Pearl* through the lens of music.

We have each written elsewhere on several aspects of using music in the English classrooms: using blues music to teach the Faust theme; writing personal narratives with music; intertextuality as it plays out with popular music; musical intertextuality; using a soundtrack approach to teach *To Kill a Mockingbird*; teaching composition with Johnny Cash; multimodal approaches to teaching English.[30] Additionally, Goering oversees a popular online resource for using music to teach literary literacy: www.LitTunes.com.

While popular in classroom settings, the empirically researched effectiveness of this strategy is less clear. To date, few studies have been completed about the effects of using music in the classroom and while teacher testimony in the articles and chapters referenced above paints a picture of how music can be used in teaching, it doesn't create an unequivocal picture of support for the strategy. In at least some circles, using music to teach English is still considered a taboo practice, one that is taken up in subversive manners in classrooms. The opportunity for music to mix with other modes of communication creates a stronger, more complete position for these ideas to become widespread.

Conclusion

Instructional methods such as multimodal intertextuality may not get all students to love literature, but the methods can help them to better understand the background, messages, and themes. Students build and enlarge their schemata through multiple print and electronic sources and apply their knowledge to the study of challenging material, and as a result become more proficient readers engaged in inquiry into significant issues in American history and culture.

One of the most pronounced voices of the Vietnam era is John Fogerty. By situating him in the teaching of literature and history classes, an opportunity presents itself to further the timeless messages of his music all the while introducing new generations of students to his work.

Notes

1. Marilyn B. Young, "Now Playing: Vietnam," *OAH Magazine of History* 18, no. 5 (2004): 22–23.

2. Ibid, 25.

3. Michael Goldberg, "Fortunate Son," *Rolling Stone*, February 4, 1993, 47.

4. Julia Kristeva, "'Nous Deux' or a (Hi)story of Intertextuality," *The Romanic Review*, 93, no. 1–2 (2002): 9.

5. Sally S. Rothenberg and Susan Watts, "Students with Learning Difficulties Meet Shakespeare: Using a Scaffolded Reading Experience," *Journal of Adolescent & Adult Literacy* 40, no. 7 (1997): 533.

6. Sharon R. Gill, "The Comprehension Matrix: A Tool for Designing Comprehension Instruction," *The Reading Teacher* 62, no. 2 (2011): 109.

7. Terri Carter, A. Hardy, and James C. Hardy, "Latin Vocabulary Acquisition: An Experiment Using Information-Processing Techniques of Chunking and Imagery," *Journal of Instructional Psychology* 28, no. 4 (2001): 225.

8. Rothenburg and Watts, 533.

9. Goldberg, 48.

10. Ibid.

11. "Vietnam War footage—Fortunate Son CCR," YouTube, http://www.youtube.com/watch?v=2ahDHwYWg8E (May 18, 2012).

12. Nancy P. Gallavan and Ellen Kottler, *Secrets to Success for Social Studies Teachers* (Thousand Oaks, CA: Corwin Press, 2008), 93.

13. Martin Luther King, Jr., "Beyond Vietnam," Speech, April 4, 1967, *Information Clearing House*, http://www.informationclearinghouse.info/article2564.htm (April 10, 2012).

14. Rothenburg and Watts, 534.

15. "Bad Moon Rising CCR Vietnam History," YouTube, http://www.youtube.com/watch?v=2Ydnka5TX8c (May 22, 2012).

16. Goldberg, 48.

17. Chris Altman, "Sketching to Create Meaning: The Story of a Second-Language Learner," *English Journal* 97, no. 5 (2008): 66–67.

18. Janine Elliott, "Summarizing With Drawings: A Reading-Comprehension Strategy," *Science Scope* 30, no. 5(2007): 26.

19. Goldberg, 48.

20. Diane Painter, "Providing Differentiated Learning Experiences Through Multigenre Projects,"*Intervention in School and Clinic* 44, no. 5 (2009): 288.

21. Ibid.

22. Divonna M. Stebick, "Informational Overload in Content Area Reading: A Professional Development Plan for Middle and High School Teachers," *Journal of Content Area Reading* 7, no. 1 (2008): 95.

23. Kristin Fontichiaro, "Nudging Toward Inquiry: Awakening and Building upon Prior Knowledge," *School Library Monthly* 27, no. 1 (2009): 12.

24. Ibid.

25. Robert Zheng, et al. "Effects of Multimedia and Schema Induced Analogical Reasoning on Science Learning," *Journal of Computer Assisted Learning* 24, no. 6 (2008): 476.

26. Carey Jewett, "Multimodal Reading and Writing on Screen," *Discourse: Studies in the Cultural Politics of Education* 26, no. 3 (2005): 316.

27. Roland Barthes, "Theory of the Text," in *Untying the Text: A Post-Structuralist Reader*, ed. Robert Young (London: Routledge, 1981), 39.

28. Carter, 228.

29. Ernest Morrell and Jeffrey M. R. Duncan-Andrade, "Promoting Academic Literacy with Urban Youth through Hip-Hop Culture," *English Journal* 91, no. 6 (2002): 89.

30. See bibliography under Copeland and Goering; Goering; Goering, et al.; Goering and Williams; Sewell; and Sewell and Denton.

PART IV

"KEEP ON CHOOGLIN'"

CHAPTER ELEVEN

∼

John Fogerty and America's Three Rock Generations

B. Lee Cooper
with research assistance from
William L. Schurk

John Fogerty and I have two things in common. We adore American music
and we are members of the pre-Baby Boomer generation. Like Pete Townshend, I have always cherished the unique qualities of "My Generation."
My father, a U.S. Marine who fought at Iwo Jima during World War II,
loved my mother, his stateside supporter who worried about him and played
and re-played "Miss You" on her phonograph. They were part of America's
Greatest Generation.[1] My folks were born during the Jazz Age of Republican political dominance, of Prohibition, and of the Charleston. They spent
their teenage years learning to do without frivolous items during the Great
Depression. For them, it was "Brother, Can You Spare a Dime?" rather than
"We're in the Money." After graduating from Hammond High School in
northwestern Indiana, they married on July 4, 1941. The terrible warfare that
had engulfed Europe since 1939 became a worldwide conflagration after the
Japanese attacked Pearl Harbor. I was born on October 4, 1942, just before
my Dad disappeared overseas for three years. He didn't return until after the
atomic annihilation of Hiroshima and Nagasaki. My sister and brother were
born in 1947 and 1948, respectively. They are Baby Boomers. Yet I remain
in limbo, neither a child of the Great Depression nor a Boomer.[2] As an adult,
I have watched other Boomers produce Generation X, who in turn spawned
the Millennials, who are now fathering (and mothering) a group of young
Americans variously labeled the Internet Generation, Homelanders, Generation 9/11, or the Dreamer Generation.[3]

Like John Fogerty, popular music was a mainstay of my early life. Audio diversity ruled. Recordings by Al Jolson, the Ink Spots, Bing Crosby, and the Mills Brothers echoed on my grandparents' antique phonographs. At local record shops I encountered the singing of Pat Boone, Little Richard, the Fontane Sisters, Bill Haley and His Comets, Jackie Wilson, Dean Martin, Jerry Lee Lewis, and Fats Domino. My mother and father listened to Patti Page, Georgia Gibbs, Perry Como, Rosemary Clooney, Eddie Fisher, and Dinah Shore. Junior high sock hops and high school dances featured the music of the Everly Brothers, Eddie Cochran, the Moonglows, Buddy Holly, and the Platters. The black-and-white television set in our living room, the source of everything from *American Bandstand* to *The Adventures of Ozzie and Harriet,* introduced the entire Cooper Family to Elvis Presley, Ricky Nelson, the Coasters, Gene Autry, Connie Francis, Roy Rogers, and Annette Funicello. Absent any older siblings, I benefited from listening to the blaring car radios of older guys who enjoyed Gene Vincent, Buddy Knox, Roy Orbison, Johnny Cash, and Billy Lee Riley. My happenstance musical education was a product of war-time birth, the rise of cover recording practices among pop, country, and R&B record artists, the increasing presence of independent Chicago radio deejays, and my sponge-like reception of all available recordings. Beyond my experiences, John Fogerty got to rummage through his older brother's country and western albums and to watch San Francisco spawn new singers and bands at a mind-numbing pace.[4] As a young adult, I took my 45s and Webcore phonograph off to college. Meanwhile, John Fogerty gathered his high school friends together and formed a band. His life story is far more interesting than mine. But we remain generational and musical soul brothers.

John Fogerty was born in Berkeley on May 28, 1945. His older brother Tom had arrived in the California-based Fogerty family four years earlier, on November 9, 1941. Music played a dominant role in their childhood lives. John, in particular, showed talent on piano, guitar, tenor saxophone, harmonica, drums, and organ. In 1959, at Portola Junior High School, the 14-year-old John formed a band with two of his classmates. Drummer Doug Clifford had been born in Oakland on April 24, 1945, and bassist Stu Cook had been born in Palo Alto on April 25, 1945. Playing gigs was fun! So much fun, in fact, that John's older brother took over the group which then played under the title of Tommy Fogerty and the Blue Velvets. Benefiting from his day-job as a shipping clerk for the San Francisco-based Fantasy Records, Tom was able to secure a recording contract for his band. Name changes occurred. The Blue Velvets morphed into the Visions, only to be re-christened the Golliwogs in order to heighten their British Invasion-like appeal. Musically and commercially nothing significant happened during the mid-'60s for the

Golliwogs. Then John and Stu entered the U.S. Army Reserves in 1966. When they returned two years later, they decided to get much more serious about a musical profession. The revived rock unit needed an appropriately outrageous moniker, though. Seeing elements of "truth" and "justice" in the given name of former high school buddy Credence Newball, the band borrowed his first name, with an extra "e" spliced in for emphasis. An Olympia Beer slogan that suggested the purity of clear water in their brewing process also seemed valuable in the renaming process. Finally, the combination of truth, purity, and renewal were molded into a one-of-a-kind band title— Creedence Clearwater Revival. As the newly named quartet practiced diligently, adopted a series of new songs, and performed at numerous Bay Area bars and clubs, it became obvious that John Fogerty had evolved into the dynamic leader of the group. Tom acknowledged the obvious. So did Doug and Stu. For the next three years, CCR ruled not just San Francisco but the entire rock music scene.[5]

Three Generations of Rock Music Performers

John Fogerty and his vibrant Creedence Clearwater Revival recording team constitute the pre-eminent illustration of transitional generation energy and hit-making power in U.S. rock music. To fully understand this statement, one must reflect upon the roots of rock and the continuity of its progress throughout the twentieth century.[6] American rock music has benefited from the energy and ingenuity of three distinct generations of singers and songwriters. Chronologically, these recording artists can be aligned by their birth dates into three musical production eras that denote creativity, transformation, and inheritance in the rock music genre. More specifically, the generations of professional musicians who contributed to establishing rock as the mainstream sound of the second half of the twentieth century can be categorized as originators (1918–1938), translators (1939–1945), and revivalists (1946–1963). In respect to generational theory, this historical birth date hypothesis contends that the children of America's Age of Normalcy and the Great Depression were crucial contributors to launching and synthesizing the blues, country, and R&B recordings that fostered the rock-and-roll music of 1953–1957. Likewise, the children of the Second World War, who were exposed at an early formative age to post-war R&B rhythms, doo-wop harmonies, rockabilly music, and rock and roll, created various strands of the '60s and '70s sounds that became known simply as rock. Finally, those future rock musicians who were born as Baby Boomers had the opportunity to experience the audio products of both the originators and the translators during their formative pre-adult years. When these artists launched their own musical careers, they functioned in a dual fashion as inheritors of a well-developed rock tradition and as revivalists of the same rhythmic patterns that had sparked the mid-'50s musical revolution.[7]

John Fogerty has a unique presence within this trio of rock music generations. The span of his recording success as the leader of CCR and later as a solo act is remarkable.[8] *Billboard* lists 20 CCR hits between 1968 and 1976, plus more than a dozen charted tunes by either John Fogerty (1972-1986) or his alter ego group the Blue Ridge Rangers (1973). But John also functions as an inter-generational conduit in respect to American musicology, political events, social trends, economic circumstances, and even geography. As Ellen Willis observed in her insightful 1980 commentary on CCR, Fogerty defied the conventions of his day at every turn. First, he was unalterably dedicated to rock and roll rather than to the Bay Area's potent mix of psychedelic sounds and acid rock. Second, he was stubbornly patriotic even as he manifested lyrical disgust about the irrationality of the Vietnam War. Third, he abstained from the local drug scene and ridiculed the pretentious mushroom visionaries that populated Berkeley and San Francisco. Fourth, he challenged the unearned privilege of the wealthy and objected to mindless government expenditures on self-serving pork barrel projects. Finally, he viewed the unproductive lethargy of hippie communes as socially irresponsible.[9] To Fogerty, Haight-Ashbury was a sad rather than joyous community. Willis is even more specific about the distinction between CCR's "Top 40" radio domination and the staunchly middle-class values that the group manifested. She writes,

> Creedence was always somewhat estranged from its generational and musical peers. Its image was of a group stubbornly loyal to unfashionable values. The geographical metaphor will do as well as any: though Creedence shared turf with the acid-rock bands, its roots were not in psychedelic San Francisco or political Berkeley but in El Cerrito, an East Bay suburb with even less cachet, if possible, than Oakland. Its members were not former folkies converted to the electric music by Bob Dylan; they had been a rock and roll band since high school. ... They were not "underground" or "avant-garde" or into drugs or given to revolutionary rhetoric. They were at home with the short, tight, hit-single aesthetic that most "serious" rock musicians scorned.[10]

Which performers constitute the three American rock music generations? If John Fogerty is indeed iconic as a translator, who are the originators and the revivalists—as well as the other translators? While it is relatively easy to develop a theoretical construct to depict musical genre expansion, it is invariably messy to shoehorn historical characters into separate categorical boxes. I freely acknowledge that my biographical illustrations are neither complete nor totally balanced in terms of future musical influence. However, this generational construct—applied strictly to U.S.-born artists who were raised within American culture between 1918 and 1963—presents musicians in the learning context of teachers and learners, leaders and followers, and dynamic participants in the historical events of their time. This approach borrows freely from the generational research and metaphors created by prominent sociologists and historians.[11] What it lacks in validity in regard to any specific artist, it more than compensates for in the perceptions gained concerning trends in general musical development. Like all hypothetical approaches, of course, it is open to criticism that will enhance the understanding of how popular music grows and changes over several decades.

Stylistic diversity was the trademark of rock's generation of originators. They were unconventional characters who delighted in experimentation with music and alcohol. Frequently lacking both higher education and formal musical training, this cadre of performers understood that music was a viable escape from hard physical labor, personal disrespect, and economic uncertainty. They shared penchants for storytelling, for camaraderie around a bottle, and for life's simple pleasures—wine, women, and song. Often denied radio access to larger audiences, these determined originators offered their blues, country, and R&B performances before small crowds at barn dances, house parties, and in bars and brothels.[12] Their variations in rhythm and lyrical content are matched by the variations of recognition they received among the American populace. What did they record? Their automobile songs included "Maybelline" and "Rocket 88"; their sexy numbers included "Work with Me Annie" and "Sixty Minute Man"; and their emotional appeals included "Please Please Please" and "I Got a Woman." There are very few women—LaVern Baker, Ruth Brown, Wanda Jackson, Etta James, Little Esther Phillips, and Tina Turner—represented among this generation of rock originators. In contrast, instrumentalists like Mickey Baker, King Curtis, Bill Doggett, Duane Eddy, Huey "Piano" Smith, Jimmy Smith, Ike Turner, and Link Wray are notably prominent. Similarly, musicians representing specific streams of regionalized or racially isolated music that eventually merged into the surging river of rock are also present. From the music of those people who are darker-than-blue came Albert Collins, Buddy Guy, John Lee Hooker, Howlin' Wolf, Elmore

James, Robert Johnson, Albert King, B. B. King, Freddie King, Little Milton, Jimmy Reed, and Muddy Waters; from the burgeoning R&B field came Hank Ballard, Jackie Brenston, James Brown, Roy Brown, Ray Charles, Sam Cooke, Harvey Fuqua, Wynonie Harris, Little Willie John, Louis Jordan, Clyde McPhatter, Johnny Otis, Lloyd Price, Big Joe Turner, and Chuck Willis; and from the country-and-western realm came Johnny Cash, Don and Phil Everly, Willie Nelson, Jerry Reed, Charlie Rich, Marty Robbins, Conway Twitty, and Hank Williams. Standing on the audio shoulders of the aforementioned musical giants, an intra-generational group of originators introduced rock and roll to America. Born between 1918 and 1938, these key figures include Chuck Berry, Johnny Burnette, Eddie Cochran, Bo Diddley, Fats Domino, Bill Haley, Ronnie Hawkins, Buddy Holly, Jerry Lee Lewis, Little Richard, Carl Perkins, Elvis Presley, Billy Lee Riley, Gene Vincent, Larry Williams, and Jackie Wilson.

The second generation of rockers is understandably less diverse than the first. These translators are children of the rhythmic revolution of the mid-'50s. The songs of Chuck, Fats, Bo, Buddy, Elvis, and Jerry Lee forged indelible soundtracks in their adolescent minds.[13] For many of those who reached puberty during mid-century, rock and roll was not just a new thing—it was everything. John Fogerty has acknowledged this feeling time and again. The first generation of rockers contributed immeasurably to the sense of rebellion, the dancing mania, and the frenzy of dating and initial sexual encounters that propelled the following generation. The translators wanted in. They wanted to make the audio magic, too. Their audio inheritance was much more than just old records on the shelf. The practice of covering classic rock hits with teenage bands eventually led to the creative process of seeking one's own distinctive rock voice. John Fogerty finally achieved this feat with CCR in 1968. While his role is emblematic in preserving, revitalizing, and expanding the rock idiom, others of the translator generation also warrant recognition for their idiosyncratic treks toward musical success. Just as R&B artists had influenced the birth of rock and roll, soul performers contributed stylistic and lyrical ideas to rock music's second generation. Among the key black American translators were Solomon Burke, Jerry Butler, Aretha Franklin, Bobby Freeman, Marvin Gaye, Curtis Mayfield, Aaron Neville, Wilson Pickett, Otis Redding, Smokey Robinson, Edwin Starr, Sly Stone, and Irma Thomas. During this period, individual musical leadership was often submerged within rock groups. From Big Brother and the Holding Company (Janis Joplin), Steppenwolf

(John Kay), and the Rascals (Felix Cavaliere) to the Righteous Brothers (Bill Medley), the Lovin' Spoonful (John Sebastian), and Simon and Garfunkel (Paul Simon), powerful and perceptive singers and songwriters tweaked rock toward the future. Of course, the generation of translators also included a range of unforgettable rock characters such as Dr. John, Bob Dylan, Jimi Hendrix, Jim Morrison, Leon Russell, Mitch Ryder, Bob Seger, Brian Wilson, Neil Young, and Frank Zappa.[14]

The rock revivalist generation parallels the Baby Boomers by chronology. Their contributions to acknowledging the rock and roll originators and to building upon and diversifying the rock music paths blazed by the translators are significant. These post-war American musicians achieved adulthood during or shortly after the Vietnam conflict, after the so-called British music invasion, and after the tragic deaths of several early rock heroes and heroines. Nevertheless, they still experienced models of rock recording, rock writing, and rock performing from the foremost artists of both the originator and the translator generations. From Chuck Berry and Jerry Lee Lewis to Bob Dylan and Bob Seger, rock's past thundered on. Once again, the youthful practice of producing cover versions of earlier rock hits served as a catechism for later prophetic audio revelations among the revivalists.[15] Not unexpectedly, a quest for rock authenticity caused noticeable fragmentation among members of this third generation of musicians.[16] They pondered, "What was the purest form or the best example of true American rock?" This debate, pursued musically by recording stars or more raucously in barroom brawls between die-hard rock fans, can be heard on the releases of Duane Allman, Greg Allman, Dave Alvin, Robert Gordon, Brian Setzer, Stevie Ray Vaughan, Hank Williams, Jr., and Kim Wilson.

For other revivalists, though, moving rock forward was simply a function of penning new songs. This diverse revivalist group includes Jackson Browne, Robert Cray, Glenn Frey, Don Henley, Carlos Santana, and Stevie Wonder. The revivalist generation strives to retain the sound and the fury of earlier rockers, but they have become international celebrities, cash cows, and media darlings in the process. Their musical success is beyond the wildest dreams of their rockabilly progenitors. Aging gracefully as the twenty-first century bids farewell to its initial decade, the third generation of rockers includes Cher, Melissa Etheridge, Billy Gibbons, Billy Joel, Al Green, Kenny Loggins, John Cougar Mellencamp, Tom Petty, Bonnie Raitt, Linda Ronstadt, David Lee Roth, Bruce Springsteen, and George Thorogood.

Table 11.1. An Alphabetical Listing of American Performing Artists Representing the Three Rock Music Generations in the United States from 1918 to 1963[17]

Originators (1918–1938)	Translators (1939–1945)	Revivalists (1946–1963)
Lavern Baker (b. 1929)	Solomon Burke (b. 1940)	Duane Allman (b. 1946)
Mickey Baker (b. 1925)	Jerry Butler (b. 1939)	Greg Allman (b. 1947)
Hank Ballard (b. 1927)	Freddy Cannon (b. 1939)	Dave Alvin (b. 1955)
Chuck Berry (b. 1926)	Felix Cavaliere (b. 1942)	Jackson Browne (b. 1948)
Jackie Brenston (b. 1930)	Jim Croce (b. 1943)	Cher (b. 1946)
James Brown (b. 1933)	Dion DiMucci (b. 1939)	Alex Chilton (b. 1950)
Roy Brown (b. 1925)	Dr. John (b. 1940)	Robert Cray (b. 1953)
Ruth Brown (b. 1928)	Bob Dylan (b. 1941)	Tinsley Ellis (b. 1957)
Dorsey Burnette (b. 1932)	Phil Everly (b. 1939)	Melissa Etheridge (b. 1961)
Johnny Burnette (b. 1934)	John Fogerty (b. 1945)	Glenn Frey (b. 1948)
Johnny Cash (b. 1932)	Tom Fogerty (b. 1941)	Anson Funderburgh (b. 1955)
Ray Charles (b. 1930)	Frankie Ford (b. 1939)	Billy Gibbons (b. 1949)
Eddie Cochran (b. 1938)	Aretha Franklin (b. 1942)	Robert Gordon (b. 1947)
Albert Collins (b. 1932)	Bobby Freeman (b. 1940)	Al Green (b. 1946)
Sam Cooke (b. 1931)	Marvin Gaye (b. 1939)	Sammy Hagar (b. 1947)
King Curtis (b. 1934)	Bobby Hatfield (b. 1940)	Don Henley (b. 1947)
Bobby Darin (b. 1936)	Jimi Hendrix (b. 1942)	Billy Joel (b. 1949)
Bo Diddley (b. 1928)	Booker T. Jones (b. 1944)	Huey Lewis (b. 1950)
Bill Doggett (b. 1916)	Janis Joplin (b. 1943)	Kenny Loggins (b. 1948)
Fats Domino (b. 1928)	John Kay (b. 1944)	John Cougar Mellencamp (b. 1951)
Duane Eddy (b. 1938)	Brenda Lee (b. 1944)	Jim Messina (b. 1947)
Don Everly (b. 1937)	Lonnie Mack (b. 1941)	Gram Parson (b. 1946)
Harvey Fuqua (b. 1924)	Curtis Mayfield (b. 1924)	Tom Petty (b. 1950)
Buddy Guy (b. 1936)	Delbert McClinton (b. 1940)	Bonnie Raitt (b. 1949)
Merle Haggard (b. 1937)	Bill Medley (b. 1940)	Linda Ronstadt (b. 1946)
Bill Haley (b. 1925)	Steve Miller (b. 1943)	David Lee Roth (b. 1955)

Wynonie Harris (b. 1915)
Dale Hawkins (b. 1936)
Ronnie Hawkins (b. 1935)
Screamin' Jay Hawkins (b. 1929)
Buddy Holly (b. 1936)
John Lee Hooker (b. 1917)
Howlin' Wolf (b. 1910)
Wanda Jackson (b. 1937)
Elmore James (b. 1918)
Etta James (b. 1938)
Little Willie John (b. 1937)
Robert Johnson (b. 1911)
Louis Jordan (b. 1908)
Chris Kenner (b. 1929)
Albert King (b. 1923)
B.B. King (b. 1925)
Ben E. King (b. 1938)
Freddie King (b. 1934)
Jerry Lee Lewis (b. 1935)
Little Milton (b. 1934)
Little Richard (b. 1932)
Clyde McPhatter (b. 1932)
Willie Mitchell (b. 1928)
Willie Nelson (b. 1933)
Roy Orbison (b. 1936)
Johnny Otis (b. 1921)
Carl Perkins (b. 1932)
Little Esther Phillips (b. 1935)

Chris Montez (b. 1943)
Jim Morrison (b. 1943)
Ricky Nelson (b. 1940)
Aaron Neville (b. 1941)
Wilson Pickett (b. 1941)
Gene Pitney (b. 1940)
Otis Redding (b. 1941)
Lou Reed (b. 1942)
Johnny Rivers (b. 1942)
Smokey Robinson (b. 1940)
Diana Ross (b. 1944)
Leon Russell (b. 1942)
Mitch Ryder (b. 1945)
Boz Scaggs (b. 1944)
John Sebastian (b. 1944)
Bob Seger (b. 1945)
Paul Simon (b. 1941)
Grace Slick (b. 1939)
Joe South (b. 1940)
Edwin Starr (b. 1942)
Stephen Stills (b. 1945)
Sly Stone (b. 1944)
B.J. Thomas (b. 1942)
Carla Thomas (b. 1942)
Irma Thomas (b. 1941)
Johnny Tillotson (b. 1939)
Ritchie Valens (b. 1941)
Brian Wilson (b. 1942)

Carlos Santana (b. 1947)
Brian Setzer (b. 1959)
Patti Smith (b. 1946)
Bruce Springsteen (b. 1949)
Billy Squier (b. 1950)
George Thorogood (b. 1952)
Travis Tritt (b. 1963)
Jimmy Vaughan (b. 1951)
Stevie Ray Vaughan (b. 1954)
Joe Walsh (b. 1947)
Hank Williams, Jr. (b. 1949)
Kim Wilson (b. 1951)
Edgar Winter (b. 1946)
Stevie Wonder (b. 1950)

(continued)

Table 11.1. *(Continued)*

Originators (1918–1938)	Translators (1939–1945)	Revivalists (1946–1963)
Elvis Presley (b. 1935)	Johnny Winter (b. 1944)	
Lloyd Price (b. 1933)	Neil Young (b. 1945)	
Jerry Reed (b. 1937)	Frank Zappa (b. 1940)	
Jimmy Reed (b. 1925)		
Charlie Rich (b. 1932)		
Billy Lee Riley (b. 1933)		
Marty Robbins (b. 1925)		
Del Shannon (b. 1937)		
Huey "Piano" Smith (b. 1934)		
Jimmy Smith (b. 1925)		
Rufus Thomas (b. 1917)		
Big Joe Turner (b. 1911)		
Ike Turner (b. 1931)		
Tina Turner (b. 1938)		
Conway Twitty (b. 1933)		
Frankie Valli (b. 1937)		
Gene Vincent (b. 1935)		
Muddy Waters (b. 1915)		
Hank Williams (b. 1923)		
Larry Williams (b. 1935)		
Otis Williams (b. 1937)		
Chuck Willis (b. 1928)		
Jackie Wilson (b. 1934)		
Bill Withers (b. 1938)		
Link Wray (b. 1929)		

The Model Rock Music Translator

Through Creedence Clearwater Revival, John Fogerty crafted his distinctive swamp rock sound. This smoky, edgy, growling audio landscape can be detected in many CCR releases. But direct experiences with Louisiana rhythms and Cajun vocal harmonies were not the source of Fogerty's bayou thunder.[18] This raw sound was invented in California recording studios by a music maven who adored country-tinged gospel, southern R&B tunes, and guitar-and-piano driven rock and roll. Wherever he encountered pop recordings, he resonated to both the words and the melodies. Whether in church, on the radio, over a jukebox, or blaring out of the tiny phonograph in his brother's bedroom, John absorbed America's mid-century soundtrack. He built a broad institutional memory and then melded that audio gumbo into a personalized musical format.[19] What emerged, as composed by John Fogerty and performed by CCR, was a unique translation of an earlier generation's rock sounds. Specifically, it was "Bad Moon Rising," "Fortunate Son," "Green River," "Have You Ever Seen the Rain?" "Proud Mary," "Sweet Hitch-Hiker," "Travelin' Band," and much, much more. The magnificent CCR songbook has attracted the attention not only of rock music fans, but also of commercially savvy cover artists. Performers as diverse in style as Jerry Reed, Sonny Charles, Ike and Tina Turner, and Solomon Burke have successfully driven the super-charged audio vehicles assembled by John Fogerty. This flattery through imitation is a signal of professional influence and personal genius, an illustration of the extended cultural meaning of a specific musical media artifact.

Table 11.2. Selected Illustrations of Cover Recordings of John Fogerty Songs by Various Performing Groups and Individual Artists, 1969–1999[20]

Song Title	Cover Artist	Date of Cover Release
1. "Bad Moon Rising"	Underground Sunshine	1969
	Ventures	1970
	Jerry Lee Lewis	1973
	Emmylou Harris	1981
	Leatherwolf	1988
	Cerrito	1989
2. "Big Train (From Memphis)"	Carl Perkins, Jerry Lee Lewis, Roy Orbison, and Johnny Cash	1986
3. "Change in the Weather"	Tesla	1991
	Buddy Guy	1993
	Love Split Love	1994
4. "Down on the Corner"	Herbie Mann	1971
	Jerry Reed	1983
	Bruce Hornsby	1998
5. "Fortunate Son"	Ventures	1969
6. "Green River"	C. W. McCall	1975
	Alabama	1982
7. "Have You Ever Seen the Rain?"	Stanley Turrentine	1975
	Bonnie Tyler	1983
	Joan Jett	1990
	Ramones	1994
	Spin Doctors	1994
8. "Lodi"	Al Wilson	1969
	Buddy Alan	1969
	Bobby Goldsboro	1970
	Tom Jones	1970
	Lobo	1974
	Tesla	1990
	Emmylou Harris	1992

9. "Proud Mary"

Artist	Year
Solomon Burke	1969
Checkmates, Ltd., featuring Anthony Armstrong Jones	1969
Tommy Roe	1969
Mongo Santamaria	1969
Spiral Staircase	1969
Conway Twitty	1969
Underground Sunshine	1969
Ventures	1969
Bobby Goldsboro	1970
Tom Jones	1970
Billy Paul	1970
Elvis Presley	1970
Boots Randolph	1970
Voices of East Harlem	1970
Jr. Walker and The All-Stars	1970
Lynn Anderson	1971
Bells	1971
Boston Pops Orchestra	1971
Ferrante and Teicher	1971
Bert Kaempfert	1971
Ike and Tina Turner	1972
Osmonds	1973
Brush Harbor	1974
Ohio Players	1988
Tina Turner	1999
Tina Turner, Elton John, and Cher	

10. "Sweet Hitch-Hiker"

Artist	Year
Sammy Hagar	1982

11. "Travelin' Band"

Artist	Year
Ed Ames	1968

12. "Who'll Stop the Rain"

Artist	Year
Bobby Vinton	1975
Ventures	1970

John Fogerty absorbed and internalized the music of a previous generation of bluesmen, cowboys, country singers, gospel choirs, rockabilly wailers, R&B artists, and folk singers. While he manufactured his own voice and composition treasury with CCR, he continued to search for potential performing material by plumbing the recordings of past masters as well as of contemporary singers. His adaptations on cover versions of hit songs were tributes to influential artists of the previous generation and salutes to members of his own generation.[21] With CCR, for example, Fogerty borrowed tunes from Ray Charles, Bo Diddley, Dale Hawkins, Little Richard, Elvis Presley (via Arthur "Big Boy" Crudup), Screamin' Jay Hawkins, and others. Beyond this recognition of artists who were born prior to the Japanese attack on Pearl Harbor, Fogerty's extended post-CCR career has been dotted with audio acknowledgments to performers from across all three rock music generations. As a gifted and prolific composer, it is obviously intentional when Fogerty adopts musical material from other performers. This isn't just filler. It is adulation. Over his long, albeit choppy, album-producing career with CCR, as the Blue Ridge Rangers, and as a solo artist, Fogerty has covered numbers by John Denver, Leadbelly, Jimmie Rodgers, Rick Nelson, the Charms, Hank Williams, Delaney and Bonnie, Rockin' Sidney, Wilson Pickett, and others. These cross-generational borrowings highlight Fogerty's role as a translator. He is a bridge between '50s rock and roll and '70s and '80s rock.

Table 11.3.   Selected Illustrations of Cover Recordings Performed by Creedence Clearwater Revival, the Blue Ridge Rangers, or by John Fogerty[22]

Song Title	Original Recording Artist	Original Date of Release	Composer
1. "Back Home Again"	John Denver	1974	John Denver
2. "Before You Accuse Me"	Bo Diddley	1957	Ellas McDaniel
3. "Cotton Fields"	Leadbelly	1947	Huddie Ledbetter
4. "Endless Sleep"	Jody Reynolds	1958	Jody Reynolds and Dolores Nance
5. "Garden Party"	Rick Nelson	1972	Rick Nelson
6. "Good Golly Miss Molly"	Little Richard	1958	Robert "Bumps" Blackwell and John Marasalco
7. "Haunted House"	Gene Simmons	1964	Robert L. Geddins
8. "Hearts of Stone"	The Charms	1955	Rudy Jackson and Eddy Ray
9. "Hello Mary Lou"	Ricky Nelson	1961	Gene Pitney and Cayet Mangiaracina
10. "Henrietta"	Jimmy Dee	1958	Fere-Hitzfeld
11. "I Ain't Never"	Webb Pierce	1959	Mel Tillis and Webb Pierce
12. "I Don't Care (Just As Long As You Love Me)"	Buck Owens	1964	Buck Owens
13. "I Heard It through the Grapevine"	Gladys Knight and the Pips	1967	Norman Whitfield
			Barrett Strong
14. "I Put A Spell on You"	Screamin' Jay Hawkins	1956	Jalacy Hawkins
15. "I'll Be There (If You Ever Want Me)"	Ray Price	1954	Ray Price and Rusty Gabbard
16. "Jambalaya (On the Bayou)"	Hank Williams	1952	Hank Williams
17. "Just Pickin'"	Freddie King	1961	Freddie King and S. Thompson

(continued)

Table 11.3. *(Continued)*

Song Title	Original Recording Artist	Original Date of Release	Composer
18. "Leave My Woman Alone"	Ray Charles	1956	Ray Charles
19. "Lonely Teardrops"	Jackie Wilson	1959	Tyran Carlo, Gwen Fuqua, and Berry Gordy, Jr.
20. "The Midnight Special"	Johnny Rivers	1965	Traditional Folk Song
21. "My Baby Left Me"	Arthur "Big Boy" Crudup	1950	Arthur Crudup
	Elvis Presley	1956	
22. "My Toot Toot"	Rockin' Sidney	1985	Sidney Simien
23. "Never Ending Song of Love"	Delaney and Bonnie	1971	Bonnie Bramlett and Delaney Bramlett
24. "The Night Time Is the Right Time"	Ray Charles	1959	Nappy Brown, Ozzie Cadena, and Lew Herman
25. "Ninety-Nine and a Half (Won't Do)"	Wilson Pickett	1966	Steve Cropper, Eddie Floyd, and Wilson Pickett
26. "Ooby Dooby"	Roy Orbison and the Teen Kings	1956	Wade Moore and Dick Penner
27. "Please Help Me, I'm Falling"	Hank Locklin	1960	Don Robertson and Hal Blair
28. "Sea Cruise"	Frankie Ford	1959	Huey "Piano" Smith
29. "She Thinks I Still Care"	George Jones	1962	Dickey Lee Lipscomb and Steve Duffy
30. "Suzie Q"	Dale Hawkins	1957	Eleanor Broadwater, Dale Hawkins, and Stanley Lewis
31. "Today I Started Loving You Again"	Merle Haggard	1968	Merle Haggard and Bonnie Owens
32. "When Will I Be Loved"	Everly Brothers	1960	Phil Everly
33. "You Rascal You"	Louis Armstrong	1931	Sam Theard
34. "You're The Reason"	Bobby Edwards	1961	Fred Henley, Terry Fell, Mildred Imes, and Bobby Edwards

Like rock music itself, John Fogerty's rhythmic journey continues. While chronologically a member of the translator generation (1939-1945), his zeal for processing a multitude of twentieth-century American recordings demonstrates the elasticity of the three rock-music generations. Recording success is complex. John Fogerty's career demonstrates that initial commercial failure (with both the Blue Velvets and the Golliwogs), legal warfare over contractual obligations and musical copyrights, and personal frustration concerning creativity and productivity can not diminish the core recording achievements of a genuinely significant artist. One wonders if recent Grammy recognition and a Rock and Roll Hall of Fame induction were as important to John Fogerty as viewing his continuing impact on rock music for future American generations.

Conclusions

Following the developmental trail of rock music from an American, age-based, generational perspective can be fruitful. This study traces the role of John Fogerty as an audio linchpin between two generations of rock-and-roll performers—the originators and the rock revivalists. Fogerty's musical generation, born during the war years, is depicted as rock translators. This latter group moved rock music forward, but always with a keen eye on the audio foundations of their craft. All three rock generations are bound together by continuing struggles concerning race, class, youth, commerce, and creativity.[23] The social and political upheavals that occurred in American life between the end of World War I and the beginning of the Vietnam conflict provide the historical setting that sparked the rise and spread of rock music. John Fogerty's career epitomizes the creative bursts and commercial frustrations of living the rock-and-roll dream. Not pursued here are the complex interactions of political climate, inventions and technological advances, and social events that prompted the birth and expansion of rock. Phillip Ennis, Richard Peterson, and other noteworthy scholars have already addressed these interrelated issues.[24]

This investigation provides a relatively simple chronological retrospective. As a member of John Fogerty's post-Depression/pre-Baby Boomer birth group, I have always been enamored with his music. But as a writer rather than a performing musician, I cannot claim to understand the personal and professional intricacies of his musical journey. A few things seem obvious, though. Fogerty benefited immensely from his immediate musical predecessors, the generation of rock-and-roll originators; he contributed mightily to his own generation of translators, who made rock music a mainstay of American life; and he remains instrumental today as a model of musical influence for the generation of revivalists who continue to spread the gospel of rock music throughout the world.

Coda

This study concentrates on John Fogerty as a critical musical force and a transitional performing and songwriting phenomenon within the context of three American-born rock generations—originators (1918–1938), translators (1939–1945), and revivalists (1946–1963). Two key issues are not addressed in this study, however. First, who are the next two generations of rock performers? While not germane to either assessing Fogerty's musical influence or to the limited chronological scope of this examination, it is reasonable to speculate that musicians born in 1964 or after have already emerged as proponents of the on-going rock tradition. Individuals like Bernard Allison (b. 1965), Billie Joe Armstrong (b. 1972), Tab Benoit (b. 1967), Beyonce (b. 1981), Tracy Chapman (b. 1964), Shemekia Copeland (b. 1979), Sue Foley (b. 1968), Janet Jackson (b. 1968), Jay-Z (b. 1969), Lady Gaga (b. 1986), Jonny Lang (b. 1981), Anton Newcombe (b. 1967), Kenny Wayne Shepherd (b. 1977), Courtney Taylor-Taylor (b. 1967), Susan Tedeschi (b. 1970), and Jeff Tweedy (b. 1967) might be candidates for membership in the post-revivalist (1964–1990) rock generation. This extended period would range from the rise of the Vietnam War to the fall of the Berlin Wall. Clearly, a generation beyond these post-revivalists, perhaps to be labeled the Internet rockers (1991–2011), is still gathering steam in public schools or preparing to enter college. But rock music DNA already courses in their blood.[25] Nevertheless, it is well beyond the scope of this study to comment about musicians that were born after the assassination of John F. Kennedy.

Second, why does this study omit references to the involvement of musicians from Great Britain, Canada, Ireland, Australia, Wales, and elsewhere in the creation, development, and extension of the rock music stream? Clearly, this may be viewed as a shortcoming of this investigation. Yet it was necessary. Foreign contributions to the growth of American popular music throughout the twentieth-century have already been well-documented.[26] But very, very few British or Canadian artists—maybe Lonnie Donegan (b. 1931), Alexis Korner (b. 1928), John Mayall (b. 1933), and Jack Scott (b. 1936)—can qualify as originators of rock and roll. Similarly, focusing strictly on American-born performers allows this generational analysis to aggregate a research population of similar location, education, common beliefs, shared cultural values, as well as age proximity.[27] Battles in the U.S. over race relations, civil rights, women's liberation, political leadership, economic distribution and taxation, and social mobility were largely distinctive and indigenous between 1918 and 1963. Today's globalism, ranging from ubiquitous use of the Internet to international fears of terrorism, is a phenomenon that has dramatically altered the creation, distribution, consumption, and continuity of modern rock music. Undeniably, the idea of a World War II generation of rock translators from beyond America's borders is factual. This influential cadre includes Randy Bachman (b. 1943), Jeff Beck (b. 1944), Eric Burdon (b. 1945), Eric Clapton (b. 1945), Joe Cocker (b. 1944), Roger Daltrey (b. 1944), Ray Davies (b. 1944), Billy Fury (b. 1941), George Harrison (b. 1943), Mick Jagger (b. 1943), Tom Jones (b. 1940), John Lennon (b. 1940), Paul McCartney (b. 1942), Jimmy Page (b. 1944), Cliff Richard (b. 1940), Keith Richards (b. 1943), Robbie Robertson (b. 1943), Dusty Springfield (b. 1939), Ringo Starr (b. 1940), Rod Stewart (b. 1945), and Pete Townshend (b. 1945).

In similar fashion, a listing of non-American rock revivalists born between 1946 and 1963 would include Bryan Adams (b. 1959), Bono (b. 1960), Burton Cummings (b. 1947), Mick Hucknall (b. 1960), Elton John (b. 1947), Freddie Mercury (b. 1946), Gary Moore (b. 1952), Robert Palmer (b. 1949), Robert Plant (b. 1948), Sting (b. 1951), and Stevie Winwood (b. 1948). Acknowledging that all of these foreign-born performers have become indelible parts of the international rock pantheon, it was still not appropriate to fold them into an American-centric generational archetype research model. Of course, for future generational studies tracing post-1964 rock music influences, international artist inclusions will be mandatory.

Notes

1. Tom Brokaw, *The Greatest Generation* (New York: Random House, 1998).

2. Richard Pells, "The Peculiar Generation," *The Chronicle Review*, March 26, 2010, B6–B8.

3. William Strauss and Neil Howe, *The Fourth Turning: An American Prophecy* (New York: Broadway Books, 1997); Angie Williams, *Intergenerational Communication across the Life Span* (Mahwah, NJ: Lawrence Erlbaum Associates, 2001).

4. Ralph J. Gleason, "John Fogerty: The Rolling Stone Interview," *Rolling Stone*, February 21, 1970, 17–24.

5. Hank Bordowitz, *Bad Moon Rising: The Unofficial History of Creedence Clearwater Revival* (Chicago: Chicago Review Press/A Cappella Books , 2007); Peter Doggett, "Creedence Clearwater Revival," *Record Collector*, November 1981, 24–32; Peter Doggett, "Creedence Clearwater Revival," *Record Collector*, October 1987, 61–64; Jerry Osborne, "Creedence Clearwater Revival," *Discoveries*, November 1988, 16-38; Ken Settle, "Creedence Clearwater Revival: The Bayou and the Backstreets," *Goldmine*, June 8, 1984, 6–18; Harry Sumrall, "Creedence Clearwater Revival," in *Pioneers of Rock and Roll* (New York: Billboard Books, 1994), 70–72; Craig Werner, "John Fogerty," *Goldmine*, July 18, 1997, 16–19, 38–62.

6. Philip Ennis, *The Seventh Stream: The Emergence of Rocknroll in American Popular Music* (Hanover, NH: Wesleyan University Press, 1992); Colin Escott, ed., *All Roots Lead to Rock: Legends of Early Rock 'n' Roll* (New York: Schirmer Books, 1999); Colin Escott, with Martin Hawkins, *Good Rockin' Tonight: Sun Records and the Birth of Rock 'n' Roll* (New York: St. Martin's Press, 1991); Colin Escott, *Roadkill on the Three-Chord Highway: Art and Trash in American Music* (New York: Routledge, 2002); Colin Escott, *Tattooed on Their Tongues: A Journey through the Backrooms of American Music* (New York: Schirmer Books, 1996); Peter Guralnick, *Last Train to Memphis: The Rise of Elvis Presley* (Boston: Little, Brown and Company, 1994); Peter Guralnick, *Lost Highway: Journeys and Arrivals of American Musicians* (Boston: Back Bay Books / Little, Brown and Company, 1999); Jeff Hannusch, *I Hear You Knockin': The Sounds of New Orleans Rhythm and Blues* (Ville Platte, LA: Swallow Press, 1985); Jeff Hannusch, *The Soul of New Orleans: A Legacy of Rhythm and Blues* (Ville Platte, LA: Swallow Press, 2001); Michael Lydon, *Rock Folk: Portraits From the Rock 'n' Roll Pantheon* (New York: Dial Press, 1971); Michael Lydon and Ellen Mandel, *Boogie Lightning: How the Music Became Electric* (New York: Da Capo Press, 1980); Greil Marcus, *Mystery Train: Images of America in Rock 'n' Roll Music*, 5th ed. (New York: Plume / Penguin Books, 2008); Randy McNutt, *Guitar Towns: A Journey to the Cross-roads of Rock 'n' Roll* (Bloomington: Indiana University Press, 2002); James Miller, *Flowers in the Dustbin: The Rise of Rock and Roll, 1947-1977* (New York: Simon and Schuster, 1999); William Ruhlmann, *Breaking Records: 100 Years of Hits* (New York: Routledge, 2004); Gene Santoro, *Highway 61 Revisited: The Tangled Roots of American Jazz, Blues, Rock, and Country Music* (New York: Oxford University Press, 2004); Arnold Shaw, *Honkers and Shouters: The Golden Years of Rhythm and Blues* (New York: Collier Books, 1978); Arnold Shaw, *The Rockin' '50s: The Decade That Transformed the Pop Music Scene* (New York: Haworth Books, 1974); Nick Tosches, *Unsung Heroes of Rock 'n' Roll*, Rev. ed. (New York: Da Capo Press, 1999).

7. Glenn C. Altschuler, *All Shook Up: How Rock 'n' Roll Changed America* (New York: Oxford University Press, 2003); Rick Coleman, *Blue Money: Fats Domino and the Lost Dawn of Rock 'n' Roll* (Cambridge, MA: Da Capo Press, 2006); Stuart Colman, *They Kept on Rockin': The Giants of Rock 'n' Roll* (Poole, Dorset, England: Blandford Press, 1982); B. Lee Cooper, "Architects of the New Orleans Sound, 1946-2006: A Bio-Bibliography," *Popular Music and Society* 30, no. 2 (May 2008): 121-161; Howard Elson, *Early Rockers* (New York: Proteus Books, 1982); David Hajdu, "Forever Young? In Some Ways, Yes," *New York Times*, May 24, 2011, A25; Herb Hendler, *Year by Year in the Rock Era: Events and Conditions Shaping the Rock Generations That Reshaped America* (Westport, CT: Greenwood Press, 1983); Barry Lazell, with Dafydd Rees and Luke Crampton, eds. *Rock Movers and Shakers* (New York: Billboard Books, 1989); George Lipsitz, *Time Passages: Collective Memory and American Popular Culture* (Minneapolis: University of Minnesota Press, 1990); Craig Morrison, *Go Cat Go! Rockabilly Music and Its Makers* (Champaign: University of Illinois Press, 1996); Walter Rimler, *Not Fade Away: A Comparison of Jazz With Rock Era Pop Song Composers* (Ann Arbor, MI: Pierian Press, 1984); Lisa Scrivani-Tidd,

Rhonda Markowitz, Chris Smith, Maryann Janosik, and Bob Gulla, *The Greenwood Encyclopedia of Rock History, 1951–2005* (Westport, CT: Greenwood Press, 2006); David Shumway, "Where Have All the Rock Stars Gone?" *The Chronicle of Higher Education,* June 22, 2007, B6–B8; William Strauss and Neil Howe, *Generations: The History of America's Future, 1584 to 2069* (New York: Morrow Books, 1991); Harry Sumrall, *Pioneers of Rock and Roll* (New York: Billboard Books, 1994).

8. Bart Bull, "Reborn On The Bayou," *Spin,* June 1985, 20–22; Dan Fort, with Steve Soest, "John Fogerty Returns," *Guitar Player,* April 1985, 54–74; Scott Isler, "John Fogerty's Triumph over Evil," *Musician,* March 1985, 32–42; Ken Sharp, "John Fogerty: From the Bayou to Centerfield and Back Again," *Goldmine,* September 15, 2006, 14–19; Ethan Smith, "John Fogerty's Road Home," *Wall Street Journal,* Dec. 16, 2005, 8; Harold Steinblatt, "Return of the Swamp King," *Guitar World,* January 2008, 92–100; Craig Werner, *Up Around the Bend: The Oral History of Creedence Clearwater Revival,* ed. Dave Marsh (New York: Spike / Avon Books, 1999).

9. Ellen Willis, "Creedence Clearwater Revival," *The Rolling Stone Illustrated History of Rock and Roll,* Rev. ed. Jim Miller, ed. (New York: Random House / Rolling Stone Press, 1980), 324–26.

10. Ibid., 324.

11. Lewis Samuel Feuer, *The Conflict of Generations: The Character and Significance of Student Movements* (New York: Basic Books, 1969); Margaret Mead, *Culture and Commitment: A Study of the Generation Gap* (Garden City, New York: American Natural History Museum Press, 1970); William Strauss and Neil Howe, *Generations*; Rex Weiner and Deanne Stillman, *Woodstock Census: The Nationwide Survey of the Sixties Generation* (New York: Viking Press, 1979).

12. B. Lee Cooper and Jim Creeth, "Present at the Creation: The Legend of Jerry Lee Lewis on Record, 1956–1963," *JEMF Quarterly* 70 (Summer 1983): 122–29; Colin Escott, with Martin Hawkins, *Good Rockin' Tonight* (New York: St. Martin's Press, 1991); Robert Palmer, *Rock and Roll: An Unruly History* (New York: Harmony Books, 1995); Tosches.

13. Hadju.

14. Dave DiMartino. *Singer-Songwriters: Pop Music's Performer-Composers, from A to Zevon* (New York: Billboard Books, 1994).

15. George Plasketes, ed., *Play It Again: Cover Songs in Popular Music* (Burlington, VT: Ashgate Publishing, 2010).

16. Kevin J. H. Dettmar and William Richey, eds. *Reading Rock and Roll: Authenticity, Appropriation, Aesthetics* (New York: Columbia University Press, 1999); Robert L. Doerschuk, ed., *Playing from the Heart: Great Musicians Talk about Their Craft* (San Francisco: Backbeat Books, 2002); Holly George-Warren and Patricia Romanowski, eds., *The Rolling Stone Encyclopedia of Rock and Roll,* 3rd ed.(New York: Fireside Books / Rolling Stone Press, 2001).

17. All birth date information has been gathered from Joel Whitburn, comp., *Hot Country Songs, 1944–2008* (Menomonee Falls, WI: Record Research, 2008); Joel Whitburn, comp., *Hot R&B Songs, 1942–2010* (Menomonee Falls, WI: Record

Research, 2010); Joel Whitburn, comp., *Top Pop Singles, 1955–2008* (Menomonee Falls, WI: Record Research, 2009).

18. Dave Thompson, *Bayou Underground: Tracing the Mythical Roots of American Popular Music* (Toronto, Ontario, Canada: ECW Press, 2010).

19. Gleason.

20. All song listings and performance dates have been gathered from Joel Whitburn, comp., *Album Cuts, 1955–2001* (Menomonee Falls, WI: Record Research, 2002; Whitburn, *Hot Country Songs*; Whitburn, *Hot R&B Songs*; Whitburn, *Top Pop Singles.*

21. B. Lee Cooper, "Charting Cultural Change, 1953–1957: Song Assimilation through Cover Recording," in Plasketes, ed., 43–76; B. Lee Cooper, "Repeating Hit Tunes, A Cappella Style: The Persuasions as Song Revivalists," *Popular Music and Society* 13 (Fall 1989): 17–27; B. Lee Cooper and Verdan D. Traylor, "Establishing Rock Standards: The Practice of Rock Revivals in Contemporary Music, 1953–1977," *Goldmine*, May 1979, 37–38.

22. All song listings and release dates are from the same Joel Whitburn volumes listed above in note 20.

23. Linda Martin and Kerry Segrave, *Anti-Rock: The Opposition to Rock 'n' Roll* (Hamden, CT: Archon Books, 1988).

24. John Broven, *Record Makers and Breakers: Voices of the Independent Rock 'n' Roll Pioneers* (Champaign: University of Illinois Press, 2009); Ennis; Ben Fong-Torres, *The Hits Just Keep on Coming: The History of Top 40 Radio* (San Francisco: Miller Freeman Books, 1998); Simon Frith, *Sound Effects: Youth, Leisure, and the Politics of Rock 'n' Roll* (New York: Pantheon Books, 1981); Charlie Gillett, *The Sound of the City: The Rise of Rock and Roll*, 2nd. ed. (New York: Da Capo Press, 1996); H. L. Goodall, Jr. *Living in the Rock N Roll Mystery: Reading Context, Self, and Others as Clues* (Carbondale, IL: Southern Illinois University Press, 1991); Jennifer C. Lena and Richard A. Peterson, "Classification as Culture: Types and Trajectories of Music Categories," *American Sociological Review* 73 (October 2008): 697–718; Richard A. Peterson, "Five Constraints on the Production of Culture: Law, Technology, Market, Organizational Structures, and Occupational Careers," in *American Popular Music–Volume One: The Nineteenth Century to Tin Pan Alley*, ed. Timothy E. Scheurer (Bowling Green, Ohio: Bowling Green State University Popular Press, 1989), 16–27; Richard A. Peterson, "Why 1955? Explaining the Advent of Rock Music," *Popular Music* 9 (January 1990): 97–116; Lawrence N. Redd, *Rock Is Rhythm and Blues: The Impact of Mass Media* (Lansing: Michigan State University Press, 1974).

25. Bob Walker, "The Song Decoders," *The New York Times Magazine*, October 18, 2009, 48–53.

26. Lester Bangs, "The British Invasion," in *The Rolling Stone Illustrated History of Rock and Roll*, rev. ed., Anthony DeCurtis and James Henke, eds., with Holly George-Warren (New York: Random House, 1992), 199–208; Dick Bradley, *Understanding Rock 'n' Roll: Popular Music in Britain, 1955–1964* (Buckingham, UK: Open University Press, 1992); Iain Chambers, *Urban Rhythms: Pop Music and Popular Cul-*

ture (New York: St. Martin's Press, 1985); Laura E. Cooper and B. Lee Cooper, "The Pendulum of Cultural Imperialism: Popular Music Interchanges between the United States and Great Britain, 1943–1967," in *Kazaaam! Splat! Ploof! The American Impact on European Popular Culture Since 1945*, eds. Sabrina P. Ramet and Gordana P. Crnkovic (Lanham, Maryland: Rowman and Littlefield, 2003), 69–82; Bill Doggett, "The British Invasion," *Record Collector*, February 1989, 19–22; Bruce Eder, "Britain before the Beatles: Guys Named Cliff, Tommy, Adam, and Billy," *Goldmine*, June 12, 1992, 50–60; Pete Frame, "British Pop, 1955–1979," *Trouser Press*, June 1983, 30-31; Brian Innes, "Clubs and Coffee Bars: Where Britain's Teenagers Found the New Music," *The History of Rock* 7 (1982): 132–134; Michael Bryan Kelly, *The Beatle Myth: The British Invasion of American Popular Culture, 1956–1969* (Jefferson, NC: McFarland and Company, 1991); Richard Pells, *Not Like Us: How Europeans Have Loved, Hated, and Transformed American Culture since World War II* (New York: Basic Books, 1997); Nicholas Schaffner, *The British Invasion: From the First Wave to the New Wave* (New York: McGraw-Hill, 1982); William L. Schurk, B. Lee Cooper, and Julie A. Cooper, "Before the Beatles: International Influences on American Popular Recordings, 1940–1963," *Popular Music and Society* 30, no. 2 (2007): 227–266; Dave Thompson, "Britain before Rock Was Not a Total Musical Wasteland," *Goldmine*, July 9, 2004, 51, 53.

27. Strauss and Howe, *Generations*; Strauss and Howe, *The Fourth Turning*; Angie Williams.

~

CHAPTER TWELVE

The Political Legacy of Fogerty: Forty Years of Parallel Messages

William J. Miller and Jeremy D. Walling

It can be argued that more than any other musician, except Bob Dylan, John Fogerty has had a lasting influence on American politics. Starting with his Creedence Clearwater Revival days in the Vietnam-era, songs such as "Bad Moon Rising," "Fortunate Son," "Who'll Stop the Rain," "Run Through the Jungle," and "Have You Ever Seen the Rain?" told the story of a generation's desperation. While the messages were not always explicit—and at times even self-imagined—the undertones were fairly clear. As he became known for his ability to sing about the politics of the time without being overtly explicit, he started to become increasingly likely to use his albums to spread a message.

After his exit from Creedence, Fogerty's early solo albums lacked underlying political tones, which was not surprising given the conclusion of Vietnam and restoration of civil society. With the release of *Eye of the Zombie* in 1986, however, Fogerty learned the danger in presenting too much explicit political commentary—mainly decreased sales and negative reviews. While his CCR albums had focused on the song instead of the message, Fogerty turned toward sloganeering and forced metaphor rather than focusing on his innate skills as a songwriter. The forced message trumped the music. Whereas his early songs took the voice of a working-class populist whose idealism never subsumed a working-class reality, this album had simply fallen victim to a lack of subtlety as the music became lost in the message.

In the aftermath of *Eye of the Zombie*, Fogerty returned to more subdued political commentaries in song. He went so far as to attempt to avoid any direct political discourse or questions with media members or fans alike. Yet, despite his stated efforts, the emergence of serious military conflicts in Iraq and Afghanistan seemed to change his stance. In 2004, Fogerty joined the Vote for Change Tour in an effort to help Democratic Senator John Kerry unseat President George W. Bush. Even on the tour, however, Fogerty appeared poised to not become too preachy. Instead, he wanted to present good music which listeners could interpret and use as they pleased.

No more than three years later, Fogerty had returned to bringing a more explicitly political tone to his lyrics. In his album *Revival*, Fogerty returned to his earlier roots and took President Bush, Secretary of Defense Don Rumsfeld, and Vice President Dick Cheney all to task by name. Unlike any efforts since *Eye of the Zombie*, he admitted a willingness to go out on a limb and directly attack those he felt were risking our nation's political future. Demonstrating another shift in direction, Fogerty turned back to his more nuanced ways in 2009 with the release of *The Blue Ridge Rangers Rides Again*, which is chock full of songs with political undertones (focused more on individuals than issues) held within well-composed lyrics. It is worth noting, however, that this album consists of cover songs except for "Change in the Weather."

In this chapter, we will trace the political nature and impact of Fogerty's songs along with his own political views. By looking at this dramatic ebb and flow, we can note a clear trajectory wherein Fogerty would remain subtle and maintain musical integrity before becoming too politically brazen, falling out of the public light for a while, and then slowly rebuilding within the same cycle. In doing so, we will demonstrate how the music of Fogerty has maintained similar messages in 2010 to his work in the late 1960s and early 1970s. Part of this is due to the largely parallel circumstances we have experienced as a country and culture, while part falls squarely on Fogerty's cycle of explicit political messaging within his writing and lyrics.

The Creedence Clearwater Revival Years: Vietnam, Protest, and a Generation in Fear

"Bad Moon Rising"

Creedence Clearwater Revival followed their first big hit "Proud Mary" with "Bad Moon Rising," equaling the earlier song's #2 U.S. chart position. The song's lyrics are positively apocalyptic, detailing earthquakes, lightning, hurricanes, and the titular ominous moon. Certainly the United States faced considerable domestic and global turmoil in the late 1960s. The assassinations of Martin Luther King and Robert Kennedy served as tragic exclamation marks to the social unrest of the era. Ongoing efforts in Vietnam, in particular the daily media reported death toll, cast a pall over the national mood. Although these events are sure worthy of the metaphorical descriptions of atmospheric weather calamities described in "Bad Moon Rising," they were not John Fogerty's inspiration for the song. In fact, Fogerty revealed to *Rolling Stone* in 1993 that he wrote the song after watching an old movie.[1] In the fantastical 1937 film *The Devil and Daniel Webster*, a farmer sells his soul to the devil and is defended in court by Daniel Webster. At one point in the film, a weather event destroys much of the town but spares the property of the man who had made the Faustian bargain. "Bad Moon Rising" was subsequently used by protesters in the Berkeley, California, People's Park riots in 1969. To be sure, the content of the lyrics reflected the mood of the times. Demonstrators co-opted the song for direct political purposes, despite the song's lack of an overt political origin.

"Fortunate Son"

Unlike "Bad Moon Rising," with its upbeat pop melody and open-to-interpretation lyrical content, "Fortunate Son" is an angry rock song with direct and clearly political content. It is both anti-Washington and anti-Vietnam while promoting blue-collar pride. Fogerty avoided the draft by electing to serve in an Army Reserve unit in 1966 and was discharged in 1967. Nevertheless, his own experience with and observations of the administration of the military draft are reflected in the content of the song. The lyrics speak of the privileged existence of the offspring of politicians and otherwise wealthy citizens. These elite individuals are fortunate, presumably due to the fact that they can avoid military service. Fogerty told *Rolling Stone*: "I remember you would hear about Tricia Nixon and David Eisenhower. ... You got the impression that these people got preferential treatment, and the whole idea of being born wealthy or being born powerful seemed to really be coming to the fore in the late-Sixties confrontation of cultures."[2] "Fortunate Son" raised the argument, then, that military conscription in the 1960s provided evidence for the consequences of class inequality. Due to its bold references to America and the flag, this anti-establishment classic is frequently misinterpreted and used as a soundtrack for patriotic events—a trait it shares with Bruce Springsteen's "Born in the U.S.A."

"Who'll Stop the Rain"

In contrast to the audacious "Fortunate Son," "Who'll Stop the Rain" is more opaque lyrically and lighter musically. Consequently, the song is highly reminiscent of the poetic protest songs of the Byrds. Lyrically, rain and clouds are the primary metaphors, representing legitimate obstacles to human progress and the efforts of "good men." An apparent reference to the Tower of Babel is followed by allusions to government solutions (e.g., a clever mention of the New Deal), all of which represent well-intentioned coordinated attempts by those in positions of authority to "stop the rain." Of course, the efforts are ultimately ineffective. The third verse of the song describes a crowd of people listening to a musical performance while the rain continues to fall, possibly an expression of the futility of such protest songs in bringing about legitimate change and an end to the rain. Although likely inspired by many of the same events that led to "Fortunate Son," "Who'll Stop the Rain" is a warmer tune that contains none of the measured rage of the earlier hit.

John Fogerty was once asked, "Does 'Who'll Stop the Rain' contain lyrically specific meanings besides the symbolic dimension?"[3] He responded that he was certainly talking about Washington when writing it. As a result, all three verses clearly allude to a sense of unending discontent, pondered by men though the ages, master planning, and the Woodstock generation. While Fogerty never directly explains what he views as the problem, he does clearly suggest that as a nation we seemed incapable of fixing it. His explanation for that assertion appears to be that only those who wish to fix a problem can.

"Run Through the Jungle"

Also on the *Cosmo's Factory* album in 1970 with "Who'll Stop the Rain" was "Run Through the Jungle." Given the title, lyrics, and time it was released, listeners fully believed the song referred to some facet of the Vietnam War. Given the nature of "Bad Moon Rising," "Fortunate Son," and "Who'll Stop the Rain," it seemed entirely plausible that the song was following suit. With references to nightmares, the devil chasing after you, millions of guns being loaded, and the land filling with smoke, it seemed a proper inference. Yet, according to a Fogerty interview with the *Los Angeles Times* in 1993, the song had nothing to do with Vietnam. While not related to the war effort, the song was still political in its discussion of gun proliferation. As Fogerty stated, "I think a lot of people thought that because of the times, but I was talking about America and the proliferation of guns, registered and otherwise. I'm a hunter and I'm not antigun, but I just thought that people were so gun-happy—and there were so many guns uncontrolled that it really was dangerous, and it's even worse now. It's interesting that it has taken 20-odd years to get a movement on that position."[4]

Such a public misperception of the meaning of the song highlights a myriad of facts regarding Fogerty's political influence. First, by the time this song had come out, Fogerty had become an important musical voice for the generation and movement. While Dylan was the clear leader, Fogerty was singing a similar message. The lyrics were misinterpreted as listeners wanted Fogerty to be their voice to the world—not a stretch here with the Vietnam suggestiveness of *jungle* in the title. Second, the lyrics were able to be misinterpreted because Fogerty was becoming less cautious in assuring the depth of his lyrics did not brazenly demonstrate his political attitudes. Rather than guarded references, the songs were sounding more explicitly political. In both scenarios, there is a definite possibility of reading too far into the meaning of a song.

"Have You Ever Seen the Rain?"

In 1971, the final CCR song with potential political undertones was released on the *Pendulum* album: "Have You Ever Seen the Rain?" Many have speculated that the lyrics directly refer to the Vietnam War as the rain could be used as a metaphor to describe the bombs falling over the country. Mark Demig—writing for *Allmusic*—instead believes the song has more general political sentiments discussing the idealism of the late 1960s falling way to events like the Kent State shootings. In this interpretation, Fogerty would be alluding to the same problems from the 1960s existing in the 1970s. However, no one is fighting for them.[5] As with "Run Through the Jungle," Fogerty himself asserts that there is no hidden political meaning present in "Have You Ever Seen the Rain?" Instead, the song deals directly with the rising tension within CCR and the imminent departure of Tom Fogerty.

Again, this song demonstrates the impact Fogerty and CCR's songs had on the late 1960s and early 1970s. While a few early songs were admittedly political, songs that came shortly thereafter were not explicitly so, yet were regularly interpreted to be. Whether Fogerty is being truthful in stating there are not explicit political messages in some of these songs can always be questioned, yet it seems clear that his music was carefully written in order to avoid overt dogmatic missives.

Fogerty as a Solo Artist: Alone with His Views

After *Pendulum*, Creedence shied away from implicit or explicit political messaging in their final album (*Mardi Gras*), which was not surprising since Fogerty himself only contributed three original songs. With the eventual breakup of CCR, Fogerty moved to a one-man show as the Blue Ridge Rangers. His first solo album—*The Blue Ridge Rangers*—had no original songs at all. The next album—*John Fogerty*—had mainly original songs but none very political. His third album—*Hoodoo*—was cancelled right before shipping due to an admitted lack of merit by Fogerty. It would be almost nine years until Fogerty returned with a solo album—*Centerfield*. This album presented a revival of sorts as tracks like "Rock and Roll Girls" and "Centerfield" expressed lyrical mastery and music that demonstrated Fogerty's joy at returning to the music scene after almost a decade without an album.

Centerfield was not, however, without some political and social influences. Two songs in particular pointed to a general concern with the direction of our country and society—"The Old Man down the Road" and "Searchlight." In "The Old Man down the Road," Fogerty describes the necessity to hide from an unsympathetic, fear-evoking character lurking. Then in "Searchlight" he describes the inability to understand the demon that led to his running. While these two songs had implicit undertones about a general statement toward society, "Mr. Greed" and "Zanz Kant Danz" explicitly screamed out against the greedy, capitalistic nature of our country. These songs, however, were directly prompted by Fogerty's own contractual disputes with Saul Zaentz (the owner and chief executive of Fogerty's old record label—Fantasy Records). Zaentz sued Fogerty for plagiarizing Fogerty's own song ("Run Through the Jungle" in "The Old Man down the Road") for which the composer did not own the copyright.

While *Centerfield* had political parallels, the next Fogerty album, which was released approximately two years later, would be the pinnacle of political brazenness. In *Eye of the Zombie*, Fogerty left the realm of a great songwriter with subtle political cues to a political musician using his guitar and voice to promote a clear set of beliefs. The public responded with negative critiques and poor chart success. Fogerty himself later recognized the shortcomings of the album, refusing to play material from the album since its corresponding tour in the mid-1980s.

No element of society is left untouched by Fogerty's reckless lyrics on the album. Within the title track, Fogerty refers to citizens as zombies aimlessly wandering with little thought put into their actions or decisions. In the third song, "Headlines," he takes aim at the American media in a shrieking lament of their efforts to describe how crazy life in America has become. The messages were not similar to his CCR days; rather than allowing listeners to read between the lines, Fogerty instead opts to unequivocally state his views of the world. Yet even these two tracks would be described as mild compared to what else follows on *Eye of the Zombie*.

In "Violence Is Golden," Fogerty brings together a discussion of military rage and sexual pomposity and exploitation. While the topics were timely and worthy of being brought to public attention, the choice in lyrics and metaphors actually works to detract from the potential power of the song. Rather than making meaningful statements, Fogerty doused "Violence Is Golden" with food references, including passing shrapnel, sprinkling explosives, and salads made of grenades. Subtlety was lacking and the thinly veiled references seemed forced and contrived—a recipe for missed opportunity.

In "Soda Pop," Fogerty returned to one of his messages from *Centerfield*, in which he rails against greed and capitalism, particularly in the music industry. However, he loses public sympathies by misplacing much of his venom on fellow musicians rather than taking aim at the corporations that create the problems. Rather than bringing sympathizers to his side, Fogerty leads listeners to wonder if he is perhaps doing too much protesting and not enough exercising of his typically high level of craftsmanship and musical prowess. Again, the message prevents the music from being well-constructed and consequently appreciated.

The final song on the troubled album—"Sail Away"—is one of the more musically pleasing songs on the album. Best described as soulful, cheery, and comparatively understated in its lyrics and message, the song leans toward the spiritual. Unfortunately for Fogerty, its placement on the album does little but present an escape route for listeners, one that involves aliens and spaceships. Only by escaping from the painful world that Fogerty has created through his lyrics and music on this album does he believe society can fully foster growth and development. Regrettably, Fogerty clearly asserts through "Sail Away" that our only option is to succumb to the perils of our surroundings and abandon hope. Thus, even one of the stronger musical tracks on the album continues with the negative, forced messaging. In this case, the placement of the track does little to help as it is the final message listeners receive from Fogerty on the album.

After the many negative responses to *Eye of the Zombie* by critics and fans alike, Fogerty returned to a musical life of solitude, away from writing and recording. It would be over a decade (1997) before he returned with a new album, attempting to correct his errors from the mid-1980s where he forgot the music and became obsessed with the message. He could not choose to cheapen his talents by resorting to simplistic metaphors in lyrics or confrontational overtures. Instead, he needed to return to his roots. With *Blue Moon Swamp*, he did just that and captured the Grammy award for best rock album. One critic described the songs and performances on the album as "richly evocative of tradition, but they're vibrant and living for the present, which makes the rockabilly, blues, country, and swampy rock & roll sound fresh."[6] None of the songs became timeless classics, but Fogerty proved that the music was what mattered. Songs were more than vehicles through which one could attempt to influence others. Yet even with the critical success of *Blue Moon Swamp*, it would again be seven years until the world was able to hear Fogerty's next album of new material.

Fogerty Returns: Kerry, Obama, and the Anti-Bush Albums

In 2004, John Fogerty returned from his latest sabbatical (this one lasting seven years) with *Déjà Vu (All Over Again)*. This album was largely considered a success by critics for remaining true to Fogerty's roots along with avoiding the flaws of *Eye of the Zombie*. That is not, however, to say that the album is void of political references and influences. The title song, for example, is actually motivated quite clearly from political events. Without being too forthcoming through the lyrics about the meaning, "Déjà Vu, All Over Again" works to create strong parallels between the Iraq and Vietnam wars. The lyrics hint at counting the dead, shipping bodies home, news coverage, mothers crying, and endless wars.

While this was the only song with clear political overtones on the album, it helps to demonstrate the ebb and flow of Fogerty's career. After all, he had been a voice of the Vietnam generation and thirty some years later was working to unseat a president he clearly failed to support. By drawing listeners to connect the conflict in Iraq with earlier similar incidents, Fogerty was working to restore the public concerns which had echoed across the nation only three decades earlier. He even proved willing to become more political in his behavior than previously in his career. Fogerty joined the Vote for Change Tour in an effort to help Democratic Senator John Kerry unseat President George W. Bush. Even on the tour, however, Fogerty appeared poised not to become too preachy. Instead, he wanted to present good music which listeners could interpret.

Rather than taking a decade off, Fogerty turned back to the recording studio and brought forth *Revival* in 2007. As with his past trajectory, his acclaimed success and ability to make societal and political comments without being directly explicit led to a more brazen follow-up that bordered on becoming more political than musical. In *Revival*, he is at his best and worst, balancing metaphorical with overtly literal songs to paint a picture of a country he worried about and its past greatness he longed for.[7] If we begin with the metaphorical lyrics, we can look at "Gunslinger." In this song, Fogerty states his concerns about how America has moved away from the characteristics and traits that once made it a great nation. Rather than working hard and getting along with neighbors, he laments that individual citizens worry about what they say and how they opt to live sheltered lives, disconnected from even those closest to them. Rather ironically, Fogerty calls for a gunslinger to attempt to redirect society. Such a person, however, serves to warn society of the need to change on its own before an outside influence (the gunslinger) appears and potentially makes life worse in a different way.

Likewise, "Don't You Wish It Was True" presents another call for rejuvenating America to better reflect its traditional core values and ideals. Fogerty wishes for a world with no armies and hate; he worries about children not having happy lives and not being able to laugh and enjoy the small favors of life. Despite being fairly nostalgic, this song is still somewhat different from the regular wishful Fogerty. Yet the central message is the same. He longs for the romantic America. His vision and memories dictate his dreams.

Not all of the songs on the album take this dreamy, Rockwellian approach to describing what our country needs. Rather, at least two songs are the most focused attacks on politicians and the country's direction that Fogerty has ever released. In "Long Dark Night," for instance, Fogerty attacks nearly every element of the Bush administration—both personally and politically. He begins by lamenting Bush's desire to take American children from their safety and throw them into the throes of war. He then turns from Bush and sets his sights on former FEMA director Mike Brown. From there, his anger is directed on Secretary of Defense Donald Rumsfeld and Vice President Dick Cheney. The underlying message is that it will be a long time before we escape from Bush's self-created disasters. While the song is clearly political in nature (and personal for a change), it lacks the musical skill that made Fogerty famous. His passion is clear, but the lyrics and music themselves are clearly maladroit. Again, Fogerty appears to be sacrificing musicianship to make a point.

"I Can't Take It No More" takes Bush to task in another direct, explicit way. While never mentioning him specifically by name, Fogerty does express his anger with the war. He accuses Bush of lying about casualties, weapons of mass destruction, and detainees. Even more pointedly, he refers to Bush's pointed messages about the war as beating a dead horse and nothing but lies. On a personal level, Fogerty beckons his musical past to refer to Bush as a fortunate son and implies that President George H.W. Bush was able to keep his son from serving in the National Guard. Again, these lyrics seem to both overshadow and empower the corresponding music. Between both "Long Dark Night" and "I Can't Take It No More," *Revival* became known as a serious epistle written and released by a man who was clearly utilizing an unquestionably powerful vehicle and medium to reach masses of potential sympathizers.

Given Fogerty's long-standing political beliefs (as easily inferred from his interviews and songs), it comes as little surprise that he was a prominent supporter of Barack Obama during his quest for the White House. Throughout his life, Fogerty admits to holding liberal beliefs, even though it makes some individuals uncomfortable that he is so staunchly political in his life and his career.[8] Speaking before President Obama was elected, Fogerty said, "I have a lot of thoughts while I'm jogging. Sometimes your mind can be very clear in a spiritual way. Anyway, yesterday while out running I said to myself, 'Are we good enough to dare elect Obama?' I think we are. It's a daring concept to say: 'Yes, we're going to change everything.' I haven't felt like that since the 1960s."[9] It was not just the opportunity to elect Obama that led Fogerty to become politically active. He had, after all, worked equally hard for John Kerry in 2004. His decisions seem to be more squarely rooted in an intense dislike of Bush and his administration. As Fogerty explained, "I grew up in a time when we were very, very proud to be Americans and we had people who seemed to be statesmen. Certainly the president seemed smarter than me in those days. I said that with obvious cynicism. I think we've arrived there again but we've arrived there after a long dark period of times when I've been literally ashamed of my country and ashamed of my government."[10]

While Fogerty's motives are well-intended, there are some clear ironies behind his statements and his music. Consider the following quote: "This award [the Nobel Peace Prize] is an affirmation of the hopefulness that is emanating from the Obama administration and really from Barack Obama himself. I'm sorry to say that the world we find ourselves in politically is so full of people shouting at each other across the center. There's so much actual hate talk. I'm sorry about that, but I choose not [to] let my heart feel that way."[11] For a man who is admonishing legislators for yelling across the center and being hateful, he seems to do the exact same in his lyrics.

In 2009, Fogerty released his most recent album, *The Blue Ridge Rangers Rides Again.* Of the twelve songs included, only one is written by Fogerty— "Change in the Weather." While this song is again not explicitly political, it does strongly suggest that our nation still has work to do—even with Obama as president—and serves as a cautionary tale attempting to drive Americans toward a greater future.

Analyzing the Political Impact and Consequences of Fogerty's Legacy

At the beginning of his career in Creedence Clearwater Revival, it seemed that the songs of John Fogerty were not inspired by politics. Instead, they were inspired by life in America during the 1960s and early 1970s. As such, politics took the songs and made them their own. Desperate generations seeking solace in anything comforting found Fogerty and believed he understood them. In fact, they seemed to believe he was telling the world about their plight through his songs. He excelled by discussing sociopolitical realities in unassuming ways. Fogerty was not telling you how to think, but he was presenting a clear explanation of his own thoughts. With time, however, he veered from this path and became less worried about his sound than about being unequivocal in his political attitudes; the cleverness gave way to a sincere anger which at times distracted critics and listeners alike. His career seemed to follow a certain trajectory. He would produce an album without attempting to be overtly political. It would be relevant to the times and struggles and consequently given political meaning. Fogerty would take this meaning, return to the studio, and come out with new songs that were far more explicit in their politics. These pieces struggled with music quality and received less than stellar reviews. Then Fogerty would disappear for a series of years before returning to work the cycle again.

There is no denying Fogerty's relevance during both the Vietnam era and the War in Iraq. His songs truly spoke to both situations and the Americans fighting to end the violence in both instances. But is it this way because of Fogerty's musical abilities in the twenty-first century or in the understood relevance of his classic works? After all, he never produced a song that citizens truly rallied around as representing the spirit of a group after the early 1970s. At the same time, however, one could easily argue that there were no protests seeking Fogerty-like songs during the decades that followed. In this time, nonetheless, Fogerty's views on politics in America became even more jaded—especially when he considered Republicans. In 2007, Fogerty sat for an interview with Joshua Klein (from *Pitchfork*) in which he discussed his political beliefs and how they developed and impacted his music.

First, Klein asked Fogerty about why *Revival* was so direct in its political statements about the Bush administration. Fogerty responded:

Look, I have very strong feelings about some things. I happen to believe—put it this way, all of our politicians, no matter what their political party and affiliation, everybody is human. Therefore, by definition, nobody is perfect. It's the nature of the game. We all make mistakes. Politicians make mistakes. . . . I just happen to feel that in this case, with this administration, it's not simply bad judgment. I think these are bad people behaving badly, very much having a sinister purpose or agenda that is very self-serving [and] selfish. Lining their own pockets, lining the pockets of their friends, and making all the rest of us pay for it, of course. That's the intensity of my own emotions and feelings about this. For the life of me, I can't remember a bunch of Democrats in recent memory who got together as a group and said—I mean, I know there was a Billy Sol Estes, and that LBJ had a couple of things that he did that were pretty much for his own good. But I can't remember such a group of people in power having the reins of power and taking the entire country to a place that makes their close friends so wealthy, so quickly.

It really seems bad. That to me is, more than the war itself, it's that agenda, that perversion of power, that I'm referring to as the "Long Dark Night."[12]

It wasn't just the Bush administration which he attacked, however. If we remember back to "Fortunate Son," we will recall that President Richard Nixon was the main assailant. As Fogerty said, this was because,

Well, it was so glaring. It was so obvious during Nixon's time that the children of privilege—the senator's son, the president's son, if he had one, or at least the president's daughter's boyfriend—they weren't going to war. They were going to have a cushy job somewhere. Whereas the poor, lower class grunt was going to be the guy in field getting shot. It made me so angry. I'm not the first guy to notice it, but it made me so angry that the rich old men make the war, and the poor young men have to fight it.[13]

When thinking about Fogerty's musical life, we see clear comparisons between Nixon and Bush along with Vietnam and Iraq. Yet few people seem to be willing to discuss the actual differences. Fogerty, however, seems to be acutely aware:

Nixon had his "golfcart army"—Halderman, Erlichman. Basically they were running around trying to protect Nixon and the whole political dirty tricks thing. It wasn't until later that Erlichman was trying to hawk ice cream or something. Whereas these guys now are doing stuff that lines their pockets now. It's so much more about power and money. The whole Halliburton thing, or Blackwater. All these different groups of people that are put right in the path of billions of dollars of American tax payers' money. If I had enough time I could have named all of those people [in the song], too! [laughs] The song would have been 400 minutes long.[14]

In Revival, Fogerty took the "Fortunate Son" label and transferred it from Nixon's daughter and Eisenhower's grandson to George W. Bush himself. Fogerty, however, expands on the basic explanation:

Put it this way: The sound of that track is a giveaway. The energy, the frustration, the anger, the intensity is a giveaway to those emotions. I've listened to the White House, the administration, and certainly George Bush for years now—we all have listened to this stuff. And my feeling is I can't take it no more! We all know he lied about the casualties for one thing. They continue to lie about the casualties on both sides. We're killing Iraqis by the hundreds of thousands—we are, or the insurgents are. We're even lying about the American casualties. If you get killed a certain way, they don't list it as died in combat. I understand if you get blown up in certain quarters of the country that's also not listed as died in combat. The total figure of deaths or casualties in Iraq doesn't get counted in the main column. ... Of course, then there are all the "civilian contractor" deaths. Just that one portion is a lie. Of course, the WMDs was a lie—I'm picking apart my song here. And the detainees? I'm talking about the detainees before the war! There's one guy we famously beat the crap out of until he said "Yes, Saddam has weapons of mass destruction!" We basically went to war with the testimony of one detainee that we tortured. Every night Bush gets on TV and says we must stay the course. We must prove we're not cowards, and we're not quitters. I've just had it! It's tired, it's old. ... It's the mess that he's created. The one that I loved was after Petraeus did his testimony—I didn't actually watch, because I was disgusted—there was a picture of him, the front page, and the headline was "Bush declares things are going so well"—because of the surge—"that we can now bring home 30,000 troops." The real truth is that we had to bring home 30,000 troops—which of course brings us back to the level we were at before the surge—or else we had to institute a draft. Those guys have all had three tours of duty now, so if he sent them back again basically there would be a revolt! The spin was that he was bringing them home because we were doing so well! God! Wow! It just makes you crazy.[15]

Most importantly, *Pitchfork* asked Fogerty whether he truly considers himself to be a protest singer. They explain that he has played protests and obviously written many of the most famous protest songs from both the Vietnam and Iraq War eras. Fogerty responds,

Only at times. I think at times the very strong feelings I have about my country coincide with my musical ability, and I'm able to actually turn it into music, a song or even hopefully a memorable song, sometimes. You may find it surprising, but I'm a very intense, proud American. I love being an American. But I come from a generation that came of age in the 60s, so that intense pride sort of comes out a little differently in me than it does in, say, John Wayne. Now that I'm a lot older, I certainly revere John Wayne as an icon. Heck, he was a cowboy, and I love cowboys. But during the Vietnam era, he was too dang right wing. He was status quo, everything's great. He was against the protesters and for the Nixon White House, and his politics I think—I think—tended to be quite conservative. He could have almost uttered the phrase "stay the course.".... I'm just made differently. Man, I just love being an American, I love my country. But it happened to me during the Nixon time, especially pre-Watergate, that as I watched Nixon for the first time in my life I felt shame. I had to analyze myself. What is this emotion? I realized that my government was separate from my country. It was the first time I ever felt ashamed of the government, not the country. I felt that the population as a whole, of which I am one member, I was proud of that. I was proud of our history, all the things that have led us to where we are and what we stood for and stand for still—I hope. But there was a distinct difference. That was the first time I could see that what the government was doing was not necessarily what my country wanted to have done. Which is probably how I feel now. That pride as an American comes out a little bit different. I can salute the flag. I can totally support the troops. And yet I am against what my president is doing with those troops.[16]

Conclusion

From his Creedence Clearwater Revival days to his time as a solo writer and artist, John Fogerty has maintained a complicated relationship with the political world. As his interview from 2007 makes clear, even he seems to be unaware of exactly how the relationship was balanced at times. There is a clear ebb and flow showing that at times Fogerty would remain subtle and place his music before the message before later becoming too politically brazen, falling out of the public light for a while, and then slowly rebuilding his career.

His messages have been fairly consistent—concerns about war, desires to return to a better time in our country's past, fears for youth, and anger with elite leaders who are allegedly out of touch with the world. It should be noted, however, that the eras where Fogerty had the greatest political impact were quite similar. Leaders like Nixon and Bush were more similar than different. The same goes for Vietnam and Iraq. With this in mind, perhaps it is not surprising that *Eye of the Zombie* was such a failure upon release. The country was not in a state of protest and our leader, President Reagan, was popular. What we are truly left with is a question about where Fogerty goes from here. His most recent album, *Revival* (2007) on which he did most of the writing was cutthroat in attacking Republicans, both generically and specifically. Using his past template, this should lead to a few years of radio silence. But with our country still struggling to fully rebound from years of political and economic turmoil, perhaps he will be back sooner to help ease the minds of a generation desperately seeking a vehicle through which they can be heard.

Notes

1. Michael Goldberg, "Fortunate Son," *Rolling Stone*, February 3, 1993, 48.

2. Ibid.

3. *Creedence Online Forum*, http://www.creedence-online.net/forum/f4-lyrics/meaning-the-lyrics-for-whoa-039-ll-stop-the-ra-202.html (June 24, 2010).

4. Robert Hilburn, "Q&A with John Fogerty," *Los Angeles Times*, January 12, 1993,http://articles.latimes.com/1993-01-12/entertainment/ca-1226_1_creedence-clearwater-revival.

5. Mark Deming, "Have You Ever Seen the Rain?" *AllMusic*, May 23, 2012, http://www.allmusic.com/song/have-you-ever-seen-the-rain-mt0001027618.

6. Stephen Thomas Erlewine, "Blue Moon Swamp," *AllMusic*, http://www.allmusic.com/album/blue-moon-swamp-mw0000022155 (May 23, 2012).

7. See Thomas Erlewine, "Revival," *AllMusic*, http://www.allmusic.com/album/revival-mw0000484972 (May 23, 2012).

8. Sean Alfano, "John Fogerty's Musical Revival," CBS *Sunday Morning*, February 11, 2009, http://www.cbsnews.com/2100-3445_162-1075791.html?pageNum=3&tag=contentMain;contentBody.

9. Mike Butler, "John Fogerty Rolls Backs the Years," *Metro*, May 23, 2012, http://www.metro.co.uk/metrolife/183900-john-fogerty-rolls-back-the-years#ixzz1xYGsdUhq.

10. Dan Reilly, "John Fogerty Calls Obama's Nobel Prize Win 'Amazing and Wonderful," *Spinner*, October 12, 2009, http://www.spinner.com/2009/10/12/john-fogerty-calls-obamas-nobel-prize-win-amazing-and-wonderfu.

11. Ibid.

12. Joshua Klein, "John Fogerty," *Pitchfork*, November 27, 2007, http://pitchfork.com/features/interviews/6737-john-fogerty.

13. Ibid.

14. Ibid.

15. Ibid.

16. Ibid.

~

CHAPTER THIRTEEN

"Rockin' All Over the World"—John Fogerty's Place in American Popular Music

Nick Baxter-Moore

No history of American popular music over the last fifty years is complete without mention, at least *some* mention, of John Fogerty. That's my position, and I'm sticking to it—and Tom Kitts, the editor of this volume, has very kindly allowed me a chapter, the concluding chapter in the book, in which to advance and defend this argument; indeed, I assume that Tom agrees with that position, at least in part—otherwise there would be no book at all to which this chapter might contribute. As songwriter, lead singer, lead guitarist, and perhaps more controversially as band leader of Creedence Clearwater Revival, one of the premier singles bands of the late 1960s, John Fogerty successfully captured the contradictions of those tumultuous times. Since CCR broke up in 1972, he has periodically reinvented himself as a solo artist, intermittently releasing albums, many critically acclaimed and/or commercially successful, which have, to a greater or lesser extent, expressed the *zeitgeist*, the spirit of the times, both musically and in socio-political terms. Other chapters in this volume have evaluated Fogerty's career and his contribution, addressing either particular eras and albums (his CCR days, his incarnation as the Blue Ridge Rangers, his comeback in the 1980s), or particular themes, such as his politics, his relationship to social class, his evocation of place. In this chapter, I attempt to provide a historical overview, considering Fogerty's location in contemporary popular culture; I chart Fogerty's career, trace his legacy, and—insofar as possible—map his place in modern American popular music.

Many of the sources on which I rely are lists; sometimes they are lists made by critics and academics, but most are popular in origin. It is one of the features of many forms of popular culture, but of popular music and sports in particular, that followers, fans, armchair quarterbacks, and would-be managers devote extraordinary amounts of time and cultural capital to the creation of Lists with a capital "L." In the film *High Fidelity* (based on Nick Hornby's book of the same name), Rob, Dick, and Barry, respectively the owner and employees of the Championship Vinyl record store, while away the idle hours between serving customers by comparing—indeed, competing to compile—lists of the Top Five Side One Track Ones, or the Top Five Songs About Death in honor of Laura's father who just dropped dead of a heart attack. Meanwhile Rob (played in the movie by John Cusack) extends the metaphor by tracking down the women involved in his All-Time Top Five Break-ups in a desperate attempt to find out who he is and why Laura has recently left him for another man.[1] Lists, in other words, often tell us much more about their compilers than their subjects, but they are an intrinsic feature of popular music culture, a form of audience participation. . . even if one can't play guitar, one still has a shot at compiling the definitive list of the Top Five Guitarists of All Time.

But it's all very well to use secondary sources to find out how other people have evaluated John Fogerty's contribution to American popular music. In this chapter, I also intend to discuss his music, his songwriting, his singing and playing, based on analysis of a text—in this case, *Revival* (2007), his most recent album of original songs. A text, in this sense, is any cultural product that is preserved in such a form that it can be observed, read, or analyzed by those who weren't present at its creation. In music, therefore, a text may be the sheet music or score of an original composition; a CD, or vinyl album, or MP3, or other digital file of a recorded performance; or a DVD, or video, or sound recording of a subsequent live performance of a song. Record reviews or concert reviews represent a different kind of text that is one step removed from the original: the experience of hearing the music is filtered through someone else's ears. Fogerty's *The Blue Ridge Rangers Rides Again* was released in 2009, but consists largely of covers of country and country-rock songs written and originally recorded by others; "Change in the Weather" is the only song on the album written by Fogerty, but even it is a cover of his own original version recorded in the studio for his 1986 album, *Eye of the Zombie*. Hence, the tracks on *Revival* remain the most recent large-scale, first-hand testament to Fogerty's songwriting, singing, guitar-playing and all-round musical abilities. . . at least, until his next studio album.[2]

In this chapter, I consider first how others have rated John Fogerty's contributions as songwriter and lyricist, singer and guitarist, as well as his all-round ability as a musician. Second, I explore his continuing relevance with particular reference to his most recent album of original songs, *Revival*. Third, in an attempt to inject some sense of balance, I consider what might have been—that is, the extent to which Fogerty's influence might have been yet more significant had he not disappeared from the popular music scene, both from recording and touring, for substantial lengths of time over the past forty years. Fogerty's career is marked as much by absence as by achievement, and those absences need to be taken into account in any consideration of his overall place in American popular music.

John Fogerty as Songwriter

A few years ago I participated in two well-attended panel discussions with colleagues Tom Kitts and Steve Hamelman at annual conferences of the Popular Culture Association and one of its regional affiliates in which we debated the Top 10 Pop/Rock Songwriters of All Time. Once in this exercise, we allowed songwriting teams; in the other debate our subjects had to be solo (singer-) songwriters. In each case we found online lists which appeared to be based on some degree of consensus, at least for the top four or five names; invariably, Bob Dylan would be #1, and Lennon-McCartney would be well up there, either as a team or as individuals, along with Jagger/Richards, Chuck Berry, perhaps Brian Wilson, and/or some of the Motown songwriters like Smokey Robinson or Holland/Dozier/Holland. Our self-appointed task at these panels was briefly to survey the Top 10 and then to propose one change in that list; that is, to drop one name and nominate a previously excluded candidate for the Top 10 Songwriters. John Fogerty never quite made our Top 10 lists, in part because of his numerous career interruptions ("sustained success and influence" was one of our criteria), but he certainly came under consideration.

DigitalDreamDoor's "100 Greatest Rock Songwriters," one of the web sites we used to create our Top 10, lists Fogerty at #49, citing his contributions to the CCR repertoire and his solo career, including such songs as "Proud Mary," "Bad Moon Rising," "Fortunate Son," and "Centerfield."[3] Despite the last reference, the *DDD* list locates Fogerty principally as an artist of the 1960s. At #49 all-time, Fogerty is in some pretty good company. Above him in the 40s are Roy Orbison, Sly Stone, Chuck D of Public Enemy, the members of the Bee Gees, Otis Redding and Steve Cropper, George Harrison, Joe Strummer and Mick Jones of the Clash, the members of Queen, and

Isaac Hayes and David Porter. Below him, in the ranks of the 50s and 60s, are such songwriters as the members of Led Zeppelin (#51), Kurt Cobain of Nirvana (#54), Michael Jackson (#55), Jim Morrison and fellow members of the Doors (#59), Sting (#60), Jimi Hendrix (#61), Don Henley and Glenn Frey of the Eagles (#64), Billy Joel (#65), and 2pac (Tupac Shakur, #68). In the 70s, lagging twenty places or more behind Fogerty, lie such influential songwriters as Elvis Costello, James Taylor, the members of REM, Jackson Browne, Cat Stevens, and—how can he possibly be rated so low at #76?— Leonard Cohen. This is tough company to keep.

In *Paste* magazine's 2006 survey to find the 100 best living songwriters, Fogerty fares even better, coming in at #34, just behind Carole King, Jerry Leiber and Mike Stoller, and Pete Townshend, and just ahead of Steve Earle, Beck, and Smokey Robinson.[4] The *Paste* write-up on Fogerty says relatively little about his songwriting *per se*, and much more about his creativity in inventing a musical persona for himself and CCR:

> Hailing from El Cerrito, Calif., John Fogerty sounded more like a 1970s Mark Twain than a California hippy. Combining tales of the Deep South with soul-meets-country chords catchy enough to land the most elusive catfish, his fierce voice wailed and growled through the swampy jams CCR created, reminiscing about his fictional boyhood on the bayous. In reality, Fogerty had only ventured as far east as Montana when "Proud Mary"—their first hit—was released. There have been over 100 covers, including the Ike and Tina Turner firebolt and the Leonard Nemoy [sic] butchering. While most of CCR's tales were dreamlike versions of the land below the Mason-Dixon line, political songs like "Fortunate Son" showed Fogerty's fierce, opinionated side, slamming affluent families whose children were excluded from the draft.[5]

Of course, the songs were part of that CCR musical persona: lyrics expressing nostalgia for better, or at least less uncertain, times; hummable melodies set in 4/4 rock and roll tempos, accompanied by often memorable guitar riffs and backed by the disciplined rhythm section of Doug Clifford and Stu Cook; a recording mix that alternated, and sometimes combined, clean rockabilly sounds with the muddiness of swamp rock; and, up front, Fogerty's distinctively accented vocals. But the songs can also be separated from the musical persona, as they often are in the many cover versions of Fogerty's songs, to which the *Paste* write-up also alludes.

The original *Paste* listing was based on a survey of fifty music journalists and musicians, perhaps the kind of people most likely to rate Fogerty's contribution as a songwriter. Surprisingly, however, when *Paste* decided to broaden the base of its study by publishing the results of a poll of over 18,000 readers on the same subject, Fogerty's position was confirmed—in fact, he even went up two places to #32, although there were some significant changes elsewhere in the rankings; the readers' poll, for example, substituted twenty-nine new artists for those on the original list.[6]

Further acclaim for Fogerty's songwriting comes from veteran music journalist Dave Marsh who, in his book *The Heart of Rock & Soul*, honors seven CCR recordings and Fogerty compositions among what he argues to be "The 1001 Greatest Singles Ever Made."[7] He lists "Bad Moon Rising," "Fortunate Son," "Green River," "Lodi," "Proud Mary," "Run Through the Jungle," and, most significantly, "Who'll Stop the Rain," ranked highest among Fogerty's songs at #26, two spots below Bruce Springsteen's "Born to Run," one after Marvin Gaye's "What's Goin' On," and three higher than the Beatles' "Ticket to Ride" (for Marsh, the highest ranked Beatles single at #29). Again, this is pretty solid company: other songs ranked in the 20s by Marsh include three Phil Spector productions—"Da Doo Ron Ron" by the Crystals, the Ronettes' "Be My Baby," and Darlene Love's "Christmas (Baby Please Come Home)"—Sam and Dave's "Hold On I'm Coming," "My Girl" by the Temptations, and Van Halen's "Jump."

Marsh's description of "Who'll Stop the Rain" relies much on the sound of the song, but also pays tribute to Fogerty's songwriting:

> The mourning in John Fogerty's voice and the elegant guitar figure on which it rides make it seem that he's expressing some specific, tangible grievance. But what's it about? Woodstock, where it poured as Creedence played? Vietnam, with America mired in mud? The clues in other Creedence songs lead to a different conclusion. Fogerty is rock and roll's version of an old testament prophet, preaching pessimism rather than damnation. "Long as I remember," he begins, with an intonation that implies he forgets nothing, clear back to the beginning. Alternately furious and heartsick, he spins a tale that includes political events, rock concerts seen from both sides of the stage, and private attempts to make sense of his life and the world.[8]

As Marsh suggests, politics, making music, and trying to make sense of both his life and the world are recurring motifs in Fogerty's songs that (as we will see further below) continue to preoccupy him, even in his most recent work.

Fogerty's songwriting prowess is recognized in magazine and internet surveys by critics, musicians, and fans alike. It has also been granted more formal acclaim. In December 1997, he received a lifetime achievement award from the National Academy of Songwriters, along with Robbie Robertson (formerly of the Band), Quincy Jones, and Ashford & Simpson.[9] Further recognition came in June 2005, when he was inducted by John Mellencamp into the Songwriters' Hall of Fame (SHOF) at a gala dinner at the Marriott Marquis Hotel in New York City. The SHOF web site emphasizes that its membership is select: "Out of the tens of thousands of successful songwriters of our era, there are fewer than 400 inductees who make up the impressive roster enshrined in the Hall of Fame." The site then lists 39 examples, approximately ten percent, of that select company, including Bob Dylan, Holland-Dozier-Holland, Leiber & Stoller, Bruce Springsteen, Paul Simon, Cynthia Weil & Barry Mann ... and John Fogerty.[10] According to the formal induction statement, Fogerty was recognized because

> enduring songs like "Proud Mary," "Bad Moon Rising," "Who'll Stop The Rain," "Lodi," "Looking Out My Back Door," "Run Through The Jungle," "Centerfield" and "Fortunate Son" are now so firmly engrained in our collective consciousness they seem to have come to us from the American soil as much as from any one man. John Fogerty recorded many of his great songs as the leader of the now legendary band Creedence Clearwater Revival. ... To this day, John Fogerty remains a genuinely great artist, one of the defining songwriters of our time.[11]

Finally, while Fogerty scores well as songwriter in internet surveys, interestingly for someone whose songs are often notable for their guitar riffs and sing-along melodies, he ranks even higher on *DigitalDreamDoor*'s list of the "100 Greatest Rock Lyricists." Rated #23 as a wordsmith, he is just behind Bob Marley, Joe Strummer (the Clash), and Warren Zevon (numbers 20–22, respectively), and just ahead of Smokey Robinson, Tom Waits, and Kurt Cobain (ranked from 24 through 26).[12] To understand why this may be the case, and since as we shall see further, below, Fogerty's achievements are often compared for better or for worse to those of Bruce Springsteen, let us give an opportunity to praise Fogerty's songwriting, especially his lyrics, to the man they call "The Boss." In his speech inducting CCR into the Rock and Roll Hall of Fame, Springsteen made special mention of Fogerty's ability to tell a complete story within the compressed space of a three-minute single:

> How can you talk about Creedence without talking about John Fogerty? ... As a songwriter only few did as much in three minutes. ... He was lyrically spare and beautiful, created a world of childhood memories and of men and women with their back to the wall, a landscape of swamps, bayous, endless rivers, gypsy women, back porches, hound dogs chasing ghosts, devils, bad moons rising, straight out of the blues tradition and turned it into a vision all his own.[13]

Elsewhere, Springsteen has lauded Fogerty as "one of the greatest singers and rock song writers of all time ... the Hank Williams of our generation."[14] I'm not sure where the Hank Williams comparison comes from;[15] perhaps Springsteen was referring to the sheer ubiquity of Fogerty's songs (and the many covers by other artists), or perhaps to his unique vocal styling.

John Fogerty as Singer

A crucial element in establishing the credentials of CCR as a roots/rock and roll band, as opposed to one of the acid-tripping, hippie progressive rock groups from California that were the band's contemporaries in the late Sixties, was John Fogerty's vocal attack. It owed a great deal more to the swamp-influenced timbres of Jerry Lee Lewis or Tony Joe White than to the softly modulated tones of north-central California. It was part Cajun, part blues, part gospel, a rasp-roughened tenor voice that enunciated in the phonemes of the Mississippi Delta. In his later career, Fogerty was not always able to reach some of the high notes, but one can always tune songs down to a lower register, even though some of the initial excitement might be lost. But the original sound, perhaps described best as "a backwoods yowl," was a seminal ingredient of CCR's iconic image that Fogerty has managed to replicate or rediscover in his solo recordings.

In its ranking of the "100 Greatest Singers of All Time," *Rolling Stone* magazine lists Fogerty at #72, just below Ronnie Spector, lead singer of the Sixties girl group the Ronettes at #69, Greg Allman of the Allman Brothers Band (#70), and reggae artist Toots Hibbert (#71), and just ahead of Dolly Parton, James Taylor, and Iggy Pop (#73 through #75).[16] Fogerty's artist profile in the magazine explains how he went about finding his voice:

> The backwoods yowl that put the fire into Creedence Clearwater Revival's gritty late-Sixties hits like "Green River" and "Proud Mary" actually was not, as the man says, "Born on the Bayou." John Fogerty's abrasive baritone [sic] didn't even come naturally at first. "In '64, I got a job playing in a club, and I had a tape recorder with me," he recalls. "I would record the whole night and then listen to myself back, and every day I would try to force myself to get that sound that was in my head." He was trying to channel the voices of blues singers like Howlin' Wolf and Bo Diddley that he heard on the radio in his hometown of El Cerrito, California. "As a kid, there was that point I realized the stuff I liked was more dangerous than the stuff my parents liked," he says. "It was that threatening sound."[17]

That "threatening sound" was the sound of the blues, filtered through the cadences of the bayous. But it wasn't so much "threatening" as fatalistic. Elsewhere in this volume, Tom Kitts has referred to Fogerty's "jeremiads" in which the Old Testament-style gloom and doom derives as much from the sound of Fogerty's voice as the lyrics he's singing. It's a point developed further by Dave Marsh in his analysis of CCR's "Who'll Stop the Rain":

> What draws you back is the grain of [Fogerty's] voice, the things it contains and expresses but cannot speak. And this voice is as far from the assurance of Elvis or Aretha as you can get. Fogerty seems confident of only two things: his doubts and his powerlessness. Hooking his audience as firmly as he's hooked himself, Fogerty makes his worries ours. … The idea that rock and roll is light-hearted good time music stops here, at the gateway to its heart of darkness.[18]

Marsh invokes the concept of "grain of voice," associated with French structuralist thinker Roland Barthes,[19] to draw attention to the additional layers of meaning imparted to a song by the sound of the singer—what Barthes would call in other contexts, the connotation of the words, their mythological connections, rather than simply the denotation, the everyday meaning—"the things it [the voice] contains and expresses but cannot speak."

Three elements of that voice make it particularly distinctive. First, there is Fogerty's "total immersion accent," an adopted mode of speech whereby a Bay-area kid sounds as if he emerged fully formed from the streets of New Orleans, "which transforms 'work' to 'woik,' among other things."[20] Second, the timbre of Fogerty's voice is equally recognizable. The "backwoods yowl" is defined as much by the tonality of the voice as by the accent or rhythms of its speech. The pitch is essentially that of a tenor—not a baritone as the *Rolling Stone* writer would suggest, although such distinctions, rooted as they are in classical or art music, have less import in analyzing the sounds of rock and roll; rather, a yowl, a cross between a yelp and howl, suggests a higher register—the sound of a wolf, or a dog, or perhaps an alley cat out on the tiles—and this is what Fogerty's voice connotes, an animalistic quality, wild, primitive, natural, above all rural, characteristics of his imagined community which is the deep south, the Delta. Third, the accent and the timbre together invoke musical mythologies of the origins of rock and roll in the blending of Appalachian and bluegrass music with blues and R&B at the meeting point of the South and the Deep South, at the place where the Delta begins, in Memphis. Fogerty's voice belongs as much in the 1950s as in the '60s or any subsequent decade; it's a sound that invokes the method of Sam Phillips's

Sun Studios. As rock journalist David Cavanagh recently stated, Fogerty's voice "remains one of the most rip-roaring rock 'n' roll instruments, seeming to come with its own slapback echo."[21]

John Fogerty as Guitarist

In *DigitalDreamDoor*'s list of the 200 Greatest Guitarists (of all genres), Fogerty is not ranked at all.[22] And in *DDD*'s somewhat more selective list of Greatest *Rock* Guitarists, he appears at #115, just behind Joe Walsh and Ted Nugent.[23] In other words, the compilers of these lists do not rate Fogerty particularly high. Perhaps given what we have already learned about the kudos attached to his songwriting prowess, his lyrics, and his status as a singer, it is unreasonable to expect that he also be ranked highly as a guitar player, but the *DDD* rankings may underestimate both his instrumental chops and appraisals of that ability accorded by amateur and professional critics alike. Admittedly, Fogerty is not another Eric Clapton or Jimi Hendrix. In CCR, in particular, he was essentially a second rhythm guitarist, alongside his brother Tom, overlaying the groove with a few riffs and licks, but his vocals, backed by the tempo laid down by Clifford and Cook, came first. CCR was primarily a singles band, devoted to telling its stories in three/four minutes. It wasn't a blues band or a jam band or an album band; it wasn't Ten Years After, featuring Alvin Lee's lightning-fast licks, or the Grateful Dead, whose history, fame, and following were focused on the meandering solo, or Led Zeppelin whose growing renown, based on the interplay between Robert Plant's vocal pyrotechnics and the guitar-playing virtuosity of Jimmy Page, was spread on the late night airwaves by album-oriented rock stations. CCR's "chooglin'" was mostly a way of marking time and having fun until the vocals came back in, not an end in itself. Hence, the band might have bookended its career with two extended jams on "I Put a Spell on You" and "I Heard It through the Grapevine," but these were exceptions rather than the rule. Their other hits, and most of their album tracks, were radio-friendly pocket narratives. Indeed, Fogerty has claimed that he didn't want to be associated with the emerging jam-band/prog-rock school of guitar-playing in the late 1960s:

> I didn't like the idea of those acid-rock, 45-minute guitar solos. I thought music should get to the point a little more quickly than that. I was a mainstream rock 'n' roll kid, and I also had a country blues ethic. Lead Belly [sic] was a big influence. I learned about him through Pete Seeger. When you listen to those guys, you're getting down to the root of the tree.[24]

If not a guitar virtuoso, even in his Creence days, Fogerty does receive, and deserve, respect as a guitarist. In 2004, *Rolling Stone* magazine published its first list of the "100 Greatest Guitarists of All Time," in which John Fogerty was ranked #40, just behind Bo Diddley, at #37, Peter Green (Fleetwood Mac, at #38), and Brian May of Queen (#39), and just ahead of Clarence White (the Byrds), Robert Fripp (King Crimson), and Eddie Hazel (Parliament/Funkadelic).[25] The artist profile on Fogerty identifies some of his principal influences: "Fogerty's taut riffing, built on the country and rockabilly innovations of Scotty Moore and James Burton, was the dynamite in CCR hits such as 'Born on the Bayou' and 'Green River.' Fogerty can also be a lethal jammer: see his extended break in CCR's '68 cover of Dale Hawkins' 'Suzie Q.'"[26]

Interviewed by Michael Goldberg of *Rolling* Stone in 1993, Fogerty delineated the four principal characteristics, for him, of a great rock-and-roll record: a great title, a great sound, a great song, and a great guitar lick. "I tried like crazy," Fogerty continued, "to come up with great guitar hooks to fashion a record around."[27] With CCR, Fogerty created some of the most memorable guitar hooks in late '60s rock and roll: the descending chord sequence in "Proud Mary" (CCA CCA CCAG FFFFD); the two-string walkdown from G that serves as a mood-setting intro to the vocal and instrumental assault on privilege and injustice that Fogerty delivers in "Fortunate Son"; the simple arpeggio on the D chord played at the tenth fret, followed by an A at the fifth, that makes the hook on "Up Around the Bend" #63 on the all-time list of greatest rock guitar riffs according to *DigitalDreamDoor*.[28]

There came a time, however, when Fogerty was no longer satisfied with his instrumental skills. In his first long hiatus from the music industry that lasted most of the seventies and the first part of the eighties, he would still go to work every day and bring his work home from the office as he attempted to master all of the instruments in a standard rock band: "Every morning, Fogerty would slip into his tiny studio in El Cerrito, CA, and practice. Guitar. Bass. Keyboards. Drums. He would go home for dinner, see his wife Martha and the three children, then practice again into the night. On weekends, he would practice again in the TV room, 'where my family could see I was actually alive, I just had to get better and better.'"[29]

Whether as a result of the work ethic stemming from working class origins that often surface in his more politically minded songs, or a form of self-deception that he was indeed still a working musician, even when he wasn't writing new songs, recording, or touring, Fogerty has spent much of the last forty years in the metaphorical "woodshed," improving his musical skills. Having played all the instruments on *Centerfield* and most of them on *Eye of the Zombie*, he went back into virtual seclusion for eleven years, before releasing *Blue Moon Swamp* in 1997, then disappearing again for seven years until he reemerged in 2004 to release *Déjà Vu All Over Again* and to participate in the Vote for Change campaign. Once again, he was not idle during either hiatus. Inspired by virtuoso dobro player Jerry Douglas (who would later make a guest appearance on "I Will Walk With You" on Fogerty's *Déjà Vu All Over Again*), he began working on slide guitar, then dobro—an instrument he had first played with CCR on "Lookin' Out My Back Door" (1970). But when it came to recording tracks for *Blue Moon Swamp*, Fogerty proved to be his own toughest critic: "I went out to play the guitar, and it was like, in five minutes I stopped the tape and I told the engineer, 'This bass player and this drummer would kick the guitar player out of this band.' It was the truth. I just wasn't at that level, so I had to go to work."[30]

Around 1998, Fogerty recalls, he finally figured out what he was trying to do: "I wanted to do the freehand thing that bluegrass guys, flatpickers, and jazz guys do, where you can just roll your hand and all these notes come out. ... And I was nowhere near that. ... I thought it might take me two or three years—it took ten to 11 years to get fluid."[31] And he has certainly attained this level, as any listening to his guitar playing on recent albums or at live performances will attest. Meanwhile, he has not only displayed a wide diversity of guitar styles in recent recordings, but also managed to hold his own with Mark Knopfler, one of the premier guitar players of the last thirty years, on the Dire Straits-influenced "Nobody's Here Anymore" from *Déjà Vu All Over Again*. Already lauded for his musicianship on the CCR recordings, Fogerty has continued to hone his skills, his musical chops, to the point at which he can, as a clever imitator and innovative inflector of guitar stylings from the last fifty years or more, portray himself as a repository of rock and roll history who nonetheless, through the contemporary cultural and political references in his lyrics, keeps one foot in the present.

Revival: Fogerty's Latest Comeback

In 1969, Creedence Clearwater Revival released three albums—*Bayou Country, Green River, Willy and the Poorboys*—all of them Top Ten hits (*Green River* was #1 in the pop album chart) and four double-sided singles which all reached the Top 3. It was a period of extraordinary creativity and plain hard work. Fogerty's last album of original songs, *Revival*, was released in October 2007, only three years after his previous release, *Déjà Vu All Over Again*. It hardly matched the output of 1969, but compared to the eleven years that elapsed between *Eye of the Zombie* (1986) and *Blue Moon Swamp* (1997), it marked a positively prolific stage in his career. The title of the new CD was both a promise—Fogerty here explores and updates a substantial chunk of rock and roll history—and a possible provocation; if the two Cs in CCR (Clifford and Cook) had reappropriated two thirds of the original band's name for Creedence Clearwater Revisited, Fogerty made sure to reclaim the Revival part. Or perhaps, given the return to Fantasy Records, his use of part of the old band name suggests a partial rapprochement with that stage in his life. But he also borrows part of the band's name and its image in the third track on *Revival*, a rollicking number called "Creedence Song." It could be a Creedence song; it chugs along at about "Suzie Q" pace, Fogerty's swampy guitar breaking into two solos, one extended, over the solid rhythm section of drummer Kenny Aronoff and bassist David Santos—it even features some playful "doo doos" to introduce the mid-song guitar solo. In it, he tells the story of "Daddy," a guitarist in a rock-and-roll band, who falls for a waitress in a diner and eventually marries her; at the conclusion to each verse, "Daddy" playing a gig, the waitress talking to a customer at the jukebox, "Daddy" asking her if he can play something for her, the newlyweds "living on rock and roll," the burden line explains that no one can go far wrong if they choose to play a little bit of a Creedence song.

There are two politically oriented songs on *Revival*, which we have come to expect of a Fogerty album. In "Long Dark Night," he excoriates the then-current Bush administration, mentioning the President, Michael Brown (head of FEMA during the Hurricane Katrina disaster), Donald Rumsfeld, and Dick Cheney, using diminutive forms ("Georgie," "Brownie," "Rummie," and "Dickie") to belittle them. The vocals are in full "backwoods howl" mode, but the song also features some fine interplay between Fogerty's guitar and an uncredited harmonica player (likely Fogerty himself). A second political rant, "I Can't Take It No More," sees Fogerty turning to a Ramones-style punk sound to attack George W. Bush, accusing him of lying about war casualties, weapons of mass destruction, the treatment of detainees—and, in another form of revival from the Creedence years—of being a "fortunate son" whose daddy wrote a check to help him evade active service in the Vietnam War. Fogerty claims to be "sick and tired" of Bush's "dirty little war" and, in the song's title, he "can't take it no more." The whole song moves to a frantic beat; all that's missing is a "hey, ho, say it ain't so," but he already did that on "She's Got Baggage" on *Déjà Vu*. And if not explicitly political, "It Ain't Right" is a timely piece of social criticism in raucous rockabilly mode, making fun of celebs and wannabes (Paris, Britney, anyone?) who ride around in big black limousines, shaking booties for the magazines, partying every weekend, before taking those big black limousines back to rehab.

Revival showcases Fogerty's talents as a guitarist. As reviewer Glen Boyd points out on Blogcritics.org:

> Fogerty has never been of those guys mentioned in the same breath as the Eric Claptons of the world. Rightfully, he is more often recognized as a songwriter. Yet his guitar sound ranks as one of a very small handful that can be instantly recognized—sometimes with a single note. ... His best guitar solos come in short blasts that rip through the air like gunfire, and always leave you wanting more. The tone is strictly dirty Cajun. Yet the delivery is all clean and economical. Not a single note is played that isn't absolutely necessary.[32]

On the gospel-tinged "The River is Waiting," for example, Fogerty's guitar playing is spare, lightly strummed chords accompanying the short stanzas, one brief solo echoing the verse melody; he is equally economical on the Tex-Mex, western swing shuffle that is "Don't You Wish It Was True," the opening track on the album. Elsewhere, he cuts loose. On "Summer of Love," he pays homage, musical and lyrical, to the era of psychedelia, even quoting from Cream's "Sunshine of Your Love" before ripping into an extended fuzzboxed solo that would not seem out of place on a Clapton or Hendrix track from that era. The fuzzbox returns on "Somebody Help Me," a quest song in which the protagonist is traveling round the world—from Kokomo and Pocatella, Idaho, to Nova Scotia, the Indian Ocean and the Great Wall of China—looking for his girl, vocals and guitar trading licks over Benmont Tench's descending riff on a Hammond B-3. And on the concluding track, "Longshot," in which the singer questions why an apparently sophisticated woman might be attracted to him, because he's not a doctor, lawyer, banker, or politician, Fogerty shapes a guitar hook and sound reminiscent of ZZ Top.

Revival also finds the singer in good voice. He can't seem to shed that adopted accent, and it's always recognizably Fogerty, but there is variation in the vocal attack appropriate to each song:

> On the rockers like "Summer of Love" and "Longshot," you are reminded once again that Fogerty is one of the great rock voices ever. ... What is easy to forget however, is that the same guy who sang screaming rockers like "Sweet Hitch Hiker" with Creedence ... also has a sense of twang that could put more than a few country singers to shame. Here on "Don't You Wish It Was True," Fogerty seems to be summoning the ghosts of both Hank Williams and Buddy Holly.[33]

Perhaps nowhere is that country sensibility more marked than on the, for me, standout song on the album, the slow ballad, "Broken Down Cowboy." Not only is it a masterly piece of lyrical songwriting, full of taut turns of phrase and magical metaphors, but Fogerty's sensitive vocal phrasing and raspy tenor is the perfect vehicle for its delivery. The guitar work isn't too shabby, either!

Last, but not least, "Broken Down Cowboy" may be the strongest song on *Revival*, but there isn't a weak one among the twelve tracks on the album (two others, "Gunslinger" and "Natural Thing," while not discussed further here for reasons of space, are both solid country rock tunes, the latter perhaps most redolent of CCR in their heyday). The CD showcases Fogerty's songwriting ability at its most consistent level. There is humor, playfulness, political spite, spirituality, irony, analogy, metaphor, and straightforward good storytelling in his words, and the tunes and arrangements are much less derivative than some of the descriptions above might suggest—Fogerty does not imitate the various musical styles represented here; rather, he alludes to them.

The album met with critical acclaim and was relatively successful commercially, peaking at #14 on the *Billboard* 200 and #4 on the *Billboard* Rock Album Chart. And Fogerty himself seemed happy with it: "It just seemed like all the records I have made since Creedence Clearwater Revival have all been sort of pushed off center. I felt like I was dancing around the outskirts of what is my true center. I really wanted to stay on the mark, right in the middle, right where rock 'n' roll is."[34] And in this last endeavor, he succeeded; *Revival* is a true rock and roll record, serving as a not-bad historical overview of its first quarter-century, from rockabilly to punk, with some gospel, psychedelic rock, country, and delta swamp-blues mixed in for good measure.

John Fogerty as Absent Presence

Speaking in 2005 of the launch of *The Long Road Home*, the compilation album which constituted, according to its subtitle, "The Ultimate John Fogerty/Creedence Collection," Glen Barros of Fogerty's new/old label, Fantasy Records, claimed of his artist, "He should have had the career of a Bruce Springsteen. If this works, that's where we'd like to get him."[35] In some ways, the comparison is not inappropriate: Springsteen and Fogerty have often been mentioned in the same breath as examples of an authentic, working-class, rock-and-roll sensibility; both men released their first solo albums in 1973; and their careers have intersected on numerous occasions over the years, sometimes controversially. It was Springsteen, for example, who inducted CCR into the Rock and Roll Hall of Fame in 1993, on the notorious evening when Fogerty refused to play with his former bandmates,

Doug Clifford and Stu Cook, at the induction ceremony, performing CCR songs instead with an all-star backing band (including Springsteen himself). Later, in the fall of 2004, Fogerty would join Springsteen and the E Street Band, among many other artists, as part of the political road show known collectively as "Vote for Change" in an unsuccessful attempt to win over swing states to vote against incumbent president, George W. Bush. Fogerty has often made guest appearances at live gigs by Springsteen and the E Street Band, they appeared together at the concert marking the 25th Anniversary of the Rock and Roll Hall of Fame in 2009, and they also duet on the old Everly Brothers song, "When Will I Be Loved" on Fogerty's 2009 album *The Blue Ridge Rangers Rides Again*.

At the same time, of course, Barros's choice of words connotes a sense of something lacking, of aspirations unfulfilled. Fogerty *should* or *could* have had a career equivalent to Springsteen's, but he hasn't. Despite the extraordinarily prolific hit-making years with CCR, and the subsequent periodic critical acclaim, recognition by his peers, and industry nominations and awards, Fogerty has not enjoyed the prolonged and sustained success, however such success is measured, typically associated with "the career of a Bruce Springsteen." Although, like Fogerty, Springsteen once broke with the E Street Band, he did so only after more than a decade of achievement, and a decade further on he reunited with the group; in the meantime, he never stopped playing the songs that launched his, and the band's, career, and he continued to tour, write, and release new albums on a regular basis. Fogerty, on the other hand, broke with Creedence Clearwater Revival only four years after the band first hit the charts, never reunited with the band (except for a couple gigs in their home town), for many years refused to play the songs that first brought him and the band to fame, and periodically dropped out of recording and touring altogether, in effect removing himself from the music business.

As a result, there is always that underlying sense of "what if?" What if Fogerty hadn't abandoned CCR when he did? What if he hadn't exiled himself from creating and playing popular music for significant periods of time? What if he hadn't been such a perfectionist? Without the apparently obsessive-compulsive and litigious personality which caused frequent interruptions to his musical career, might John Fogerty have come to occupy an even higher place in the pantheon of American rock musicians? On the other hand, we might ask ourselves, without those personality traits, might he have amounted to anything at all? On such questions, we can only speculate, and we will.

Let's start with missed opportunities. First, Creedence Clearwater Revival might have been the most successful singles band in 1969–70, but relatively few who weren't there would know that the group was one of the headliners of the Woodstock festival of August 1969, "three days of peace and music" that became, in the mythology of the sixties, one of the defining events, and for some the cultural culmination of that decade. That mythology was cemented, at least for subsequent generations, in film and sound recordings from the festival, but the performance of CCR is conspicuously absent from such records. Hence, Fogerty can say "At Woodstock, I felt totally part of my generation. We *smoked* at Woodstock but it's amazing how many people don't know we were one of the headliners."[36] But whose fault was that?

CCR was one of the first bands to sign on to the Woodstock Music and Art Fair some four months in advance, and subsequently its commitment became a lever used by the organizers to recruit other big-name artists.[37] The band was rewarded with the headline spot on Saturday evening, but, such were the organizational delays that they didn't get on stage until the small hours of Sunday morning, after an hour-long, problem-filled set by the Grateful Dead. The technical problems persisted during CCR's set, affecting the band's sound. According to Fogerty:

> We didn't do very well at Woodstock because of the time segment and also because we followed the Grateful Dead, and therefore everybody was asleep. It seemed like we didn't go on until two a.m. Even though in my mind we made the leap into superstardom that weekend, you'd never know it from the [film] footage. All that does is show us in a poor light at a time when we were the number one band in the world. Why should we show ourselves that way?[38]

Twenty-five years on, in 1994, Fogerty again spurned the opportunity to be shown in a Woodstock film when "The Director's Cut" of the original footage was released. According to Stu Cook, "John threatened to sue Warner Bros. Pictures if any image of him was included. WB didn't want their big release stained by a lawsuit from a guy they knew to be litigious, so the offer to be included in the director's cut of the film was withdrawn."[39] Fogerty wasn't able to prevent four Creedence tracks from being included in the 4-CD box set (*Woodstock: Three Days of Peace and Music*) released in 1994 by Atlantic Records, also to celebrate the 25th Anniversary. Nonetheless, a couple generations of music fans had already grown up to the mythology of Woodstock without access to any recorded evidence that CCR had performed his songs there.

Second, Fogerty's long-time unwillingness to play the songs he had written for CCR, alongside his perfectionist streak which limited his output of solo recordings, has deprived audiences of seeing him perform live for substantial numbers of years. The reluctance to play the Creedence-era songs is well-documented,[40] attributable in large measure to his ongoing legal disputes with Fantasy Records and his unwillingness to help Saul Zaentz, and subsequently his former CCR bandmates, make any more money. But Fogerty also became alienated from his songs; indeed, having traded away the rights to the songs to allow him to break his contract with Fantasy, they weren't in some sense really *his* anymore. "I had so much anger," he told David Cavanagh. "I was afraid that I'd start singing 'Proud Mary' and go off on a tirade. If one of my songs came on the car radio, I'd change the station. That's why I couldn't play those songs. I didn't want that person standing in front of an audience."[41] Later, he would change his mind, as a result, he has claimed in interviews, of a conversation with Bob Dylan who told him that "if he didn't play 'Proud Mary' himself, people will think it's an Ike and Tina Turner song."[42]

Meanwhile, for some twenty-five years, Fogerty refused to acknowledge those songs as his; and, while he undoubtedly experienced loss and pain and confusion in rejecting his "musical offspring," ego and obsession were also partly responsible. But the loss for his fans and music fans in general was doubly acute: first, Fogerty was so consumed by his resentment towards Fantasy, Zaentz, and his former bandmates, so caught up in the legal struggles, that he was unable to write new songs, to record, to tour, for substantial periods of time; second, when he did record a respectable comeback album in *Centerfield* in the mid-1980s, he found that without the CCR songs, he had insufficient material to tour, so fans had no live concerts until he returned to the studio to produce (perhaps in too much of a hurry) *Eye of the Zombie*; and then, when he did finally go out on the road, fans were still unable to hear many of his finest compositions. Of course, from the mid-nineties on, they could hear those songs played by Creedence Clearwater Revisited, but not sung by the man who actually wrote them.

Third, Fogerty's perfectionism and his desire to control his musical output (fed, in part, by the legal disputes and bitterness towards Zaentz) have further limited access to his music for fans and casual listeners alike. This is because Fogerty destroys every tape, every take of every track, that doesn't make it onto an album. "I save nothing," he told Alberto Gausch in 1997. "If it's not good, I'm not going to want to listen to it. I destroy it. It's an old habit of mine. Look what happened to Buddy Holly and Jimi Hendrix: they have released all they could find. Every artist has albums and songs that are not good, and I don't want that to be heard." Then the argument took a familiar tack. "Imagine if I hadn't destroyed all my material when I was with Creedence. Those guys ... would be selling it already. They even did it with material from our beginnings when we were kids."[43] Once again artistic integrity duels with, and is possibly outdone by, resentment at his former bandmates and record label in presenting reasons for a particular course of action.

Of course, Fogerty has a perfect right to dispose of his intellectual and artistic property as he sees fit; and certainly some artists have been embarrassed or, figuratively, have rolled in their graves when greedy record labels put together retrospective CD compilations of studio outtakes, alternative mixes, and poorly recorded live performances. But, in the right hands (usually those of the artist), archived recording material can be repackaged in a way that satisfies all parties—the artist, existing fans, new listeners, music critics, and scholars. Since I have already used Bruce Springsteen as a reference point, let me do so again: in 2010, the release of a remastered version of Springsteen's 1978 album, *Darkness on the Edge of Town,*was accompanied by a new documentary film on the making of the album, called *The Promise: The Making of "Darkness on the Edge of Town,"* and by a double CD set (also called *The Promise*[44]) of outtakes and alternative versions recorded during the making of *Darkness*. Some songs on *The Promise* would probably have been worthy of release at the time as singles or as part of another album, had they been recorded by an artist less choosy or conscious of his reputation than Springsteen; other tracks simply provide a window to Springsteen's songwriting method, or the process of recording in general, and it is the latter categories that concern me here. Had Springsteen adopted Fogerty's policy of destroying the recordings of every song, or every version of a song, that does not make it onto an album, his fans—along with casual listeners, music critics, and scholars—would have been deprived of access to a wealth of new material. Springsteen is well-known to be a perfectionist, a hard taskmaster, something of a control freak, but Fogerty seems to outdo him on every count, at a cost to his fans, to his own place in the history of American popular music, and, most likely, to his own well-being.

Conclusion

I have attempted in this chapter to assess John Fogerty's place in American popular music—as a songwriter, singer, and guitar player. I have referred along the way to many of his successes, both commercial and critical. There have been other awards not previously mentioned: Grammy nominations and wins (most notably, the Grammy for Best Rock Album for *Blue Moon Swamp* in 2008); a star on the Hollywood Walk of Fame at 7000 Hollywood Blvd (1998); named as a "BMI [Broadcast Music Industry] Icon" at the BMI's 58th Annual Pop Awards in London, May 2010,[45] and, also in 2010—perhaps most unusually for a rock star—induction into the Baseball Hall of Fame at Cooperstown, NY, for his song "Centerfield." On the other hand, I have not discussed Fogerty's attributes as a bandleader or manager,[46] while suggesting at least three ways in which his behavior—most notably his recurring absences from the music scene, from recording, performing, or touring, for extended periods of time—has likely detracted from his overall reputation and standing within popular consciousness and the views of critics alike. I have argued here that John Fogerty is a great American songwriter, a great rock (and country) vocalist, and a great guitarist capable of matching the best instrumentalists in diverse genres of popular music. But Fogerty is also a complex individual with a fragile psyche who has often been his own worst enemy. His demons may have helped make him a great artist, but they have also diminished his productivity. The example of *Revival* suggests that the sagacity and serenity of advanced middle age might allow Fogerty's creative side to prevail over his (self-) destructive tendencies. He still has time to consolidate his place in American music.

Notes

1. Nick Hornby, *High Fidelity* (London: Victor Gollancz, 1995). *High Fidelity*, dir. Stephen Frears, Working Title Films/Touchstone Pictures, 2000.

2. At time of writing, Fogerty is currently working on a new album, provisionally titled *Wrote a Song for Everyone* and slated for release in fall 2012. The album will reportedly include a number of re-recordings of Fogerty's older songs as duets (Jennifer Hudson, the Foo Fighters, My Morning Jacket, Keith Urban, Bob Seger, Bread Paisley, Miranda Lambert, and Alan Jackson are among the guest artists).

3. "100 Greatest Rock Songwriters," *DigitalDreamDoor.com*, March 3, 2004, last updated, August 23, 2007, http://digitaldreamdoor.com/pages/best_songwriters.html (January 20, 2012).

4. "Paste 100 Best Living Songwriters," *Paste Magazine.com*, June 5, 2006, http://www.pastemagazine.com/articles/2006/06/pastes-100-best-living-songwriters.html (January 18, 2012).

5. Leila Regan-Porter, "John Fogerty," in "Paste's 100 Best Living Songwriters: The List," *Paste Magazine.com*, June 5, 2006, http://www.pastemagazine.com/articles/2006/07/pastes-100-best-living-songwriters-3140.html (January 18, 2012).

6. See "Paste's 100 Best Living Songwriters: The Readers' Poll," *Paste Magazine.com*, http://www.pastemagazine.com/action/article/3004/feature/music/pastes_100_best_living_songwriters_the_readers_poll (January 18, 2012).

7. Dave Marsh, *The Heart of Rock & Soul: The 1001 Greatest Singles Ever Made* (New York: New American Library, 1989).

8. Ibid, 24–25.

9. Hank Bordowitz, *Bad Moon Rising: The Unauthorized History of Creedence Clearwater Revival* (Chicago: Chicago Review Press/A Cappella Books, 2007), 289.

10. "About the Songwriters Hall of Fame," http://www.songwritershalloffame.org/about/1001 (January 19, 2012).

11. Statement honoring Fogerty's induction into the Songwriters' Hall of Fame, June 2005, http://www.songwritershalloffame.org/ceremony/C3126 (January 19, 2012).

12. *DigitalDreamDoor.com*, "100 Greatest Lyricists of Rock 'n' Roll," http://www.digitaldreamdoor.com/pages/best_lyricists.html (February 26, 2012).

13. Bruce Springsteen, induction speech, Rock and Roll Hall of Fame ceremonies 1993, qtd. in Bordowitz, 256

14. Bruce Springsteen, introducing John Fogerty at a performance at the Rock and Roll Hall of Fame 25th Anniversary Concert, Madison Square Gardens, NYC, October 2009.

15. Springsteen is not the only one to invoke this comparison. In a 1985 *Time* magazine article, Jay Cocks made the same analogy among several to describe Fogerty's all-round ability: "He [Fogerty] was, in short, a great American songwriter with the clean-cut narrative gifts of Chuck Berry, the honesty of a Hank Williams, and the rave-up musical skills of a perfesser in a Saturday night juke joint." Jay Cocks, "Music: High Tide on the Green River," *Time*, January 28, 1985, 78.

16. "100 Greatest Singers of All Time," *Rolling Stone* http://www.rollingstone.com/music/lists/100-greatest-singers-of-all-time-19691231/john-fogerty-19691231 (February 26, 2012).

17. "100 Greatest Singers of All Time—John Fogerty," *Rolling Stone*, http://www.rollingstone.com/music/lists/100-greatest-singers-of-all-time-19691231/john-fogerty-19691231#ixzz1rmVqxM9V (February 26, 2012).

18. Marsh, 25. Elsewhere in the same book, Marsh compares Fogerty, "pop music's … greatest fatalist," to Phil Spector as pop's "truest romantic" and Roy Orbison as its "ultimate stoic" (19).

19. Roland Barthes, "The Grain of the Voice," in *Image, Music, Text*, trans. Stephen Heath (New York: Hill and Wang, 1977), 179–89.

20. Marsh, 89.

21. David Cavanagh, "Bad Blood Rising: Creedence Clearwater Revival," *Uncut*, February 2012, 46.

22. "100 Greatest Guitarists," *DigitalDreamDoor.com*, http://www.digital dreamdoor.com/pages/best_guitar-all.html (April 28, 2012).

23. "100 Greatest Rock Guitarists," *DigitalDreamDoor.com*, http://www.digital dream door.com/pages/best_newguitar.html (April 28, 2012).

24. Cavanagh, 49.

25. "100 Greatest Guitarists of All Time: David Fricke's Picks." *Rolling Stone*, http://www.rollingstone.com/music/lists/100-greatest-guitarists-of-all-time-19691231 (February 8, 2012).

26. "100 Greatest Guitarists of All Time—John Fogerty," *Rolling Stone*, http://www.rollingstone.com/music/lists/100-greatest-guitarists-of-all-time-19691231/john-fogerty-19691231 (February 8, 2012).

27. Michael Goldberg, "Fortunate Son," *Rolling Stone*, February 4, 1993, http://riverrising.tripod.com/john-interviews/rollingstone3.html (May 27, 2012).

28. "100 Greatest Rock Guitar Riffs," *DigitalDreamDoor.com*, http://www.digital dreamdoor.com/pages/best_guitarriff.html. "Fortunate Son" ranks #146 on the list of the Top 200 riffs (note that *DigitalDreamDoor* lists rarely stop at 100, irrespective of what the title promises); "Proud Mary" sits at #169. Of course, "Smoke on the Water" is #1! (March 3, 2012).

29. Cocks, 78.

30. John Fogerty, interviewed by Edna Gundersen, "With *Blue Moon Swamp*, a John Fogerty Revival," *USA Today*, May 19, 1997, qtd. in Bordowitz, 266.

31. Jeffrey Pepper Rogers, "John Fogerty," *Acoustic Guitar*, http://www.acguitar .com/articles/default.aspx?articleid=25309 (March 1, 2012).

32. Glen Boyd, "Music Review: John Fogerty—*Revival*," Blogcritics, September 9, 2007, 1-2, http://blogcritics.org/music/article/music-review-john-fogerty-revival (May 27, 2012).

33. Boyd, 2.

34. Dave White, "CD Review: The revival of John Fogerty," http://classicrock .about.com/od/artistsgm/fr/fogerty_revival.htm (May 27, 2012).

35. "John Fogerty's Road Home," *Wall Street Journal*, December 16, 2005.

36. Cavanagh, 48.

37. "Once Creedence signed, everyone else jumped in line and all the other big acts came on." CCR drummer Doug Clifford in Ken Levy, "Stricken from the Record." *San Francisco Examiner*, August 9, 1994, qtd. in Bordowitz, 64.

38. Pete Fornatale, "Woodstock 1969: High Times." *Guitar World*, September 15, 2009. http://www.guitarworld.com/woodstock-1969-high-times?page=0,3 (February 9, 2012).

39. Bordowitz, 268.

40. See Bordowitz, for example.

41. Cavanagh, 46.

42. David Hinckley, "Still Rockin' Our World: Fogerty's Concert Is on PBS," *New York Daily News*, May 13, 2006, http://articles.newyorkdailynews.com/2006-05-13/ entertainment/18334384_1_songs-blue-moon-nights-long-road-home (May 30, 2012).

43. Bordowitz, 280.

44. The full title of the CD release was *The Promise—The Lost Sessions: Darkness on the Edge of Town* (Sony Music, 2010).

45. BMI (Broadcast Music Industry) Icons are selected for their "unique and indelible influence on generations of music makers." As a BMI Icon, Fogerty joined ranks that include Gamble & Huff, Kris Kristofferson, the Jacksons, the Bee Gees, Paul Simon, Brian Wilson, Willie Nelson, James Brown, Carlos Santana, and Dolly Parton, among others. "John Fogerty named BMI Icon at 58th Annual BMI Pop Music Awards," http://www.bmi.com/news/entry/548139 (November 23, 2011).

46. See especially reports of Fogerty's former bandmates' assessments of his managerial and contract-negotiation skills in Bordowitz, *passim*, and Cavanagh, 54–55.

Bibliography

"Affective Key Characteristics." *Music Theory*. From Christian Schubart, *Ideen zu einer Aesthetik der Tonkunst*, 1806. Translated by Rita Steblin. http://www.wmich .edu/mus-theo/courses/keys.html (March 1, 2012).

Alfano, Sean. "John Fogerty's Musical Revival." John Blackstone, interviewer. *CBS Sunday Morning*, February 11, 2009, http://www.cbsnews.com/2100-3445_162 -1075791.html?pageNum=3&tag=contentMain;contentBody.

Altman, Chris. "Sketching to Create Meaning: The Story of a Second-Language Learner." *English Journal* 97, no. 5 (2008): 64–68.

Altschuler, Glenn C. *All Shook Up: How Rock 'n' Roll Changed America*. New York: Oxford University Press, 2003.

Anatomy of a Hit. Directed by Richard Moore. Ralph Gleason/KQED, 1963.Television.

Augustine, Saint. *Confessions*. 397–398 A.D. Translated by Henry Chadwick. New York and Oxford: Oxford University Press, 1998.

Azerrad, Michael. *Our Band Could Be Your Life: Scenes from the American Indie Underground 1981–1991*. Boston: Back Bay, 2002.

Bangs, Lester. "The British Invasion." In *The Rolling Stone Illustrated History of Rock and Roll*, eds. Anthony DeCurtis and James Henke, with Holly George-Warren, 199–208. New York: Random House, 1992.

——. *Psychotic Reactors and Carburetor Dung*. New York: Alfred A. Knopf, 1988.

Barbaro, Michael. "Santorum Makes Case for Religion in Public Sphere." *New York Times* February 27, 2012, A1.

Barrows, Cliff, Donald Hustad, and William Franklin Graham. *Crusader Hymns and Hymn Stories: Crusade Hymn Stories*. Minneapolis: Billy Graham Evangelistic Association, 1967.

Barthes, Roland. "The Grain of the Voice." In *Image, Music, Text*, trans. Stephen Heath, 179–89. New York: Hill and Wang, 1977.

———. "Theory of the Text." In *Untying the Text: A Post-Structuralist Reader*, ed. Robert Young, 31-47. London: Routledge, 1981.

Bauder, David. "Fogerty is back with Fantasy." Associated Press, October 28, 2005, http://news.google.com/newspapers?nid=1298&dat=20051028&id=ZzEzAAAAI BAJ&sjid=1AgGAAAAIBAJ&pg=6699,8381401.

Bellah, Robert N. *Beyond Belief: Essays on Religion in a Post-Traditionalist World*. Berkeley: University of California Press, 1991.

———. "Civil Religion in America." *Daedalus* 96, no.1 (Winter 1967): 1–21.

Bendix, Reinhard. *Max Weber: An Intellectual Portrait*. Berkeley: University of California Press, 1977.

Bercovitch, Sacvan. *The American Jeremiad*. Madison: University of Wisconsin Press, 1978.

Beschizza, Rob. "Compact Disc Is 25 Years Old." *Wired.com*, August 18, 2007, http://www.wired.com/gadgetlab/2007/08/compact-disk-is/.

Bono. Introduction to *The Book of Psalms*. Edinburgh: Canongate, 1999.

Bordowitz, Hank. *Bad Moon Rising: The Unauthorized History of Creedence Clearwater Revival*. Chicago: Chicago Review Press/A Cappella Books, 2007.

Bottege, Brian A., Enrique Rueda, Timothy S. Grant, Ana C. Stephens, and Perry T. Laroque. "Anchoring Problem-Solving and Computation Instruction in Context-Rich Learning Environments." *Exceptional Children* 76, no. 1 (2010): 417–37.

Boyd, Glen. "Music Review: John Fogerty—*Revival*." Blogcritics, September 9, 2007, 1–2, http://blogcritics.org/music/article/music-review-john-fogerty-revival (May 27, 2012).

Bradley, Dick. *Understanding Rock 'n' Roll: Popular Music in Britain, 1955–1964*. Buckingham, UK: Open University Press, 1992.

Brogan, Daniel. "Getting Past John Fogerty." *Creem*, January 1987, 7.

Brokaw, Tom. *The Greatest Generation*. New York: Random House, 1998.

Broven, John. *Record Makers and Breakers: Voices of the Independent Rock 'n' Roll Pioneers*. Champaign: University of Illinois Press, 2009.

Brown, Mark. "Q&A with John Fogerty."*Rocky Mountain News*, September 29, 2007, http://m.rockymountainnews.com/news/2007/Sep/29/qa-with-john-fogerty/.

Brueggemann, Walter. *The Message of the Psalms: A Theological Commentary*. Minneapolis, MN: Fortress, 1985.

Bull, Bart. "Reborn on the Bayou." *Spin*, June 1985, 20–22.

Burridge, Kenelm. *New Heaven, New Earth: A Study of Millenarian Activities*. London: Blackwell, 1980.

Butler, Mike. "John Fogerty Rolls Backs the Years." *Metro*, May 23, 2012, http://www.metro.co.uk/metrolife/183900-john-fogerty-rolls-back-the-years#ixzz1xYGsdUhq.

"California Labor Code Section 2855 and Recording Artists' Contracts." *Harvard Law Review* 116, no. 8 (June 2003): 2632.

Carter, Steven. "The Beatles and Freshman English." *College Composition and Communication* 20 (1969): 228–32.

Carter, Terri, C. A. Hardy, and James C. Hardy. "Latin Vocabulary Acquisition: An Experiment Using Information-Processing Techniques of Chunking and Imagery." *Journal of Instructional Psychology* 28, no. 4 (2001): 225.

Cash, Wilbur J. *The Mind of the South.* New York: Alfred A. Knopf, 1940.

Caswell, Roger. "A Musical Journey through John Steinbeck's 'The Pearl': Emotion, Engagement, and Comprehension." *Journal of Adolescent and Adult Literacy* 49, no. 1 (2005): 62–67.

Cavanagh, David. "Bad Blood Rising: Creedence Clearwater Revival." *Uncut*, February 2012, 44–55.

Chambers, Iain. *Urban Rhythms: Pop Music and Popular Culture.* New York: St. Martin's Press, 1985.

Christgau, Robert. "Christgau Consumer Guide." *Creem*, February 1987: 21.

Cocks, Jay. "Music High Tide on the Green River," *Time*, January 28, 1985, 78.

Cohen, Debra Rae. "Creedence Clearwater's Revival's Rock & Roll: It's a Gift." *Rolling Stone*, June 11, 1981, 55.

Coleman, Rick. *Blue Monday: Fats Domino and the Lost Dawn of Rock 'n' Roll.* Cambridge, MA: Da Capo Press, 2006.

Collis, Clark. "John Fogerty Talks about Being Honored by the Baseball Hall of Fame—and Having George W. Bush as a Fan." *Music Mix*, May 2010, http://music-mix.ew.com/2010/05/25/john-fogerty-centerfield-baseball (May 19, 2011).

Colman, Stuart. *The Kept on Rockin': The Giants of Rock 'n' Roll.* Poole, Dorset, UK: Blandford Press, 1982.

Cooper, B. Lee. "Architects of the New Orleans Sound, 1946–2006: A Bio-Bibliography," *Popular Music and Society* 30, no. 2 (May 2008): 121–61.

———. "Charting Cultural Change, 1953–1957: Song Assimilation through Cover Recording." In *Play It Again: Cover Songs in Popular Music*, ed. George Plasketes, 43–76, Burlington, VT: Ashgate, 2010.

———. "Repeating Hit Tunes, A Cappella Style: The Persuasions as Song Revivalists, 1967–1982." *Popular Music and Society* 13 (Fall 1989): 17–27.

———, and Jim Creeth. "Present at the Creation: The Legend of Jerry Lee Lewis on Record, 1956–1963." *JEMF Quarterly* 70 (Summer 1983): 122–29.

———, and Verdan D. Traylor. "Establishing Rock Standards: The Practice of Record Revivals in Contemporary Music, 1953–1977." *Goldmine*, May 1979, 37–38.

Cooper, Laura E., and B. Lee Cooper. "The Pendulum of Cultural Imperialism: Popular Music Interchanges between the United States and Great Britain, 1943–1967." In *Kazaaam! Splat! Ploof! The American Impact on European Popular Culture Since 1945*, eds. Sabrina P. Ramet and Gordana P. Crnkovic, 69–82. Lanham, MD: Rowman and Littlefield, 2003.

Cooper, Peter. "John Fogerty Considers Long Career, Nashville's Influence." *The Tennessean* Nov. 19, 2009, http://blogs.tennessean.com/tunein/2009/11/19/john-fogerty-considers-long-career-nashvilles-influence/.

Cook, Stu. E-mail message to Hank Bordowitz, 1996.

Copeland, Matt, and Chris Goering. "Blues You Can Use: Teaching the Faust Theme through Music, Literature, and Film." *Journal of Adolescent and Adult Literacy* 46, no. 5 (2003): 436–41.

"Creedence & Run-DMC Top NARM Best Sellers at Independent Confab." *Variety*, November 4, 1987, 71.

"Creedence's Fogerty to Revive Career." *Rolling Stone*, July 7, 1983, 41.

Crèvecoeur, J. Hector "What Is an American?" *Letters from an American Farmer*, 1782, xroads.virginia.edu/letters from an American farmer.

Crowe, Cameron. "John's Clearwater Credo: Proud Fogerty Post-Creedence." *Rolling Stone*, May 6, 1976, 8+.

Davies, Phil. "Tom Fogerty." In *This Is My Story*, 1993, http://www.rockabilly.nl/references/messages/tom_fogerty.htm (June 18, 2012).

DeCurtis, Anthony. "Fogerty eyes the apocalypse." *Rolling Stone*, November 20, 1986, 121+.

———. "John Fogerty Is Closer to Peace with a Label." *New York Times*, November 1, 2005, E1.

Deming, Mark. "Have You Ever Seen the Rain?" *AllMusic*, May 23, 2012, http://www.allmusic.com/song/have-you-ever-seen-the-rain-mt0001027618.

Dettmar, Kevin J. H., and William Richey, eds. *Reading Rock and Roll: Authenticity, Appropriation, Aesthetics*. New York: Columbia University Press, 1999.

Dickinson, Gail and Emily J. Summers. "(Re)Anchored, Video-Centered Engagement: The Transferability of Preservice Training to Practice." *Contemporary Issues in Technology and Teacher Education* 10 no. 1 (2010): 106–18.

DiMartino, Dave. *Singer-Songwriters: Pop Music's Performer-Composers, from A to Zevon*. New York: Billboard Books, 1994.

Doerschuk, Robert L., ed. *Playing from the Heart: Great Musicians Talk about Their Craft*. San Francisco: Backbeat Books, 2002.

Doggett, Peter. "The British Invasion." *Record Collector*, February 1989, 19–22.

———. "Creedence Clearwater Revival." *Record Collector*, November 1981, 24–32.

———. "Creedence Clearwater Revival." *Record Collector*, October 1987, 61–64.

Dulles, John Foster. "Dulles Cautions Europe to Ratify Army Treat Soon." *New York Times*, December 15, 1953, 14.

Durham, David L. *California's Geographic Names: A Gazetteer of Historic and Modern Names of the State*. Sanger, CA: Quill Driver Books, 1998.

Dylan, Bob. *Chronicles, Volume One*. New York: Simon and Schuster, 2004.

Ebeling, Richard M. "What Makes an American?" *The Future of Freedom Foundation: Freedom Daily*, May 2001, www.fff.org/freedom.

Eder, Bruce. "Britain before the Beatles: Guys Named Cliff, Tommy, Adam, and Billy." *Goldmine*, June 12, 1992, 50+.

Edmonds, Ben. "The Velvet Underground." In *All Yesterday's Parties: The Velvet Underground in Print 1966–1971*, ed. Clinton Heylin, 211–19. Cambridge, MA: Da Capo, 2006.

Eisenhower, Dwight David. "The Chance for Peace." Speech. April 16, 1953, http://www.presidency.ucsb.edu/ws/index.php?pid=9819#axzz1rf3YPqdP (April 12, 2012).

Elliott, Janine. "Summarizing with Drawings: A Reading-Comprehension Strategy." *Science Scope* 30, no. 5 (2007) 26–31.

Elson, Howard. *Early Rockers*. New York: Proteus Books, 1982.

Ennis, Philip. *The Seventh Stream: The Emergence of Rocknroll in American Popular Music*. Hanover, NH: Wesleyan University Press, 1992.

Erlewine, Stephen Thomas. Rev. of *Blue Moon Swamp*. AllMusic, May 23, 2012, http://www.allmusic.com/album/blue-moon-swamp-mw0000022155.

———. Rev. of *Revival*. AllMusic, May 23, 2012, http://www.allmusic.com/album/revival-mw0000484972.

———. Rev. of *Willy and the Poor Boys*. Allmusic, November 1, 2004, http://www.allmusic.com/album/willy-and-the-poor-boys-mw0000193432.

Escott, Colin, ed., *All Roots Lead to Rock: Legends of Early Rock 'n' Roll*. New York: Schirmer Books, 1999.

———. *Good Rockin' Tonight: Sun Records and the Birth of Rock 'n' Roll*. New York: St. Martin's Press, 1991.

———. *Roadkill on the Three-Chord Highway: Art and Trash in American Popular Music*. New York: Routledge, 2002.

———. *Tattooed on Their Tongues: A Journey through the Backrooms of American Music*. New York: Schirmer Books, 1996.

Eskow, John. "Christina Aguilera and the Hideous Cult of Oversouling." *Huffington Post*, February 8, 2011, http://www.huffingtonpost.com/john-eskow/christina-aguilera-and-th_b_819979.html.

Feuer, Lewis Samuel. *The Conflict of Generations: The Character and Significance of Student Movements*. New York: Basic Books, 1969.

Fielder, Leslie A. *Love and Death in the American Novel*. New York: Criterion, 1960.

Fogerty, Bob. Interview by Hank Bordowitz, 1997.

"Fogerty Performs Centerfield, 7/25/10." *MLB.com*. "Baseball Video Highlights & Clips." http://mlb.mlb.com/video/play.jsp?content_id=10264413 7/25/10.

Fogerty, Tom. Interview by Hank Bordowitz, 1981.

Fong-Torres, Ben. *The Hits Just Keep on Coming: The History of Top 40 Radio*. San Francisco: Miller Freeman Books, 1998.

Fontenot, Robert "Top 10 Patriotic Oldies." *About.com*, http://oldies.about.com/od/buyersguides/tp/patrioticoldies.htm (May 21, 2011).

Fontichiaro, Kristin. "Nudging Toward Inquiry: Awakening and Building upon Prior Knowledge." *School Library Monthly* 27, no. 1 (2009): 12–13.

Fornatale, Pete. *Back to the Garden: The Story of Woodstock and How It Changed a Generation*. New York: Touchstone, Simon and Schuster, 2009.

———. "Woodstock 1969: High Times." *Guitar World*, September 15, 2009, http://www.guitarworld.com/woodstocl-1969-high-times?page=0,3.

Forte, Dan, with Steve Soest. "John Fogerty Returns." *Guitar Player*, April 1985, 54+.

"Fortunate Son Meaning." *Shmoop*. http://www.shmoop.com/fortunate-son/meaning .html (June 25, 2012).

"The Fortunate Son Returns." *San Francisco Chronicle*, May 11, 1997, 38.3.

Fox, Pamela, and Barbara Ching, eds. *Old Roots, New Routes: The Cultural Politics of Alt.Country Music*. Ann Arbor: University of Michigan Press, 2008.

Frame, Pete. "British Pop, 1955–1979." *Trouser Press*, June 1983, 30–31.

Freud, Sigmund. *The Uncanny*. 1911. Translated by David McClintock. London and New York: Penguin Modern Classics, 2003.

Frith, Simon. *Sound Effects: Youth, Leisure, and the Politics of Rock 'n' Roll*. New York: Pantheon Books, 1981.

Fulmer, Sara M., and Jan Frijters. "A Review of Self-Report and Alternative Approaches in the Measurement of Student Motivation." *Educational Psychology Review* 21, no. 3 (2009): 219–46.

Gallavan, Nancy P., and Ellen Kottler. *Secrets to Success for Social Studies Teachers*. Thousand Oaks, CA: Corwin Press, 2008.

Garth-McCullough, Ruanda "Untapped Cultural Support: The Influence of Culturally Bound Prior Knowledge on Comprehension Performance." *Reading Horizons* 49 no. 1 (2008): 1–30.

George-Warren, Holly, and Patricia Romanowski, eds. *The Rolling Stone Encyclopedia of Rock and Roll*. 3rd edition. New York: Fireside Books/ Rolling Stone Press, 2001.

Gill, Sharon R. "The Comprehension Matrix: A Tool for Designing Comprehension Instruction." *The Reading Teacher* 62, no. 2 (2011): 106–13.

Gillett, Charlie. *The Sound of the City: The Rise of Rock and Roll*. 2nd edition. New York: Da Capo Press, 1996.

Gleason, Ralph J. "John Fogerty: The Rolling Stone Interview." *Rolling Stone*, February 21, 1970, 17–24.

Goering, Christian Z. "Music and the Personal Narrative: The Dual Track to Meaningful Writing." *The Quarterly* 26, no. 4 (2004): 11–17.

———. "Open Books, Open Ears, and Open Minds: The Grapes of Wrath, the 'Broken Plow,' and the *LitTunes* Approach." In *Dialogue: Reflections on Steinbeck's The Grapes of Wrath*, Ed. Michael J. Meyer, 801–17. Amsterdam, Netherlands: Rodopi. 2009.

Goering, Christian Z. and Bradley J. Burenheide. "Exploring the Role of Music in Secondary English and History Classrooms through Personal Practical Theory." *SRATE Journal* 19, no.2 (2010): 44–51.

Goering, Christian Z., Katherine Collier, Scott Koenig, John O. O'berski, Stephanie Pierce, & Kelly Riley. "Musical Intertextuality in Action: A Directed Reading of *Of Mice and Men*. In *The Essential Criticism of Of Mice and Men*. Ed. Michael J. Meyer. Lanham, MD: Scarecrow, 2009.

Goering, Christian Z. and Cindy Williams. "A Soundtrack Approach to Teaching *To Kill a Mockingbird*." In *Harper Lee's To Kill a Mockingbird: New Essays on an American Classic*. Ed. Michael J. Meyer, 36–53. Lanham, MD: Scarecrow, 2010.

Goldberg, Michael. "Fogerty Returns to the Stage," *Rolling Stone*, March 14, 1985, 12+.

———. "Fogerty wins unusual self-plagiarism suit," *Rolling Stone*, January 12, 1989, 15.

———. "Fortunate Son." *Rolling Stone*, February 4, 1993, 46–48+.

———. "John Fogerty alters album: 'Zanz' becomes 'Vanz.'" *Rolling Stone*, March 28, 1985, 34.

———. "On the Road Again," *Rolling Stone*, October 9, 1986, 24, 26.

Goodall, Jr., H. L. *Living in the Rock N Roll Mystery: Reading Context, Self, and Others as Clues*. Carbondale: Southern Illinois University Press, 1991.

Goodwin, Ana Parker. "Seven Reasons for Writer's Block." *Bitterroot Mountain*, Oct. 26, 2009, www.bitterrootmountainllc.com.

Gundersen, Edna. "With *Blue Moon Swamp*, a John Fogerty Revival." *USA Today*, May 19, 1997.

Guralnick, Peter. *Last Train to Memphis: The Rise of Elvis Presley*. Boston: Little, Brown and Company, 1994.

———. *Lost Highway: Journeys and Arrivals of American Musicians*. 1979. Boston: Back Bay Books/ Little, Brown, and Company, 1999.

Guthrie, William P. *The Later Thirty Years War: From the Battle of Wittstock to the Treaty of Westphalia*. New York: Greenwood, 2003.

Hailikari, Telle, Nina Katajavuori, and Sari Lindblom-Ylanne. "The Relevance of Prior Knowledge in Learning and Instructional Design." *American Journal of Pharmaceutical Education* 72, no. 5 (2008): 1–5.

Hajdu, David. "Forever Young? In Some Ways, Yes." *New York Times*, May 24, 2011, A25.

Hannusch, Jeff. *I Hear You Knockin': The Sounds of New Orleans Rhythm and Blues*. Ville Platte, LA: Swallow Press, 1985.

———. *The Soul of New Orleans: A Legacy of Rhythm and Blues*. Ville Platte, LA: Swallow Press, 2001.

Haymes, Max. *Railroadin' Some: Railroads in the Early Blues*. Eden Prairie, MN: Gazelle Distribution, 2006.

Hendler, Herb. *Year by Year in the Rock Era: Events and Conditions Shaping the Rock Generations That Reshaped America*. Westport, CT: Greenwood Press, 1983.

Henke, James. "John Fogerty." *Rolling Stone*, November 5, 1987: 146+.

High Fidelity. Dir. Stephen Frears. Working Title Films/Touchstone Pictures, 2000.

Hilburn, Robert. "Fogerty's Nightmare Is Over." *Los Angeles Times*, January 6, 1985: 54.

———. "Q&A with John Fogerty." *Los Angeles Times*, January 12, 1993, http://articles. latimes.com/1993-01-12/entertainment/ca-1226_1_creedence-clearwater-revival.

Hinckley, David. "Still Rockin' Our World: Fogerty's Concert Is on PBS." *New York Daily News*, May 13, 2006, http://articles.newyorkdailynews.com/2006-05-13/entertainment/ 18334384_1_songs-blue-moon-nights-long-road-home (May 30, 2012).

Hoffman, Ivan. "The Price of Popcorn, the Personal Services Contract." 2006, http:// www.ivanhoffman.com/personal.html (October 25, 2011).

Hollowell, John. *Inside Creedence*. New York: Bantam Books, 1971.

Hornby, Nick. *High Fidelity*. London: Victor Gollancz, 1995.

Hoskyns, Barney. *Lowside of the Road: A Life of Tom Waits*. New York: Broadway, 2009.

Hurwitz, Matt. "Classic Tracks: Creedence Clearwater Revival 'Fortunate Son.'" *Mix Magazine: Professional Audio and Music Production*, March 1, 2009, http://mixonline.com/recording/tracking/classic-tracks-creedence-clearwater-revival-fortunate//index1.html, 2.

Innes, Brian. "Clubs and Coffee Bars: Where Britain's Teenagers Found the New Music." *History of Rock* 7 (1982): 132–34.

Isler, Scott. "Fogerty vs. Fogerty." *Musician*, February 1989, 12+.

———. "John Fogerty's Triumph over Evil." *Musician*, March 1985, 32+.

Jacobson, Jeffery. E-mail message to Hank Bordowitz. November 24, 2011.

Jaffee, Larry. "K-Tel's Place in the Music Industry: Where Have All the One-Hit Wonders Gone?" *Popular Music and Society* 10, no. 4 (1986): 43–50, http://www.rocksbackpages.com/article.html?ArticleID=19219.

James, Etta. Interview by Hank Bordowitz, 1988.

James, Gary. "Gary James' Interview with Doug Clifford of Creedence Clearwater Revival." *Classicbands.com*, http://www.classicbands.com/CCRInterview.html (April 24, 2012).

Jekielek, Jon, and Ira Scott Meyerowitz. "Unreasonable Duration of Recording Agreement." *MJlawfirm.com*. February 18, 2009, http://mjlawfirm.com/entertainment-law/unreasonable-duration-of-recording-agreements/ (October 25, 2011).

Jewitt, Carey. "Multimodal Reading and Writing on Screen." *Discourse: Studies in the Cultural Politics of Education*. 26, no. 3 (2005): 315–32.

"Job Performance Ratings for President Reagan." Roper Center: Public Opinion Archives, http://webapps.ropercenter.uconn.edu/CFIDE/roper/presidential/webroot/presidential_rating_detail.cfm?allRate=True&presidentName=Reagan (May 2, 2011).

"John Fogerty Named BMI Icon at 58th Annual BMI Pop Music Awards." http://www.bmi.com/news/entry/548139 (November 23, 2011).

"John Fogerty Quotes." http://www.brainyquote.com/quotes/authors/j/john_fogerty.html (April 24, 2012).

"John Fogerty Revisiting Creedence Hits on New Duets Set." *KHITS96 Classic Hits*, http://www.k-hits.com/musicnews/Story.aspx?ID=1681428 (April 4, 2012).

Jones, Allan. "Centre Points." *Melody Maker* February 2, 1985.

Kelly, Michael Bryan. *The Beatle Myth: The British Invasion of American Popular Music, 1956-1969*. Jefferson, North Carolina: McFarland, 1991.

Kelin, Joshua. "John Fogerty." *Pitchfork*, November 27, 2007, http://pitchfork.com/features/interviews/6737-john-fogerty.

Kemp, Mark. *Dixie Lullabye: A Story of Music, Race and Beginnings in a New South*. New York: The Free Press, 2004.

Kennedy, John F. "An Address to the Greater Houston Ministerial Association." Speech, September 12, 1960, http://www.npr.org/templates/story/story.php?storyId=16920600 (April 10, 2012).

King, Jr., Martin Luther. "Beyond Vietnam." Speech, Riverside Church, NY, April 4, 1967. *Information Clearing House*. http://www.informationclearinghouse.info/article2564.htm (April 10, 2012).

———. "How Long." Speech, Montgomery, AL, March 25, 1965. http://www.youtube
.com/watch?v=TAYITODNvlM (March 1, 2012).

———. "I Have a Dream." Speech, Washington, D.C., August 28, 1963. In *A Testament of Hope: The Essential Writings of Martin Luther King, Jr.*, ed. James M. Washington, 217–20. New York: Harper and Row, 1986.

Kissner, Emily. "How Do We Know What We Know? A Look at Schemas." *Science Scope* 33, no.1 (2009): 48–50.

Klein, Joshua. "Interviews: John Fogerty." *Pitchfork*, November 27, 2007, pitchfork
.com/features/interviews John Fogerty.

Koch, Adrienne, ed. *The American Enlightenment: The Shaping of the American Experiment and a Free Society.* "Letter from John Adams to Count Sarsfield," February 3, 1786. New York: George Braziller, Inc., 1965.

Kristeva, Julia. "'Nous Deux' or a (Hi)story of Intertextuality." *The Romanic Review* 93, no. 1–2 (2002): 7–13.

Landau, Jon. Rev. of *Mardi Gras. Rolling Stone*, May 25, 1972, 63.

Lawrence, Mark Atwood. *The Vietnam War: A Concise International History.* New York: Oxford University Press, 2010.

Lazell, Barry, with Dafydd Rees and Luke Crampton, eds. *Rock Movers and Shakers.* New York: Billboard Books, 1989.

Lena, Jennifer C., and Richard A. Peterson. "Classification As Culture: Types and Trajectories of Music Categories." *American Sociological Review* 73 (October 2008): 697–718.

Levitin, Daniel J. "Blue Moon Rising: The John Fogerty Interview." *Audio Magazine*, January 1998, 1–12.

Levy, Ken. "Stricken from the Record." *San Francisco Examiner*, August 9, 1994.

Lewis, R. W. B. *The American Adam: Innocence, Tragedy and Tradition in the Nineteenth Century.* Chicago: University of Chicago Press, 1965.

Light, Alan. "Stars Add New Tunes to Country King's Lyrics." *New York Times*, September 23, 2011, http://www.nytimes.com/2011/09/25/arts/music/bob-dylan
-assembles-the-lost-notebooks-of-hank-williams.html?pagewanted=all.

Lipsitz, George. *Time Passages: Collective Memory And American Popular Culture.* Minneapolis: University of Minnesota Press, 1990.

Loder, Kurt. "Fogerty Still Hits with Power." Rev. of *Centerfield. Rolling Stone*, January 31, 1985: 47–48.

Lomax, John Avery and Alan Lomax. *American Ballads and Folk Songs.* Mineola, New York: Courier and Dover Publications, 1994.

Lydon, Michael, and Ellen Mandel. *Boogie Lightning: How the Music Became Electric.* New York: Da Capo Press, 1980.

———. *Rock Folk: Portraits from the Rock 'n' Roll Pantheon.* New York: Dial Press, 1971.

Marcus, Greil. *Invisible Republic: Bob Dylan's Basement Tapes.* New York: Henry Holt, 1997, reprinted as *The Old, Weird America: The World of Bob Dylan's Basement Tapes.*

———. *Mystery Train: Images of America in Rock 'n' Roll Music.* 5th ed. New York: Plume/ Penguin Books, 2008.

———. *Ranters and Crowd Pleasers: Punk in Pop Music*. New York: Doubleday, 1993.

Marsh, Dave. *The Heart of Rock & Soul: The 1001 Greatest Singles Ever Made*. New York: New American Library, 1989.

———. "Where Has John Fogerty Gone?" *Musician, Player, and Listener*, April 1981, 12–13.

Martin, Linda, and Kerry Segrave. *Anti-Rock: The Opposition to Rock 'n' Roll*. Hamden, CT: Archon Books, 1988.

Marx, Leo. *The Machine in the Garden: Technology and the American Ideal in America*. New York: Oxford University Press, 1964.

Matsumoto, Jon. "Where Did the Rest of Creedence Go?" *Los Angeles Times*, January 6, 1985: 55.

Matthews, Mitford M., ed. *A Dictionary of Americanisms*. Chicago: University of Chicago Press, 1951.

Mazor, Barry. "John Fogerty Twangs Again." *Wall Street Journal*, September 29, 2009. http://online.wsj.com/article/SB10001424052970203440104574402840540253868.html.

MCA Records, Inc. Plaintiff and Respondent v. Olivia Newton-John, Defendent and Appellant. Civ. No. 54177, March 2, 1979, Court of Appeal of California, Second Appellate District, Division Two, LexisNexis.

McCullaugh, Jim. "Claymation Creator Molds Fogerty Clip." *Billboard*, July 13, 1985. *Billboard Archives*, http://www.billboard.com/archive#/achive.

McDaniel, Elias. "Bo Diddley." Interview by Hank Bordowitz, 1996.

McDougal, Dennis. "The Trials of John Fogerty Singer, Executive Locked in Decade-Old Legal Feud." *Los Angeles Times*, November 15, 1988: 1.

McNutt, Randy. *Guitar Towns: A Journey to the Crossroads of Rock 'n' Roll*. Bloomington: Indiana University Press, 2002.

Mead, Margaret. *Culture and Commitment: A Study of the Generation Gap*. Garden City, NY: American Museum of Natural History Press, 1970.

Milburn, Michael. "Selling Shakespeare." *The English Journal* 92, no. 1 (2002): 74–79.

Miller, James. *Flowers in the Dustbin: The Rise of Rock and Roll, 1947–1977*. New York: Simon and Schuster, 1999.

Miller, Jim. "Another Clearwater Revival." *Newsweek*, February 18, 1985: 89.

Moore, Allan, ed. *The Cambridge Companion to Blues and Gospel Music*. Cambridge: Cambridge University Press, 2002.

Morrell, Ernest, and Jeffrey M. R. Duncan-Andrade. "Promoting Academic Literacy with Urban Youth through Hip-Hop Culture." *English Journal* 91, no. 6 (2002): 88–92.

Morrison, Craig. *Go Cat Go! Rockabilly Music and Its Makers*. Champaign: University of Illinois Press, 1996.

Music Outfitters. http://www.musicoutfitters.com/ (February 3, 2012).

Neuhaus, Richard John. *The Naked Public Square*. Grand Rapids: Eerdmans, 1984.

Olsen, Eric. "Huge Jazz News: Concord Buys Fantasy." *BC Music*, December 2, 2004, http://blogcritics.org/music/article/huge-jazz-news-concord-buys-fantasy/.

"100 Greatest Guitarists." *DigitalDreamDoor.com*, http://www.digitaldreamdoor.com/pages/best_guitar-all.html (April 28, 2012).

"100 Greatest Guitarists of All Time—John Fogerty." *Rolling Stone*, http://www.rollingstone.com/music/lists/100-greatest-guitarists-of-all-time-19691231/john-fogerty-19691231 (February 8, 2012).

"100 Greatest Lyricists of Rock 'n' Roll." *DigitalDreamDoor.com*, http://www.digitaldreamdoor.com/pages/best_lyricists.html (February 26, 2012).

"100 Greatest Rock Guitarists." *DigitalDreamDoor.com*, http://www.digitaldreamdoor.com/pages/best_newguitar.html (April 28, 2012).

"100 Greatest Rock Guitar Riffs." *DigitalDreamDoor.com*, http://www.digitaldreamdoor.com/pages/best_guitarriff.html. 'Fortunate Son' ranks #146 (March 3, 2012).

"100 Greatest Rock Songwriters." *DigitalDreamDoor.com*, March 3, 2004, last updated, August 23, 2007, http://digitaldreamdoor.com/pages/best_songwriters.html (January 20, 2012).

"100 Greatest Singers of All Time." *Rolling Stone*, http://www.rollingstone.com/music/lists/100-greatest-singers-of-all-time-19691231/john-fogerty-19691231 (February 26, 2012).

"100 Greatest Singers of All Time—John Fogerty." *Rolling Stone*, http://www.rollingstone.com/music/lists/100-greatest-singers-of-all-time-19691231/john-fogerty-19691231#ixzz1rmVqxM9V (February 26, 2012).

Osborne, Jerry. "Creedence Clearwater Revival." *Discoveries* 1 (November 1988): 16–38.

Painter, Diane D. "Providing Differentiated Learning Experiences through Multigenre Projects." *Intervention in School and Clinic* 44, no. 5 (2009): 288–93.

Palao, Alec. "Pre-Creedence: The First Decade." *Creedence Clearwater Revival*. Booklet accompanying box set, 19–34. Fantasy Records, 2001.

Palmer, Robert. "Pop: Show by Fogerty in Memphis." *New York Times*, March 30, 1986, sec. 1, 9.

———. *Rock and Roll: An Unruly History*. New York: Harmony Book, 1995.

Parker, John. "Special Report: Burgeoning Bourgeoisie." *The Economist*, February 12, 2009, http://www.economist.com/node/13063298.

"Paste's 100 Best Living Songwriters." *Paste Magazine.com*, June 5, 2006, http://www.pastemagazine.com/articles/2006/06/pastes-100-best-living-songwriters.html (January 18, 2012).

"Paste's 100 Best Living Songwriters: The Readers' Poll." *Paste Magazine.com*, http://www.pastemagazine.com/action/article/3004/feature/music/pastes_100_best_living_songwriters_the_readers_poll (January 18, 2012).

Pells, Richard. *Not Like Us: How Europeans Have Loved, Hated, and Transformed American Culture since World War II*. New York: Basic Books, 1997.

———. "The Peculiar Generation." *The Chronicle Review* 56 (March 26, 2010): B6–B8.

Peterson, Richard A. "Five Constraints on the Production of Culture: Law, Technology, Market, Organizational Structures, and Occupational Careers." In *American Popular Music—Volume One: The Nineteenth Century to Tin Pan*

Alley, ed. Timothy E. Scheurer, 16-27. Bowling Green, OH: Bowling Green State University Popular Press, 1989.

———. "Why 1955? Explaining the Advent of Rock Music." *Popular Music* 9 (January 1990): 97–116.

Plasketes, George, ed. *Play It Again: Cover Songs In Popular Music*. Burlington, VT: Ashgate, 2010.

Posten, Bruce R. "Will the real Harry Angstrom please stand up?" *readingeagle.com*, February 1, 2009, http://readingeagle.com/article.aspx?id=123669.

"Proud Mary." *All Music Guide*, http://www.allmusic.com/search/track/Proud+Mary/ order:default-asc (October 28, 2011).

"Recording Contract." Creedence Clearwater Revival and Fantasy Records. June 5, 1969.

Redd, Lawrence N. *Rock Is Rhythm and Blues: The Impact of Mass Media*. East Lansing: Michigan State University Press, 1974.

Regan-Porter, Leila. "John Fogerty." In "Paste's 100 Best Living Songwriters: The List," *Paste Magazine.com*, June 5, 2006, http://www.pastemagazine.com/articles/ 2006/07/pastes-100-best-living-songwriters-3140.html (January 18, 2012).

Reich, Charles. *The Greening of America*. New York: Bantam, 1971.

Reilly, Dan. "John Fogerty Calls Obama's Nobel Prize Win 'Amazing and Wonderful.'" *Spinner*. October 12, 2009. http://www.spinner.com/2009/10/12/john -fogerty-calls-obamas-nobel-prize-win-amazing-and-wonderfu.

Reynolds, Simon. *Totally Wired: Postpunk Interviews and Overviews*. New York: Soft Skull, 2010.

Ricoeur, Paul. *Time and Narrative, Volume 2*. Translated by Kathleen McLaughlin and David Pellauer. Chicago and London: University of Chicago Press, 1985.

Rieder, Jonathan. "The Rise of the Silent Majority." In *The Rise and Fall of the New Deal Order*, eds. Steve Fraser and Gary Gerstle, 243–68. Princeton: Princeton University Press, 1989.

Rimler, Walter. *Not Fade Away: A Comparison of Jazz Age with Rock Era Pop Song Composers*. Ann Arbor, Michigan: Pierian Press, 1984.

Rodgers, Jeffrey Pepper. "John Fogerty Interview." *Acoustic Guitar*, January 2010, 1–7.

Romano, Tom. *Blending Genre, Altering Style: Writing Multigenre Papers*. Portsmouth, NH: Boynton/Cook, 2000.

Rome, Adam. *The Bulldozer in the Countryside: Suburban Sprawl and the Rise of American Environmentalism*. New York: Cambridge University Press, 2001.

Rood, George. "Holiday Expands Recording Sales." *New York Times*, Dec. 19, 1965, F12.

Rose, David, ed., *Social Research Update* 9 (July 1995).

Rosen, Steven. "The Popdose Interview: Doug Clifford." *Popdose*, June 23, 2009, http://popdose.com/the-popdose-interview-doug-clifford/ (April 24, 2012).

Rothenberg, Sally S., and Susan Watts. "Students with Learning Difficulties Meet Shakespeare: Using a Scaffolded Reading Experience." *Journal of Adolescent & Adult Literacy* 40, no. 7 (1997): 532–39.

Ruhlmann, William. *Breaking Records: 100 Years of Hits*. New York: Routledge, 2004.

Santoro, Gene. *Dancing in Your Head: Jazz, Blues, Rock, and Beyond*. New York and Oxford: Oxford University Press, 1994.

———. *Highway 61 Revisited: The Tangled Roots of American Jazz, Blues, Rock, and Country Music*. New York: Oxford University Press, 2004.

Scaggs, Austin. "Born on the Bayou: Creedence Clearwater Revival, 1969." In "100 Greatest Guitar Songs," *Rolling Stone*, June 12, 2008, 57.

Schaffner, Nicholas. *The British Invasion: From the First Wave to the New Wave*. New York: McGraw-Hill, 1982.

School District of Abington Township, Pennsylvania V. Schempp. In *Documents of American History, Volume II*, edited by Henry Steele Commager, 678–80. Englewood Cliffs, NJ: Prentice-Hall, 1973.

Schumacher, E.F. *Small Is Beautiful: Economics as if People Mattered*. London: Blond and Briggs, 1973.

Schurk, William L., B. Lee Cooper, and Julie A. Cooper. "Before the Beatles: International Influences on American Popular Recordings, 1940–1963." *Popular Music and Society* 30, no. 2 (May 2007): 227–66.

Scrivani-Tidd, Lisa, Rhonda Markowitz, Chris Smith, Maryann Janosik, and Bob Gulla. *The Greenwood Encyclopedia of Rock History, 1951-2005*. 6 vols. Westport, CT: Greenwood Press, 2006.

Selvin, Joel. "John Fogerty on Threshold of Big Comeback." *San Francisco Chronicle*, January 6, 1985: 17.

Serafino, Kathleen, and Terry Cicchelli. "Cognitive Theories, Prior Knowledge, and Anchored Instruction on Mathematical Problem Solving and Transfer." *Education and Urban Society* 36, no. 1 (2003): 79–93.

Settle, Ken. "Creedence Clearwater Revival: The Bayou and the Backstreets." *Goldmine*, June 8, 1984, 6–18.

Sewell, William C. "Composing with the Man in Black: Using the Music of Johnny Cash to Teach Writing." *LitTunes.com* (June 22, 2012).

Sewell, William C., and Shawn Denton. "Multimodal Literacies in the Secondary English Classroom." *English Journal* 100, no. 5 (2011): 61–65.

Sharp, Ken. "John Fogerty: From the Bayou to Centerfield and Back Again." *Goldmine*, September 15, 2006, 14–19.

Shaw, Arnold. *Honkers and Shouters: The Golden Years of Rhythm and Blues*. New York: Collier Books, 1978.

———. *The Rockin' '50s: The Decade That Transformed the Pop Music Scene*. New York: Haworth Books, 1974.

Sheffield, Rob. "Creedence Clearwater Revival: Green River." *Rolling Stone*. May 11, 2000, 134.

Shumway, David. "Where Have All the Rock Stars Gone?" *The Chronicle of Higher Education*, June 22, 2007, B6–B8.

Shyu, Cindy Hsin-Yih. "Using Video-Based Anchored Instruction to Enhance Learning: Taiwan's Experience." *British Journal of Educational Technology* 31, no. 1 (2000): 57–69.

Skaggs, Merrill. *The Folk of Southern Fiction*. Athens: University of Georgia Press, 1973.

Smith, Ethan. "John Fogerty's Road Home." *Wall Street Journal*, December 16, 2005, 8.

Soocher, Stan. Interview by Hank Bordowitz, November 3, 2011.

Spencer, John Michael. *Blues and Evil*. Knoxville: University of Tennessee Press, 1993.

Springsteen, Bruce. "On Creedence Clearwater Revival." Speech from the Rock and Roll Hall of Fame Induction Ceremony, January 1993. In *The Rock and Roll Hall of Fame: The First 25 Years*, ed. Holly George-Warren, 78–79. New York: Collins, 2009.

"Stargazer in a Puddle." *Bones* (season 2, episode 21, May 16, 2007). TV.

Stebick, Divonna M. "Informational Overload in Content Area Reading: A Professional Development Plan for Middle and High School Teachers." *Journal of Content Area Reading* 7, no. 1 (2008): 87–113.

Steblin, Rita. *A History of Key Characteristics in the 18th and Early 19th Centuries*. Ann Arbor: UMI Research Press, 1983.

Steinblatt, Harold. "Return of the Swamp King." *Guitar World*, January 2008, 92–100.

Steiner, Rudolph. *The Inner Nature of Music and the Experience of Tone: Selected Lectures from the Work of Rudolph Steiner*. London: Rudolph Steiner Press, 1983.

Strauss, Neil. "The Pop Life: A Lurking Album Is Freed." *New York Times*, May 21, 1997, C13.

Strauss, William, and Neil Howe. *The Fourth Turning: An American Prophecy*. New York: Broadway Books, 1997.

———. *Generations: The History of America's Future, 1584 to 2069*. New York: Morrow Books, 1991.

Suddath, Claire. "A Brief History of the Middle Class." *Time*, February 27, 2009, http://www.time.com/time/nation/article/0,8599,1882147,00.html.

Sumrall, Harry. "Creedence Clearwater Revival," In *Pioneers of Rock and Roll*. 70–72. New York: Billboard Books, 1994.

Sutherland, Sam. "Rock Recluse Fogerty Returns." *Billboard*, February 2, 1985, 66–68.

Swenson, John. Rev. of *Centerfield*. *Saturday Review*, March/April 1985, 70.

Takaki, Ronald. *A Different Mirror: A History of Multicultural America*. New York: Little, Brown and Company, 1993.

Theiss, Evelyn. "My Lai photographer Ron Haeberle exposed a Vietnam massacre 40 years ago today in *The Plain Dealer*." *cleveland.com*. November 20, 2009, http://www.cleveland.com/living/index.ssf/2009/11/plain_dealer_published_first_i.html.

Thirty-eight Annual Grammy Awards, Shrine Auditorium. February 28, 1996. Los Angeles, CA, http://www.youtube.com/watch?v=AHEYs0CMe4U.

Thompson, Art. "John Fogerty Summons His Creedence-Era Spirit on Revival." *Guitar Player*, February 2008, 1–9.

Thompson, Dave. *Bayou Underground: Tracing the Mythical Roots of American Popular Music*. Toronto: ECW Press, 2010.

———. "Britain before Rock Was Not a Total Musical Wasteland." *Goldmine*, July 9, 2004, 51, 53.

Thompson, Debra S. "Creating Developmentally Appropriate Curriculum for Young Children: An Integrated Thematic Unit Plan Format." 1993, Microform, ERIC Clearinghouse.

"TK's Factory: 'Born on the Bayou.'" *TK's Factory.* http://www.backonstage.halmstad .net/tk/fogindex.htm (October 31, 2011).

Tobias, Sigmund. "Interest, Prior Knowledge, and Learning." *Review of Educational Research* 64, no. 1 (1994): 37–54.

Tolleson, Robin. "John Fogerty Wins Lawsuit." *Billboard*, January 19, 1988, 71.

Tosches, Nick. *Unsung Heroes of Rock 'n' Roll.* Rev. ed. New York: Da Capo Press, 1999.

Twain, Mark. *The Adventures of Huckleberry Finn.* 1885. New York: Oxford University Press, 2001.

———. *Life on the Mississippi.* 1883. New York: Oxford University Press, 1990.

Updike, John. *Rabbit, Run.* New York: Alfred A. Knopf, 1960.

Walker, Bob. "The Song Decoders." *New York Times Magazine*, October 18, 2009, 48–53.

Walsh, Jim. *The Replacements: All Over but the Shouting.* Minneapolis: Voyageur, 2007.

Walters, Barry. "Creedence: Back to the Bayou." *Rolling Stone*, October 2, 2008, 74.

Weber, Max. "Science as a Vocation." In *From Max Weber: Essays in Sociology.* London: Routledge, 2007.

Weiner, Rex, and Deanne Stillman. *Woodstock Census: The Nationwide Survey of the Sixties Generation.* New York: Viking Press, 1979.

Werner, Craig. "John Fogerty." *Goldmine*, July 18, 1997, 16–19, 38–62.

———. *Up Around the Bend: The Oral History of Creedence Clearwater Revival.* New York: Spike/Avon Books, 1999.

Whitburn, Joel, comp. *Album Cuts, 1955-2001.* Menomonee Falls, WI: Record Research, 2002.

———. *Hot Country Songs, 1944–2008.* Menomonee Falls, WI: Record Research, 2008.

———. *Hot R&B Songs, 1942–2010.* Menomonee Falls, WI: Record Research, 2010.

———. *Top Pop Singles, 1955–2008.* Menomonee Falls, WI: Record Research, 2009.

White, Dave. "CD Review: The Revival of John Fogerty." *About.com Classic Rock*, http://classicrock.about.com/od/artistsgm/fr/fogerty_revival.htm (May 27, 2012).

Wiehardt, Ginny. "Top 10 Tips for Overcoming Writer's Block," *About.com: Fiction Writing*, http://fictionwriting.about.com/o/writingroadblock/tp/block.htm (December 4, 2011).

Williams, Angie. *Intergenerational Communication across the Life Span.* Mahwah, NJ: Lawrence Erlbaum Associates, 2001.

Williams, Roger. "Mr. Cotton's Letter Examined and Answered." 1644. In *The Bloudy Tenent of Persecution, for Cause of Conscience Discussed.* 375. London: Adamant Media, 2005.

Willis, Ellen. "Creedence Clearwater Revival." In *The Rolling Stone Illustrated History of Rock and Roll*, ed. Anthony DeCurtis, James Henke, and Holly George-Warren, 449. New York: Random House, 1992.

———. "Creedence Clearwater Revival." In *The Rolling Stone Illustrated History of Rock and Roll*, ed. Jim Miller, 324-26. New York: Random House/Rolling Stone Press, 1980.

Winthrop, John. "A Model of Christian Charity." 1630. http://religiousfreedom.lib .virginia.edu/sacred/charity.html (May 24, 2012).

Woodward, C. Vann. *Origins of the New South.* 1931. Baton Rouge: Louisiana State University Press, 1971.

Young, Marilyn B. "Now Playing: Vietnam." *OAH Magazine of History* 18, no. 5 (2004): 22–26.

"Zaentz Heads Fantasy Sales."*Billboard*, March 12, 1955, 26.

Zeller, Craig. Rev. of *Eye of the Zombie. Creem*, February 1987, 15–16.

Zheng, Robert. Z., Wanda Yang, Dean Garcia, and Eugene P. McCadden. "Effects of Multimedia and Schema Induced Analogical Reasoning on Science Learning." *Journal of Computer Assisted Learning* 24, no. 6 (2008): 474–82.

Zinn, Howard. *A People's History of the United States: 1492–Present.* New York: HarperCollins, 2003.

~

General Index

Black, Bill, 121
Black 47, xi
Blackstone, John, 30
The Blasters, 75
Blues Image, 75
Blue Moon Swamp (Fogerty), 35, 116, 117, 126, 130, 181, 201, 208
Blue Ridge Rangers (Fogerty), xiv, 35, 101–2, 112, 117, 122, 154, 167
Blue Ridge Rangers Rides Again (Fogerty), 102, 109, 116, 117, 122, 126, 176, 179, 184, 192
The Blue Velvets, xii, 73, 88, 152, 167
Bonham, John, 6
Booker T. & the MGs, 128
The Book of Psalms, 64
Bordowitz, Hank, xv, 85
Born in the U.S.A. (Springsteen), 114
The Bottle Rockets, 82n1
Bowie, David, 20
Boyd, Glen, 203
Brown, Michael, 183, 202
Browne, Jackson, 157, 194
Brubeck, Dave, 88
Bruce, Jack, 6
Bruce, Lenny, 88, 96
Burgess, Sonny, 5
Burning Spear, 119
Burton, James, 18, 200
Bush, George, H. W., 183
Bush, George W., 32, 79, 116, 138, 176, 182–83, 202, 205
Butterfield, Paul, 76
The Byrds, 177
Byrne, Chris, xi

California Labor Code Section 2855, "Seven Year Statute," 90
Camper Van Beethoven, 73
Carter, Steven, 135, 145
"Casey at the Bat," 122
Cash, Johnny, 121, 145, 152, 156
Cash, Wilbur J., 46

Caswell, Roger, 145
Cavanagh, David, 199, 207
Centerfield (Fogerty), xv, 34, 35, 109, 113, 114, 115, 117–24, 127, 128, 129, 177, 179, 181, 200, 207
Chapin, Harry, 27, 75
Charles, Ray, 43, 72, 156, 164
Cheney, Dick, 176, 183, 202
Chess Records, 86–88
Chess, Leonard, 86
Ching, Barbara, 82n1
Chooglin' (CCR), 130n2
Christgau, Robert, 127
Chronicle (CCR), 119, 130n2
Chronicle 2 (CCR), 130n2
Chuck D (Public Enemy), 193
Clapton, Eric, 169, 199, 203
The Clash, 74, 111
Clifford, Doug, xii, xiii–xiv, 4, 5, 6, 17, 18, 19, 21, 24, 32, 33, 36, 42, 45, 88–89, 96–97, 118, 123, 152, 153, 194, 199, 202, 205
Clinton, William Jefferson, 25
Cobain, Kurt, 194, 196
Cocks, Jay, 114, 210n15
Cody, Buffalo Bill, 28
Cohan, George M., 104
Cohen, Debra Rae, 111–12
Cohen, Leonard, 194
Collins, Phil, 114
Coltrane, John 88, 96
Columbia Records, 85
The Concert (CCR), 111, 119, 130n2
Concord Records, 35, 96
Cook, Herman, Esq., 87
Cook, Stu, xii, xiii–xiv, 5, 6, 24, 36, 42, 45, 76, 87–89, 95–97, 118, 123, 152, 153, 194, 199, 202, 205, 206
Cooper, B. Lee, xv, 151–52, 167
Cooper, Charles and Kathleen, 151–52
Cosmo's Factory (CCR), 41, 78–79, 80, 116, 178
Cosmo's Factory (band), 96

Song Index

~

About the Editor and Contributors

Nick Baxter-Moore, PhD, Associate Professor in the Department of Communication, Popular Culture and Film at Brock University, Ontario, is the author of recent articles and chapters on the Englishness of Ray Davies and the Kinks, Canadian singer-songwriter Stan Rogers, local music stores, and the architecture of Canadian wineries. His current research focuses on the live music and concert sector, brand names in music lyrics, and the political dimensions of popular music. He is president of the Popular Culture Association of Canada and editor of the *Canadian Journal of Popular Culture*.

Hank Bordowitz is the author of *Bad Moon Rising: The Unauthorized History of Creedence Clearwater Revival* (first published in 1998, updated in 2007). His many other books include *Dirty Little Secrets of the Record Business: Why So Much Music You Hear Sucks*; *Billy Joel: The Life and Times of an Angry Young Man*; *U2 Reader: A Quarter Century of Commentary*; *The Bruce Springsteen Scrapbook*; *Every Little Thing Gonna Be Alright: The Bob Marley Reader*; *Noise of the World: Non-Western Musicians in Their Own Words*, and *Turning Points in Rock and Roll*. He is currently curating the forthcoming *Led Zeppelin on Led Zeppelin* (2013) for A Cappella Press. He has taught music and the music business at Ramapo College, Baruch College (CUNY), Western Illinois University, and several others.

B. Lee Cooper, PhD, is a freelance writer and popular music critic. Over the past 40 years he has been a professor of history and American culture, a dean of students, a provost and vice president for academic affairs, and a university president. He is the author of more than 500 book and record reviews and over 150 articles that have appeared in 40 different scholarly journals and music magazines. He has also published 15 books, including *A Resource Guide to Themes in Contemporary Song Lyrics, 1950-1985*; *Rock Music in American Popular Culture*, 3 vols.; *The Popular Music Handbook*; and *New Orleans Music: Legacy and Survival*. In 1983 he received the ASCAP-Deems Taylor Award for excellence in music research after publication of *Images of American Society in Popular Music*.

Christian Z. Goering, PhD, Associate Professor of English Education at the University of Arkansas, has published some twenty-five articles and chapters in such journals as *American Secondary Education*, *Journal of Adolescent and Adult Literacy*, and *English Journal*, and in books such as *Harper Lee's To Kill a Mockingbird: New Essays on an American Classic*; *Essential Criticism of Of Mice and Men*, and *Reclaiming the Rural: Essays on Literacy, Rhetoric, and Pedagogy*.

Timothy Gray, PhD, Professor of English and American Studies at the College of Staten Island, City University of New York is the author of *Gary Snyder and the Pacific Rim* (2006), *Urban Pastoral* (2010), and *Reading Roots Rock Writing* (forthcoming), all published by the University of Iowa Press. He also has a chapbook of poems, *Moonchild*, forthcoming from Foothills Publishing.

Thomas M. Kitts, PhD, Professor of English and Chair of the Division of English and Speech at St. John's University, NY, is the author of *Ray Davies: Not Like Everybody Else*, *The Theatrical Life of George Henry Boker*, and *Gypsies: An East Village Opera* (a play). With Michael Kraus, he co-edited *Living on a Thin Line: Crossing Aesthetic Borders with the Kinks*, and with Gary Burns, he co-edits *Popular Music and Society*. He is also the author of many essays, book chapters, reviews, and instructor manuals. He recently edited the anthology *Literature and Work*.

Robert McParland, PhD, Associate Professor of English and Humanities at Felician College, NJ, is a singer-songwriter, playwright, novelist, and teacher. He is the author of *Music and Literary Modernism*, *Dickens and Melodrama*, *Charles Dickens's American Audience*, *Music—The Speech of Angels*, *The Healing Magic of Music*, *How to Write about Joseph Conrad*, and two collections of short fiction.

Stephen Paul Miller, PhD, Professor of English at St. John's University, NY, and a former Senior Fulbright Scholar at Jagiellonian University in Krakow, Poland, is the author of several books including *The Seventies Now: Culture as Surveillance* (Duke University Press) and several poetry books including *There's Only One God and You're Not It* (Marsh Hawk Press), *Being with a Bullet* (Talisman), *Fort Dad* (Marsh Hawk Press), *Art Is Boring for the Same Reason We Stayed in Vietnam* (Domestic), *The Bee Flies in May* (Marsh Hawk Press), and *Skinny Eighth Avenue* (Marsh Hawk Press). He also co-edited, with Daniel Morris, *Radical Poetics and Secular Jewish Culture* (University of Alabama Press), and, with Terence Diggory, *The Scene of My Selves: New Work on New York School Poets* (National Poetry Foundation). His work has appeared in *New American Writing, Best American Poetry, The Contemporary Narrative Poem: Critical Crosscurrents*, and many other publications.

William J. Miller, PhD, Assistant Professor of Public Administration at Flagler College, earned his doctorate from the University of Akron. He focuses his studies on campaigns and elections, public opinion toward public policy (domestic and international), and the pedagogy of political science. His research appears in the *Journal of Political Science Education, Journal of Political Marketing, Studies in Conflict and Terrorism*, and *Journal of Common Market Studies*. Book chapters have appeared in Stephen Craig and David Hill's *The Electoral Challenge* (CQ Press) and John Ishiyama and Marijke Breuning's *Twenty-First-Century Political Science* (Sage). He is the editor of *Tea Party Effects on 2010 U.S. Senate Elections: Stuck in the Middle to Lose*, along with *The Election's Mine—I Draw the Lines: Redistricting in the American States*.

Lawrence Pitilli, an Associate Professor of Speech at St. John's University, NY, has presented papers and written book reviews in the area of popular culture with a focus on music. He has worked as a musician and has composed music and lyrics for Off Broadway, Off Off Broadway, and Street Theater productions. In addition, he has been a country music category winner and Grand Prize winner in the Music City Song Festival in Nashville, Tennessee. He resides in Brooklyn, New York.

Jeff Sellars, PhD, teaches philosophy and humanities in Northern California and Southern Oregon. His creative endeavors include art, film, fiction, and music. His current academic research centers mainly on theological aesthetics and the study of music, literature, and film. He is the editor of *Light Shining in a Dark Place: Discovering Theology through Film* and the founder and senior editor of *Imaginatio et Ratio: A Journal of Theology and the Arts*.

William C. Sewell, PhD, Assistant Professor of Education at the University of Central Missouri, has published articles in such journals as *English Journal, Wisconsin English Journal,* and *The Journal of Media Literacy and Education,* among others.

Jake Sudderth is the author of *The St. Ann's Kid: A Seattle Memoir* and the forthcoming "Footprints of Freedom, Mifflin Wistar Gibbs and the Pursuit of Equality across North America" in *Before Obama: A Reappraisal of Black Reconstruction Era Politics.*

Theodore Louis Trost, PhD, Professor and Chair of the Department of Religious Studies at the University of Alabama, is the author of *Douglas Horton and the Ecumenical Impulse in American Religion,* editor of *The African Diaspora and the Study of Religion,* and many book chapters, essays, and reviews. He is also a songwriter, vocalist, and producer of several albums for WreckLoose Recordings.

Jeremy D. Walling, PhD, Associate Professor of Political Science at Southeast Missouri State University, received his doctorate from the University of Kansas and his MPA from Missouri State University. He studies state politics and intergovernmental relations, American national institutions, and public administration ethics and accountability. His work has appeared in *The Constitutionalism of American States, The Handbook of Administrative Ethics,* and *Public Personnel Management,* the last two with H. George Frederickson. He is currently working with William J. Miller on *The Election's Mine—I Draw the Lines: Redistricting in the American States.*